GRAND INQUESTS

Also by William H. Rehnquist:

The Supreme Court: How It Was, How It Is

GRAND INQUESTS

The Historic Impeachments of Justice
Samuel Chase and President Andrew Johnson

William H. Rehnquist

WILLIAM MORROW AND COMPANY, INC.
New York

It is the policy of William Morrow and Company, Inc., and its imprints and affiliates, recognizing the importance of preserving what has been written, to print the books we publish on acid-free paper, and we exert our best efforts to that end.

Library of Congress Cataloging-in-Publication Data

Rehnquist, William H., 1924—
    Grand inquests: the historic impeachments of Justice Samuel Chase
and President Andrew Johnson / William H. Rehnquist.
      p.   cm.
    ISBN 0-688-05142-1
    1. Chase, Samuel, 1741-1811—Impeachments. 2. Johnson, Andrew,
1808-1875—Impeachment. 3. Impeachments—United States—History.
I. Title.
E302.6.C4R44   1992
353.03'6—dc20   91-31681
                                                                 CIP

Printed in the United States of America

First Edition

1 2 3 4 5 6 7 8 9 10

BOOK DESIGN BY LISA STOKES

To Nan

–Preface–

One need only note the way in which the framers arranged the text of the United States Constitution to realize that they were concerned about the separation of powers within the new federal government which they were creating. Each of the three powers of government—legislative, executive, and judicial—is dealt with in a separate article. Article I grants legislative power to Congress, Article II grants the executive power to the president, and Article III vests the judicial power in the federal courts.

The framers were particularly concerned about the possibility of overreaching and bullying by the legislative branch—Congress—against the other branches. To that end, they established the terms of office of the president and of the judges in the Constitution itself, where they could not be changed by Congress. The president was to be elected for a term of four years. The judges were appointed by the president, subject to Senate confirmation, to serve "during good behavior." Congress was forbidden to diminish the compensation of either the president or the judges during their terms.

But those who wrote the Constitution realized that there could also be malfeasance by high officials of the government, and so they borrowed from England the concept of impeachment and removal of such officials. Article I of the Constitution confers upon the House the sole power to impeach, and on the Senate the sole power to try impeachments. Article II provides:

> The President, Vice President, and all civil officers of the United States, shall be removed from Office on Im-

peachment for, and Conviction of, Treason, Bribery, or other high Crimes and Misdemeanors.

The framers were sufficiently practical to know that no charter of government could possibly anticipate every future contingency, and they therefore left considerable room for "play in the joints." Nor did they try to foresee exactly how each of the many powers and checks and balances they conferred and established would work out in particular situations. That was of necessity left to future generations.

This book is about two episodes in American history in which the country witnessed a visible demonstration of play in the joints between constitutional provisions. In 1804 Justice Samuel Chase of the Supreme Court of the United States was impeached, and in 1805 he was tried by the United States Senate. In 1868 President Andrew Johnson was impeached, and in that same year he, too, was tried by the Senate. The outcome of each of these trials was of extraordinary importance to the American system of government. If Samuel Chase had been convicted, the future independence of the president could have been jeopardized. It was the United States Senate which in each case made these fundamental decisions. This book is the story of those two trials.

As in the case with my previous book, *The Supreme Court: How It Was, How It Is,* I have presented some of the ideas contained in these chapters at the University of Arizona College of Law, the University of Michigan Law School, and Northwestern University Law School, and I am grateful to these law schools for having afforded me the opportunity to develop these themes. Robby Lantz of the Lantz Office not only encouraged me to develop the ideas embodied in the book, but faithfully read and helpfully commented on the work and progress. My editor at William Morrow and Company, Lisa Drew, has again made just the sort of suggestions that have greatly improved the clarity and organization of the work without ever trenching on the author's execution of his plan.

My secretary, Janet Barnes, has again cheerfully and willingly used the word processor to bring the manuscript for the book into being, and Mark Miskovsky has been an invaluable help in many ways in helping put the book together. The staff of the library of the Supreme Court of the United States, headed by Librarian Shelley Dowling, has been more than cooperative in filling my requests for a wide number of volumes, many of which were not in the Supreme Court library. Gail Galloway, the curator of the Supreme Court, has assisted in obtaining pictures of members of the Court contained in this volume. Alan Fern, director of the National Portrait Gallery, has been equally helpful in assisting me to obtain from the National Portrait Gallery other pictures used in this volume.

I have also received helpful comments from Professor G. Edward White of the University of Virginia Law School, Professor Stephen B. Presser of the Northwestern University Law School, and Chief Judge Gilbert Merritt of the United States Court of Appeals for the Sixth Circuit.

My wife, Nan, has again been the "editor of first resort" with every chapter of this manuscript. Her suggestions often led to substantial revisions in the way I presented the material, because to me she represents the interested and informed nonlawyer for whom the book is written. Working with her on the book has made it a true labor of love.

GRAND INQUESTS

–1–

"Oyez! Oyez! Oyez!—All persons are commanded to keep silence on pain of imprisonment, while the grand inquest of the nation is exhibiting to the Senate of the United States, sitting as a Court of Impeachments, articles of impeachment against Samuel Chase, Associate Justice of the Supreme Court of the United States."

With this solemn warning from the sergeant-at-arms of the United States Senate, the trial of Samuel Chase began on February 4, 1805. The Senate chamber where the trial would take place was outfitted in a manner deemed equal to the occasion. On each side of the presiding officer's chair at one end of the chamber were two rows of benches with desks, entirely covered with crimson cloth. Here would sit the thirty-four senators who would pass judgment on Chase. Two from each of the thirteen original states, and two each from the more recently admitted states of Vermont, Tennessee, Kentucky, and Ohio.

Three rows of benches, arranged in tiers, ran from the wall toward the center of the room. They were covered with green cloth and would be occupied by members of the House of Representatives, the body that had impeached Chase. To their right a small enclosure had been constructed for use of the members of President Jefferson's Cabinet.

On either side of the aisle leading from the presiding officer's chair to the doorway were a table and chairs covered with blue cloth; one was occupied by the managers prosecuting the case for the House of Representatives, and the other by the lawyers conducting Chase's defense. In the rear of the room was the permanent gallery to which the general public was customarily admitted. But for this event a temporary gallery, facing the crimson-covered desks of the senators, had been constructed. The seats in this gallery were covered with green cloth and would be filled during the trial with ladies who turned out in large numbers to see the event.

The spectators who attended the trial were drawn there not only because of its drama, but also because of the lack of most other forms of entertainment in the nation's capital in the year 1805. Washington was then a raw new city in a wilderness along the Potomac River. For the first year of its existence, the capital city of the United States had been the city of New York, and then for the next ten years it had been Philadelphia. But Congress had provided that as of 1800 the capital should be moved to a ten-mile-square district located on land along the Potomac River which had been ceded by the states of Maryland and Virginia.

There were two established cities in this new district—Georgetown, on the Maryland side, with a population of about three thousand, and Alexandria, on the Virginia side, with a population of about five thousand. But the "city" of Washington itself was scarcely a village. Jenkins Hill, located in roughly the center of the district, had been chosen as the site of the Capitol building. By 1805 only the north or Senate wing had been completed. The House of Representatives occupied a temporary brick structure to the south known as the "oven." Nearly two miles away, at the other end of Pennsylvania Avenue, stood what was then called the President's House and is now called the White House. A list of Washington buildings drawn up in November 1801 showed a total of 621 houses standing on private land; the city had a population of a little more than three thousand. One incident that occurred during the disputed election of 1800—when the Republicans had defeated the incumbent President John Adams for reelection but it was uncertain whether Thomas Jefferson or Aaron Burr would be president—shows the contrast between the Washington scene of that day and of the present time far more dramatically than any set of statistics. Thomas Jefferson and John Adams met and discussed the election dispute, which under the Constitution had been thrown into the House of Representatives; the occasion for their meeting was that they bumped into one another as each was walking along Pennsylvania Avenue!

Because of the peculiar system of electoral voting provided for by the United States Constitution, the duly chosen presidential electors from each state did not vote separately for president and vice-president, but simply cast a vote for each of two candidates. The person receiving the most electoral votes became president, and the runner-up became vice-president. In each of the first three elections—1789, 1792, 1796—this system had worked as it was supposed to: One candidate received more votes than any of the others, and was declared president. But the election of 1800 exposed a flaw in the system. Both Jefferson—who was intended by most of the Republican voters to be their presidential candidate, and Burr—who was intended by most to be their vice-presidential candidate, received seventy-three electoral votes. The Constitution provided that in such a situation the presidential election should be thrown into the House of Representatives, where each state was entitled to cast one vote. The Federalist members of the House, although their party had lost the presidential election, were in a position to decide whether Jefferson or Burr should become the next president. After thirty-five indecisive ballots taken during a hectic period of several days, Alexander Hamilton finally persuaded enough of his fellow Federalists that Jefferson was preferable to Burr. The House then elected the former as president by the votes of nine states. This imbroglio led to the adoption in 1804 of the Twelfth Amendment to the United States Constitution, whereby presidential electors were required to vote separately for president and for vice-president.

Albert Gallatin, appointed by President Jefferson as secretary of the treasury in 1801, said upon his arrival in the city to take up the duties of his office:

> Our local situation is far from being pleasant or even convenient. Around the Capital are 7 or 8 boarding houses, 1 taylor, 1 shoemaker, 1 printer, and washing woman, a grocery shop, a pamphlet and stationery shop, a small dry goods shop and an oyster house. This makes the whole of the federal city as connected with the Capital.

There were several racecourses in or about the city, but its only theater was located in a part of Blodgett's Hotel. A permanent theater building was then under construction and would open later in the year. The *National Intelligencer* newspaper had begun publishing in Washington in 1801; it was published three times a week and an annual subscription cost five dollars.

Aaron Burr, vice-president of the United States and president of the Senate, would preside over the Chase trial. It was he who had decked out the Senate chamber in its colorful garb, seeking to re-create as nearly as possible on this side of the Atlantic Ocean the appearance of the House of Lords at the time of the impeachment trial of Warren Hastings in England at the end of the eighteenth century. Burr was short of stature, erect, with piercing black eyes. He himself was a fugitive from justice at this time. During the preceding summer he had shot and killed Alexander Hamilton in a duel at Weehawken, New Jersey, and indictments had been issued against him in both that state and New York. This fact caused one contemporary wag to remark that whereas in most courts the murderer was arraigned before the judge, in this court the judge was arraigned before the murderer! But none of this in any way interfered with the elegant bearing of the vice-president as he made ready to officiate at the trial.

Burr came from an ancestry notable for intellectual achievement; his father was a theologian and the second president of the College of New Jersey, which later became Princeton University; his maternal grandfather was Jonathan Edwards, the greatest of the New England theologians. Aaron Burr graduated with honors from Princeton at sixteen years of age, and upon the outbreak of the Revolutionary War he served with distinction in Benedict Arnold's expedition against Quebec. After his military service, he moved to New York and was admitted to the bar of that state, where he and Alexander Hamilton became both rivals for clients and political adversaries. From 1791 to 1797 he represented New York in the United States Senate. Through shrewdness and diligent application he mastered the labyrinthine politics of the Empire State, assuring the electoral votes of that state for the Republican nominee for president in 1800 and procuring his own endorsement as that party's candidate for vice-president. In so doing he also procured the undying enmity of Hamilton.

Jefferson no sooner became president than he began to antagonize Burr by allowing a rival Republican faction in New York State, headed by Governor George Clinton, to control that state's federal patronage. Burr was not included in the councils of Jefferson's first administration, and was unceremoniously dumped as a vice-presidential candidate in the election of 1804. He sought the New York governorship that year but was defeated, in part by Hamilton's opposition. In a series of letters published during the campaign, Hamilton described Burr as a "dangerous man and one who ought not to be trusted with the reins of government." Burr challenged Hamilton to a duel, and on July 11, 1804, on the New Jersey heights opposite New York City, he shot and mortally wounded Hamilton.

As the impeachment trial of Chase approached, Jefferson suddenly became very attentive to his outgoing vice-president. Burr's stepson, his brother-in-law, and his good friend General James Wilkinson were appointed to three important offices in the new government of the Louisiana Territory. Burr himself was repeatedly invited to dine with Jefferson at the President's House. Senator William Giles, who was a leading supporter of the movement to impeach Chase, circulated a petition to the governor of New Jersey requesting that the indictment against Burr for murder be dropped, and secured the signatures of a large number of Republican senators.

Burr does not appear to have been seduced by these blandishments. According to the account of one newspaper by no means friendly to Burr, "He conducted [the trial] with the dignity and impartiality of an angel, but with the rigor of a devil." This is not to suggest that he was at all friendly to the accused. When Chase entered the box, the sergeant-at-arms brought him a chair, but Burr, thinking of the English practice by which the prisoner was required to stand in the dock, ordered it to be taken away. But when the white-haired justice, then sixty-four years of age and badly troubled by gout, requested that the chair be returned, Burr acquiesced.

Senator William Plumer of New Hampshire, in his daily diary entries, indicates that Burr may have been something of a martinet in the eyes of the senators over whom he presided at the trial.

"Mr. Burr is remarkably testy—he acts more of the tyrant—is impatient, passionate—scolds—he is in a rage because we do not sit longer."[1]

"Just as the time for adjourning to morrow was to be put . . .

Mr. Burr said he wished to inform the Senate of some irregularities that he had observed in the Court.

"Some of the Senators as he said during the trial and while a witness was under examination walked between him and the Managers—others ate apples—and some eat cake in their seats.

"Mr. Pickering said he eat an apple—but it was at the time when the President had retired from the chair. Burr replied he did not mean him—he did not see him.

"Mr. Wright said he eat cake—he had a just right to do so—he was faint—but he disturbed nobody—he never would submit to be schooled and catechised in this manner.

"At this instance a motion was made by Bradley, who also had eaten cake, for an adjournment. Burr told Wright he was not in order—sit down. The Senate adjourned and I left Burr and Wright scolding.

"Really, *Master Burr*, you need a ferule or birch to enforce your lectures on polite behavior!"[2]

Presiding over the Chase trial would be Aaron Burr's swan song as a public official. Immediately after the conclusion of the trial of Chase, he would disappear into the western wilderness on an adventure, the purpose of which still puzzles historians. He would emerge two years later from that wilderness in the custody of United States marshals, being transported to Richmond, Virginia, to be tried for treason before John Marshall sitting as a circuit judge.

Aaron Burr is one of the truly enigmatic figures in American history. He may well have been the equal in talent and personal charm of his great contemporary rival, Alexander Hamilton. But for all his flaws, Hamilton was a patriot, with a deep loyalty to his country. Burr was at heart an opportunist, and the judgment of history has not been kind to him.

Samuel Chase, who stood to lose his office as an associate justice of the Supreme Court of the United States if convicted by the Senate, was more than six feet tall and correspondingly broad; his complexion was brownish-red in color, earning him the nickname of "Old Bacon Face." He was hearty, gruff, and sarcastic; one would rather have him as a dinner companion than as a judge in one's case.

Born in Somerset County, on the Eastern Shore of Maryland, at the age of eighteen he went to Annapolis to study law. He was an early and spirited participant in the American Revolution. He was one of the organizers of the Sons of Liberty in 1774 and in that same year was a Maryland delegate to the first Continental Congress. Largely through his efforts the Maryland legislature had instructed its delegation to the Continental Congress to vote for complete independence from England in July 1776. Chase was one of the Maryland signers of the Declaration of Independence, but twelve years later opposed Maryland's ratification of the Constitution because it contained no bill of rights.

Chase had had a distinguished and successful career at the bar, and in 1791 became chief judge of the Maryland General Court. In 1796 he was appointed by George Washington to the Supreme Court of the United States. His legal ability was recognized by all, but his impetuous nature made him something of a stormy petrel. Joseph Story described him as the "living image" of Samuel Johnson, "in person, in manners, in unwieldy strength, and severity of reproof, in real tenderness of heart; and above all in intellect."[3] One of the federal district judges with whom Chase sat had a more negative reaction:

> Of all others, I like the least to be coupled with him. I never sat with him without pain, as he was forever getting into some intemperate and unnecessary squabble. If I am to be immolated, let it be with some other victim or for my own sins.[4]

At this time, and for many years thereafter, the justices of the Supreme Court of the United States performed two separate roles. For a small part of the year they were appellate judges sitting together in Washington, D.C., as the Supreme Court of the United States. But for the rest of the year they were circuit justices assigned to hold court and hear cases in a particular geographic part of the nation. In these instances they sat with a federal district judge assigned to that particular court; hence Judge Peters's reference to being "coupled" with Chase.

Although Chase had started out as an anti-Federalist or Republican, he was converted to Federalism shortly after the adoption of the Constitution and brought to that commitment the intense dedication with which he held all of his beliefs. Even before Jefferson was elected president, his conduct of trials in the case of John Fries in Philadelphia and James T. Callender in Richmond had drawn criticism from the Republican press. The term of the Supreme Court scheduled for August 1800 had to be delayed because Justice Chase remained in his home state of Maryland to campaign for the reelection of John Adams as president. The *Aurora*, a Republican mouthpiece, expostulated: "The Supreme Court adjourning from day to day and the business of the Nation being held up until Chase shall have disgorged himself. O Tempora O Mores! . . ."[5]

In May 1803, while charging a grand jury in Baltimore, Chase spoke disparagingly of some Republican policies, sharply criticized at least one act of Congress passed after Jefferson became president, and also criticized proposed changes in the Maryland state constitution. Henry Adams, in his *History of the United States of America*, says of Chase:

> Unluckily Chase's temper knew no laws of caution. He belonged to the old class of conservatives who thought that judges, clergymen, and all others in authority should guide and warn the people.[6]

When Jefferson, now president, learned of this happening, he wrote to Joseph Nicholson of Maryland, one of the leaders of the House of Representatives:

> Ought this seditious and official attack on the principles of our Constitution, and on the proceedings of a State, to go unpunished? And to whom so pointedly as yourself will the public look for the necessary measures? I ask these questions for your consideration, for myself it is better that I should not interfere.[7]

Jefferson, ever the master of indirection, was mindful of the constitutional provision that placed the initiative in such matters with the House of Representatives:

> The House of Representatives . . . shall have the sole Power of Impeachment. [Article 1, Section 2, Clause 5].

> . . . [A]ll civil officers of the United States, shall be
> removed from Office on Impeachment for, and Convic-
> tion of, Treason, Bribery, or other high Crimes and Mis-
> demeanors. [Article II, Section 4]

The Republican leaders in the House of Representatives in due
course followed the suggestion of their leader. The House voted
impeachment on eight separate charges against Chase, but only
three were serious enough to merit close attention today.

Chase chose as the principal counsel to assist in his defense at
the trial his longtime friend and fellow Marylander Luther Martin. Luther Martin is one of the great lawyers in American history, and also one of the great iconoclasts of the American legal
profession. Joseph Story, shortly before his appointment to the
Supreme Court of the United States, watched Luther Martin arguing a case before the Supreme Court and described him in these
terms:

> He is about middle size, a little bald, with a common
> forehead, pointed nose, inexpressive eyes, large mouth,
> and well-formed chin. His dress is slovenly . . . you
> should hear of Luther Martin's fame from those who have
> known him long and intimately, but you should not see
> him.[8]

Martin was the first attorney general of Maryland, and served
in that office for more than twenty-eight years. He was both a
member of the Continental Congress and one of Maryland's delegates to the Constitutional Convention. He does not seem to have
made a favorable impression on other delegates at the Convention;
it may be that his forensic talents were better suited to jury arguments than to constitutional debates. William Pierce of Georgia, who wrote sketches of the delegates, described Martin in these
words:

> Mr. Martin was educated for the Bar, and is Attorney
> General of Maryland. This gentleman possesses a good
> deal of information, but has a very bad delivery, and so

extremely prolix, that he never speaks without tiring the patience of all who hear him.[9]

Oliver Ellsworth reported that Martin "so exhausted the politeness of the Convention" that it "at length prepared to slumber" whenever he rose.[10]

Martin had his share of causes célèbres in addition to his defense of Samuel Chase. He would be the principal defense counsel for Aaron Burr when the latter was tried for treason in Richmond two years later. Martin was counsel in a number of cases in the Supreme Court of the United States, including two that produced notable opinions from Chief Justice John Marshall: *Fletcher* v. *Peck*,[11] and *M'Culloch* v. *Maryland*.[12] Martin was on the losing side in both of these cases.

He had a marked weakness for the bottle, being referred to colloquially by his enemies in Baltimore as "lawyer Brandy Bottle." But at least in the short run, intoxication does not seem to have impaired his performance in court. He was described by the American historian Henry Adams as "the rollicking, witty, audacious Attorney-General of Maryland; . . . drunken, generous, slovenly, grand; bull-dog of Federalism . . . the notorious reprobate genuis."[13]

A few years after successfully defending Chase, Martin appeared before him as circuit judge sitting in Baltimore. Martin was visibly intoxicated. His biographer describes the incident thus:

> [Chase] said, "I am surprised that you can so prostitute your talents." Martin, drawing himself up as straight as he could, replied to Chase, "Sir, I never prostituted my talents except when I defended you and Colonel Burr," at which, turning to the jury, he added confidentially, "A couple of the greatest rascals in the world." Chase angrily instructed the clerk to draw up a citation of Martin for contempt of court, but when it was presented for his signature, that choleric old man, recollecting their forty-year friendship and all that he owed Martin, put the quill pen back in its holder, saying "this hand could never sign a citation against Luther Martin."[14]

Martin suffered a paralytic stroke shortly after his argument before the Supreme Court in the case of *M'Culloch* v. *Maryland* in 1819, but he lived on for seven years helpless, without family, and without means of support. The Maryland legislature took notice of his condition and unanimously enacted a truly remarkable statute: Every lawyer admitted to practice in the state of Maryland was required to pay annually to the clerk of the court in the county in which he practiced the sum of five dollars, which sums were turned over to trustees to use for the benefit of Martin.

Martin was assisted in conducting the Chase defense by four other lawyers of national reputation: Robert Goodloe Harper, Joseph Hopkinson, Phillip Barton Key, and Charles Lee. The leader for the House managers in support of the charges was John Randolph of Roanoke, a rara avis of the same order as Luther Martin.

Randolph represented the extreme states' rights and agrarian point of view among the Jeffersonian Republicans. Born into one of the most prominent Virginia families, he inherited from his father extensive land on the Staunton River in Charlotte County, Virginia, which he eventually developed into the plantation known as "Roanoke." His education was desultory, and as a young man his principal interests seemed to be horses and horse racing. But he was elected to Congress at the age of twenty-six, and when the Jeffersonians gained control of Congress in 1801 he became in effect the administration leader in the House of Representatives. But Randolph was too dogmatic and too egotistical to automatically follow Jefferson's lead; shortly after the latter's election he wrote:

> In this quarter we think that the great work has only begun: and that without *substantial reform*, we shall have little reason to congratulate ourselves on the mere change of *men*.[15]

He was brilliant, talented, capricious; Senator Plumer described him as one who had "the appearance of a beardless boy more than a full-grown man."[16] The consummate Southern tobacco planter, he patrolled the House of Representatives in boots and spurs with a whip in his hand.

It has generally been thought that he was not well suited to the task of managing the impeachment trial in the Senate because he had not been trained as a lawyer. He had his own kind of insightful brilliance, but it was undisciplined and erratic, better suited to the stump or to legislative debates than to legal argument. Dumas Malone says of him:

> Since there never was another like him, he must be described as an incomparable orator. For hours on end his shrill flute-like voice irritated and fascinated, pouring upon his audience shafts of biting wit, literary allusions, epigrams, parables, and figures of speech redolent of the countryside. . . . Dauntless in spirit though he was, he now seems one of the most pathetic as well as one of the most brilliant figures that ever strutted and fretted his hour upon the American public stage.[17]

Randolph would be assisted in prosecuting the charges before the Senate by several of his fellow House members, including future attorney general of the United States Caesar Rodney of Delaware.

The Senate of the United States in 1805 was not, by and large, a particularly distinguished body. Two of its members kept diaries—John Quincy Adams of Massachusetts, who would be elected president of the United States twenty years later, and William H. Plumer of New Hampshire. Both were Federalists, and it is understandable that their diaries frequently reflect a Federalist point of view when describing the proceedings. The leader of the administration forces in the Senate was William Branch Giles of Virginia. He had entered Congress in 1790, and was identified from the beginning of his career in that body as a champion of the anti-Federalist or Republican point of view. He sought to censure Hamilton in his conduct of the Treasury Department, bitterly opposed the ratification of Jay's Treaty, and even hinted at a desire for disunion during the Adams administration. Giles was the principal author of a doctrine that regarded impeachment as a strictly political device for removing public officials who were out of tune with the prevailing political tides in the country. John Quincy Adams described Giles's views as stated to him in a conversation:

Impeachment was not a criminal prosecution . . . and a removal by impeachment was nothing more than a declaration by Congress to this effect: you hold dangerous opinions, and if you are suffered to carry them into effect, you will work the destruction of the Union. We want your offices for the purpose of giving them to men who will fill them better.[18]

It was Giles, Plumer, Adams, and their thirty-one senatorial colleagues who would now hear the evidence for and against Chase on the charges against him: his conduct during the trial of John Fries, his conduct during the trial of James Callender, and his charge to the Baltimore grand jury. Each of these charges had strong political, even philosophical, connotations—connotations that cannot be fully understood without some reference to the first twelve years of our government under the Constitution.

-2-

*T*hirty years earlier—in 1775—there had been no United States of America: only thirteen English colonies strung out along the Atlantic seaboard from Savannah, Georgia, to Portsmouth, New Hampshire. But on April 19 of that year, at Lexington and Concord, the "embattled farmers stood, and fired the shot heard round the world." The Revolutionary War they started ended eight years later when the Treaty of Paris recognized American independence. At the beginning of that war the colonies were loosely banded together in the Continental Congress, which was more like a League of Nations than a government: It had, for example, no taxing authority and could merely request the individual colonies to pay their share of the cost of the American military effort. Such a system was obviously inadequate for the needs of the emerging nation, and in 1781 the Articles of Confederation were ratified by the states. The name "United States of America," first used in the Declaration of Independence, was officially adopted for the new government. The Articles provided for a Congress in which each state was represented, but each state—large or small— had but one vote. Congress was given the authority to borrow money, raise armies, establish a postal service, and deal with the Indians. But noticeably lacking were the powers to levy taxes and regulate interstate and foreign commerce, and any mechanism for the enforcement of the powers that *were* given to Congress. Amendment of the Articles to grant more power to the central government was made all but impossible by the requirement of unanimous consent of the states to any such change.

Thus the Articles of Confederation, though a step in the right direction, were soon seen by many as nothing more than that. New York levied taxes on goods coming through its port destined for other states, and even on vessels bound for other states that stopped there in transit. When Shays's Rebellion broke out in Massachusetts in 1786, that state appealed to the central government for help, but Congress was unable to respond. Pursuant to a call from delegates from five states, who attended a convention in Annapolis in 1786, the states elected delegates to the Constitutional Convention which met at Philadelphia from May until September 1787. The Constitution framed by that body established a federal government consisting of three branches—the legislative, the executive, and the judicial—and granted to that government limited but very important powers: the power to levy taxes, the power to regulate interstate and foreign commerce, the power to declare war. Article VI declared:

> This Constitution, and the Laws of the United States which shall be made in Pursuance thereof; and all treaties made . . . under the Authority of the United States, shall be the supreme Law of the Land . . . any Thing in the Constitution or Laws of any State to the Contrary notwithstanding.

The Constitution would create a federal government that was within its limited sphere independent of the states, and capable of acting directly upon the individual citizen. Officials of the executive and judicial branches of the government would be authorized to enforce its laws. Such a long step in the direction of a central government for what had been thirteen separate colonies did not please everyone, and the issue of ratification of the Constitution was hotly debated in many of the states. The proponents of ratification were called Federalists; they feared that the weak national government then in place would atrophy if it was not strengthened. The opponents of ratification were naturally called anti-Federalists; they feared tyranny from the new central government if the Constitution was ratified.

Nine of the thirteen states were required to ratify before the Constitution would go into effect, and in June 1788 New Hampshire became the ninth state to ratify. But among the four states that had not yet ratified, Federalist success in Virginia and New York was necessary if the new government was to get off the ground in any practical sense of the word. Both of these states stretched from the Atlantic Ocean to the Appalachians and beyond in a way that no other state did. If Virginia failed to ratify, her territory would separate the southern states from the middle states. If New York failed to ratify, her territory would separate the New England states from the middle states.

The Virginia Convention, after weeks of debate, ratified in June 1788 by the narrow margin of 89 to 79. But New York was still not heard from. In that state Alexander Hamilton, John Jay, and James Madison penned a series of eighty-five essays extolling the merits of the Constitution. Most of them were published in the New York daily newspapers; later collected under the title *The Federalist*, they remain arguably the outstanding single American contribution to political philosophy. In July 1788 New York ratified by a vote of 30 to 27.

The closeness of the vote in New York and Virginia—and in Massachusetts, which ratified by a vote of 187 to 168—shows that there was a good deal of anti-Federalist sentiment in the United States at this time. While most of those who had opposed ratification accepted the new government like good losers, the underlying issues that separated the Federalists from the anti-Federalists during the ratification debates did not disappear with the establishment of the new government. Surfacing again in different forms, they would remain an important factor in the political life of the new nation.

On April 30, 1789, George Washington stepped onto the balcony of Federal Hall in New York City and took the oath prescribed by the Constitution itself for the chief executive: "I do solemnly swear that I will faithfully execute the office of President of the United States and will, to the best of my ability, preserve, protect, and defend the Constitution of the United States." So far as personnel was concerned, the new government was starting from scratch. The government of the Articles of Confederation was one of the few to truly "wither away" (in the words of Karl Marx); there were fewer than a dozen of its employees on hand at the end. Such elementary questions as the manner in which the president should be addressed had to be decided. John Adams, who had been elected vice-president, had acquired from his diplomatic service abroad a fondness for titles, and he proposed that the president be referred to as "His Highness the President of the United States of America and the Protector of the Rights of the Same." Fortunately, the House of Representatives rejected this European affectation, and the chief executive was simply referred to as "The President of the United States" or "The President." But Adams's detractors, mindful of his tendency to corpulence, thereafter referred to him behind his back as "His Rotundity."

Congress almost immediately created four Cabinet-level positions: secretary of state, secretary of the treasury, secretary of war, and attorney general. President Washington named General Henry Knox of Massachusetts as secretary of war and Edmund Randolph of Virginia as attorney general. Neither of them played a prominent role in the Cabinet. But the exact opposite was true of the other two appointees.

Washington appointed as his secretary of state Thomas Jefferson, surely the most versatile in talents, and the most catholic in interests, of this country's great political figures. Jefferson's forebears had been among the early settlers of Virginia, and his father, Peter, owned land along the James River in that state. Peter had married Jane Randolph, of the ubiquitous Virginia Randolphs, in 1739, and four years later Thomas Jefferson was born of this union. By that time the family had moved west to Albemarle County, on the eastern slope of the Blue Ridge Mountains.

Jefferson was educated by a private tutor and at a private school until he was sixteen years old, when he enrolled in the College of William and Mary at Williamsburg. After two years of studies there, Jefferson began the study of law with George Wythe, probably the best-known legal scholar in Virginia and perhaps throughout the colonies.

He was admitted to the practice of law, and seems to have divided his time between that enterprise and the family home in Albemarle County. Fond of distant mountain vistas, before he was twenty-five years old, he located on the crest of a hill a suitable site for a future home, which he would name Monticello.

At the age of twenty-eight he married Martha Wayles Skelton, a young widow who was also of the Virginia gentry. She died ten years later, after having borne two children, and Jefferson remained a widower for the rest of his long life.

He was elected to the House of Burgesses, the colonial legislature of Virginia, and took an increasing interest in the affairs of that body as relations between Virginia and the mother country worsened. He was chosen as one of the delegates from Virginia to the Continental Congress, and while a member of that body drafted the Declaration of Independence, which was approved by the Congress on July 4, 1776. He served as wartime governor of Virginia, fleeing the new capital of Richmond with what some thought was unseemly haste when the British under Benedict Arnold captured the city. In 1784 Congress had appointed him American minister to France, and there he had remained throughout the drafting of the Constitution and the debates over its ratification. Indeed, he did not actually return from France until March 1790, to take up his duties as secretary of state.

Washington chose Alexander Hamilton to be his secretary of the Treasury. Hamilton was born in 1757 on the Island of Nevis in the British West Indies to a father and mother who were living together but not married. John Adams tartly described him as the "bastard brat of a Scots peddler." The father deserted the family when Hamilton and his younger brother were children, and Alexander received only scanty schooling on the island of St. Croix. At the age of twelve he became an apprentice clerk for a wealthy merchant on that island, and distinguished himself by his aptitude for figures and feel for the business. Three years later relatives and friends raised enough money to send him to the mainland to finish his education. He enrolled at King's College in New York—later to be called Columbia—but at the age of nineteen obtained a commission as captain in a New York artillery company raised to fight the British. In March 1777 Hamilton—then twenty years of age—was raised to the rank of lieutenant colonel and made an aide-de-camp to the Commander in Chief. From this time forth Hamilton became something of a protégé of George Washington.

During his service with Washington, Hamilton met Elizabeth Schuyler, the daughter of General Phillip Schuyler. The Schuylers at this time were one of the great families of New York, ranking with the Rensselaers, the Van Cortlandts, and the Livingstons; Phillip Schuyler was a fourth-generation descendant of Dutch patroons whose landholdings in the neighborhood of Albany were on a baronial scale. Hamilton was very much of a ladies' man, and an alliance with the Schuyler family would be of great benefit to an orphan with no family fortune. Alexander Hamilton and Betsy Schuyler, both aged twenty-three, were married in Albany in December 1780.

Hamilton left the army after a spat with Washington in early 1781, but later that year Washington generously awarded him the command of a battalion in time for the Battle of Yorktown. Hamilton performed with conspicuous bravery at that battle in October 1781, after which the British commander, Cornwallis, surrendered his forces to the Americans.

With the war over, Hamilton decided to study law, and after a few months of diligent application he was admitted to practice in New York. His outstanding ability soon took him to the top of the profession, but professional success did not prevent him from attending to public affairs. He was elected a delegate to the Continental Congress from New York, and was one of the moving figures behind the Annapolis Convention in 1786, which in turn issued the call for a Constitutional Convention. He was again a delegate from New York, though not an active participant, in the Philadelphia Convention in 1787. At the time he took office as Washington's secretary of the treasury in September 1789, he was but thirty-two years old.

No sooner had he assumed his duties than the House of Representatives passed a resolution directing him to devise a plan for the "adequate support of the public credit." The continually deteriorating financial affairs of the government under the Confederation had been one of the main reasons for adopting the Constitution, and the new government had no more pressing assignment than the task of putting the country on a sound monetary footing. Though Hamilton had no experience or training in public finance, he threw himself into his new assignment with all of his customary diligence and zeal.

More than one question was involved. No one doubted that the debts the national government had incurred since the outbreak of the Revolution must be assumed and discharged, but there was considerable disagreement over the manner in which this should be done. That portion of the debt held by foreign creditors—chiefly

French and Dutch—presented little problem; if the United States was to obtain credit abroad in the future, it must pay off these debts to their present holders. But that part of the debt held by domestic creditors—citizens of the United States—presented a more difficult problem. Many of the original certificates of debt had been given during the war and afterward to soldiers in payment of wages, or to merchants in payment for supplies needed by the army. Many of these creditors were necessitous, and could not hold the certificates indefinitely in the hope that they should be someday redeemed at face value. Many of them had been forced to sell their certificates to investors and speculators, who purchased them at tremendous discounts, ranging as low as twelve cents on the dollar. There was no doubt that the new government should redeem these certificates at face value, but the dispute arose as to whether all of the face value should be paid to the present holders or some effort made to apportion the face amount between previous holders and the present holders.

Another distinct question was posed by the existence of the public debts of many of the states, which had been incurred in their efforts to assist in the prosecution of the war. Should they be assumed by the new national government? Understandably, those states with large debts felt that they should, and those states that had managed better financially felt that they should not.

In January 1790 Hamilton advised the House of Representatives that he had prepared a plan for the support of public credit, and would be pleased to deliver it in person later that month. This proposal created a great stir in the House of Representatives, not because of the contents of the report but because of the proposal that it be delivered in person. A large majority, fearing that the eloquence of the new secretary might overwhelm the House, insisted that the report be delivered not orally but in writing. Thus was lost to the American system of government the valuable "question period" which later developed in the English Parliament, in which members of that body submit questions to Cabinet members and the latter reply to them in person on the floor of the House. The result, ironically, from the point of view of Congress, was that members of the president's Cabinet—completely excluded from any participation in the deliberations of Congress—became totally attached to the executive branch. Today Cabinet members testify before committees of Congress, but such proceedings are quite different from the British question period.

Hamilton's report proposed that the portion of the national debt owned by domestic as well as by foreign creditors should be paid at full face value to its present holders. Appealing arguments were made on both sides during the debates in Congress. Those who wished to see the debt paid to the present holders pointed out the extraordinary difficulty in identifying and locating the original recipients of the debt certificates, and the even greater difficulty of ascertaining the price for which they had sold them. Any general formula of apportionment between former holders and present holders would suffer from the same sort of imprecise adjustment of equities from which Hamilton's formula suffered, albeit to a lesser degree. The opponents pointed out that Hamilton's plan would reward wealthy speculators at the expense of deserving soldiers and merchants who had supplied the government with the sinews of war at a time when its need had been desperate. Indeed, following the publication of Hamilton's report, speculation proceeded apace, with more than one congressman and several of Hamilton's relatives hastening to buy up certificates of debt in places where the contents of the report had not yet been made public. Hamilton himself, however, did not profit from any of this speculation.

The debate on this issue represented the first break between Hamilton and James Madison, congressman from Virginia, who had fought side by side for ratification of the Constitution when they authored *The Federalist*. Madison offered a compromise whereby the present holders would be paid the highest price for which the certificates had sold in the market, and the remainder would go to the original holders. His proposal denied any compensation to the intermediate holders of a certificate who might have purchased it from the original holder and then later sold it to a present holder.

But the debate in the House was not solely about how the payment of the debt should be apportioned among domestic holders. Hamilton's plan did not call for a simple levy of taxes to pay off the debt and have done with it. Instead it called for a *funding* of the debt by the issuance of new evidences of indebtedness, which would be publicly sold. New permanent taxes would be levied to provide for the periodic payment of interest and principal on this debt. To those agrarian Democrats who at the time of the Chase impeachment would constitute the "Old Republican" segment of Jefferson's followers, the idea of a permanent public debt was anathema. To Hamilton it was a means of giving the propertied class a stake in the success of the new government. The funding bill passed the House in late February 1790.

Hamilton's report had also proposed that the national government should fully assume all the debts of the state governments. These would be merged with the national debt and funded and paid off in the same manner. The secretary advanced not only the equitable argument that these state debts had been largely incurred in a national endeavor, but the desirability of giving the states a stake in the success of the new national government. Representatives from states such as Massachusetts, which had incurred a heavy debt, enthusiastically supported the proposal. But representatives from states such as Georgia, which had not engaged in heavy borrowing, and whose relatively small debt was largely in the hands of Northern speculators, opposed it.

The debate on assumption began in the House of Representatives in February 1790 and did not end until it passed that body by a vote of 34 to 28 in late July. It had originally been defeated in the House in April by a vote of 31 to 29, but Hamilton immediately busied himself to rescue his plan from this setback. He stopped Jefferson on the street in New York one day as he was about to go in to see the president, and the two walked back and forth outside the president's door for half an hour. Jefferson, returned only the previous month from France, would later claim that he was duped by Hamilton. But at the time he acceded to the latter's plea that the members of the administration should act in concert, and that Jefferson should use his influence with the Virginia delegation to change some of their votes. Jefferson arranged a dinner at which Hamilton would have an opportunity to present his views to some of the Southern representatives. At this dinner it was agreed that Hamilton and his followers would support the placement of the new capital along the banks of the Potomac on land ceded by Maryland and Virginia, and that two Virginia congressmen representing Potomac River constituencies would change their votes on the assumption bill.

The bill was brought up again in the House and carried narrowly there, and by a wider margin in the Senate. Another bill was enacted providing that the national capital should be moved from New York to Philadelphia at the end of 1790, and after remaining in Philadelphia for ten years should be permanently moved to the site of a new federal district on either side of the Potomac River. Two essential parts of Hamilton's financial program for the new nation were now in place, but he had at least two more proposals to submit to the next Congress. Meanwhile, the fissure in the political landscape that would soon separate Jefferson and Madison from Washington, Hamilton, and Adams had made its appearance. When it came to the question of whether or not the Constitution should be ratified, all of these were Federalists; but as the first administration of George Washington took its course, the difference between them would become sharper.

In December 1790 Hamilton laid before the House of Representatives a report proposing that Congress create a national bank. The capital stock would be $10 million, divided into twenty-five thousand shares. The United States would purchase one fifth of the shares, while the balance would be open to private subscription. The government would therefore have only minority representation on the Board of Directors, which was exactly what Hamilton wanted; he looked to the interests of the private stockholders as a guarantee of prudent management. The bank would be empowered to issue notes, which would be legal tender for all obligations of the United States. The bank would be chartered for a period of twenty years, and it would be authorized to establish branch banks in the various states.

The report provoked immediate controversy, with Northern mercantile interests viewing it favorably and Southern agrarian interests denouncing it. In the House of Representatives James Madison—speaking with great authority as the "father of the Constitution"—presented a careful, logical argument to prove that the Constitution did not authorize Congress to charter a bank. Article I, defining the powers that Congress should have, said nothing at all about chartering banks; and the Constitution should be construed strictly, since the entire national government was a creature of power delegated from the people. Fisher Ames, an able supporter of the administration from Massachusetts, replied to Madison the following day. The framers could not possibly have set forth in the grant to Congress every conceivable step Congress might wish to take in implementing a particular policy, and foreseeing this very problem, the framers had granted to Congress, in addition to enumerated powers, the authority "to make all laws which shall be necessary and proper for carrying into execution the foregoing powers. . . ." Surely the chartering of a bank could be justified as a device to carry into effect the power to borrow money, which was expressly conferred by the Constitution.

The bank bill was passed first by the Senate and then, after considerably more debate, by the House. But Washington hesitated to sign the bill because of doubts in his own mind about the authority of Congress to charter a bank. He asked Edmund Randolph, his attorney general, for an opinion, and Randolph advised him that the bill was not constitutional. Washington then asked Jefferson, who provided an opinion based largely on Madison's arguments in the House. Once Congress went beyond its enumerated powers, where would be the stopping point? As to the argument that the creation of a bank was "necessary and proper," it was clear that the power to borrow money and the power to collect taxes could all be carried into execution without the creation of a bank; therefore, while a bank might be convenient, it was not necessary.

Washington then turned to Hamilton, and Hamilton rose to the occasion as might be expected. Sitting up all night to draft his argument supporting the constitutionality of the bank, he urged that the "necessary and proper" clause did not require that a thing be absolutely indispensable, but only "needful, requisite, incidental, useful, or conducive to." Surely the creation of a bank met these criteria in connection with the congressional authority to lay and collect taxes, for its notes would provide a convenient medium of exchange in which taxes could be paid.

Washington accepted Hamilton's arguments, and signed the bill. Nearly thirty years later, in the great constitutional case of *M'Culloch* v. *Maryland*,[1] John Marshall would speak for the Court in upholding the constitutionality of the bank chartered by Congress, saying:

> We admit . . . that the powers of the government are limited, and that its limits are not to be transcended. But

we think the sound construction of the Constitution must allow to the national legislature that discretion, with respect to the means by which the powers it confers are to be carried into execution, which will enable that body to perform the high duties assigned to it, in the manner most beneficial to the people. Let the end be legitimate, let it be within the scope of the Constitution, and all means which are appropriate, which are plainly adopted to that end, which are not prohibited, but consist with the letter and spirit of the Constitution, are constitutional. . . .

Hamilton had yet another arrow in his public-finance quiver, and that was the Report on Manufactures that he submitted to the House of Representatives in December 1791. This report urged Congress to affirmatively encourage manufacturing, primarily through the use of protective tariffs although he also recommended monetary bounties, exemption from import duties on essential raw materials, and the encouragement of invention.

These ideas were anathema to Jefferson and the agrarian interests who supported him. Encouragement of manufacturing by the government would lead to the congregation of people in large cities, where they would be shut up in factories and become simply hired hands. He saw agriculture as the true foundation of the nation, and public sentiment on this issue agreed with him rather than with Hamilton. Congress took no action on the Report of Manufactures.

In the presidential election of 1792, Washington again received all the electoral votes for president, but the electoral votes for vice-president were split between John Adams, who received the majority, and Jefferson. This split vote was further evidence of the increasing political division in the United States. Washington and Hamilton represented the views of the party that came to be called Federalist: They emphasized the importance of an aristocracy of talent and wealth, believed in a strong central government, and favored Great Britain as an ally as opposed to France. Thomas Jefferson and James Madison represented the views of what came to be called the Democratic-Republican party, or simply the Republican party: They favored democracy, states' rights, and France over Great Britain. Both of the principal antagonists left Washington's Cabinet before the end of his second administration; Jefferson resigned at the end of 1793, and Hamilton stepped down at the beginning of 1795. Jefferson would return to public office, first as vice-president in 1797, and then as president for two terms beginning in 1801. But Hamilton's retirement from public office was permanent, though he continued to take an active role behind the scenes in the affairs of the government.

Hamilton's vision of the nation and its future was flawed in many respects, but so was Jefferson's. Hamilton had no geographical concept of what the United States might eventually be; he saw it basically as a nation lying along the Atlantic seaboard, and had little interest in or knowledge of the vast territory that lay west of the Appalachian Mountains. He had little sympathy with what Abraham Lincoln would call "government of the people, by the people, and for the people," a political philosophy that would be a dominant theme of Western civilization throughout the coming century. In each of these respects Jefferson was his better.

But Jefferson and his adherents, with their strong belief in states' rights and their insistence on strict construction of the powers of the national government, believed essentially in what Professor Carl Friedrich called the "night watchman" theory of the state: The government should preserve order, collect the small amount of taxes needed to sustain itself, and generally leave people alone. This was plausible doctrine in the eighteenth century, but it would not do for the years to come. In contrast, Hamilton saw the necessity of a relatively strong central government, and the necessity of that government's attaching to itself the financial and mercantile interests of the country. He understood the infant concept of public finance as did no one else in his time: The government should create a national bank in order to establish a medium of exchange for the country and to have some agency that would be able to regulate the expansion and contraction of the nation's credit. The debts incurred in the prosecution of the Revolutionary War must be assumed and paid off by the new national government in order that it might have credit on which to borrow in the future. The government should by its fiscal policies affirmatively encourage the growth of manufacturing so that the country would not be permanently dependent on the importation of manufactured goods from other countries.

There is an imposing statue of Hamilton on the south side of the Treasury Building in Washington, D.C. On the side facing the building is inscribed:

> *He smote the rock*
> *Of the national resources,*
> *And abundant streams*
> *Of revenue gushed forth.*
> *He touched the dead corpse*
> *Of the public credit, and*
> *It sprung upon its feet.*

The inscription is a fitting memorial to one who was not only the most gifted secretary of the treasury in our history, but one of the great political economists of all times.

-3-

*F*oreign relations also occupied the attention of the young republic during the first years of its existence. England and France, for obvious reasons, were the two most important players in the game of world politics as far as the United States was concerned. England had not only been the "mother country" until 1783, but was the principal trading partner of the United States. France had been a vital ally against England during the Revolutionary War, and was the dominant power on the continent of Europe.

The French Revolution, with its cry of "liberty, equality, fraternity," took place only a few months after George Washington had taken the oath of office as the first president of the United States. A wave of sympathy—"Gallomania," it was called by some—swept the United States. Not only had France been our ally, but many felt that the American might have inspired the French revolution. Many shared the exuberant view of the English poet Wordsworth:

> *Bliss was it in that dawn to be alive,*
> *But to be young was very heaven!*

The salutation "Citizen" was substituted for "Mister" in addressing men, because the latter was thought to have aristocratic connotations. The name of a Boston street was changed from "Royal Exchange Place" to "Equality Court." People wore French tricolors in their buttonholes.

At the same time, relations with England remained on an uneven keel. That country had not deigned to accredit a diplomatic representative to the United States until 1791, when George Hammond was sent as minister to the United States. The failure of England to carry out her promise, made in the Treaty of Paris in 1783, impeded the establishment of normal diplomatic relations.

Thomas Jefferson had assumed his duties as secretary of state in the spring of 1790, returning from a mission of six years as United States minister to France. His sympathies were on the side of the French. Alexander Hamilton, on the other hand, sympathized with the English. Although Jefferson, as secretary of state, was responsible for the conduct of foreign relations, Hamilton proved to be an inveterate meddler in this area. These internal frictions were brought to a head when France declared war on England in February 1793. Thus began more than twenty years of European conflict, which would end only when Napoleon was routed at the Battle of Waterloo in 1815. The Francophile element in this country urged that the United States should go to war in aid of France, just as France had come to our aid during the Revolution.

But events inside France itself moved rapidly after the declaration of war, in a manner that dimmed the luster of the French Revolution in the eyes of many Americans. First Louis XVI and then Marie Antoinette were guillotined, and the Reign of Terror began. Many who had been ardent supporters of France took a second look at the situation, and George Washington issued a neutrality proclamation declaring the intention of the United States to stay out of the hostilities. England by a series of "orders in council" authorized the seizure of United States ships carrying cargoes to either France or French colonies in the West Indies. France retaliated by announcing its intention to seize United States ships carrying cargoes for England. Both countries proceeded to enforce these decrees at the expense of American neutral shipping.

Early in 1794 the English foreign secretary modified the orders in council in favor of American shipping, and Washington chose the occasion to send an envoy extraordinary to England. He nominated John Jay, Chief Justice of the United States, to perform this important mission. Jay sailed for England in the spring of

1794, and finally signed the treaty with England that bears his name in November of that year.

The United States bargained from weakness in the negotiations, and the Jay Treaty showed it. The only important gain for the United States was a new promise on the part of the English to surrender their posts on the northern borders of the United States. The disputed boundary between Maine and New Brunswick, the satisfaction of English debts, and compensation for the seizures of American vessels by English men-of-war were all referred to arbitration. The United States won no concessions at all with respect to the rights of neutral shipping.

The Federalists were disappointed with the treaty, and the Republicans were outraged by it. Washington sensibly viewed it as the best settlement that could be had, and pushed for ratification; the Senate consented by a close vote in June 1795. War with England over the rights of neutral vessels was thus postponed for seventeen years, to a time when the United States would be on a footing much closer to equality with that country.

In 1796 George Washington declined to stand for a third term as president, and in the election of that year, John Adams, the candidate of the Federalists, won the presidency over Thomas Jefferson by the narrow margin of 71 votes to 68 in the Electoral College. Whoever succeeded Washington in the presidency would have a very difficult act to follow. Washington did not have the intellectual attainments of Jefferson or Hamilton, nor did he have the encyclopedic knowledge of Adams. But he had a stature—almost a majesty—which none of the other three had. He also was possessed of extraordinarily good judgment based upon instinctive shrewdness, which served him and the nation well during his terms as president. He had an ability to make use of men of talents greater than his own, such as Jefferson and Hamilton, and yet remain master in his own house. The fact that the first eight years of the new government passed in relative peace, tranquillity, and prosperity was itself a remarkable accomplishment, and for this his countrymen were indebted to George Washington as to no one else.

John Adams was far better educated than Washington, but he lacked his shrewd instincts as well as Jefferson's common touch. Benjamin Franklin said of Adams that he was "always honest, often great, but sometimes mad." He and his wife, Abigail, were prickly; they resented Philadelphia society's continuing its annual celebration of Washington's birthday after Adams had succeeded him. They could not understand that Washington had been feted not just because he was currently president, but because he was seen as the "father of his country." It was a small matter, but one that gives considerable insight into Adams's shortcomings as a national leader.

Adams chose to keep in office Washington's entire Cabinet, with the result that three of its principal members were secretly loyal to Alexander Hamilton rather than to him. No sooner had he taken office than he was forced to deal with the spoliations on American maritime commerce of the increasingly aggressive French Navy, and with the considerable number of diehard Francophiles within the United States. Adams, seeking to solve these difficulties through diplomacy, appointed a mission to France consisting of Elbridge Gerry, John Marshall, and Charles Cotesworth Pinckney. This mission arrived in Paris in the fall of 1797, but the members of the ruling Directory refused to receive the American envoys.

Instead, the French foreign minister, Prince Talleyrand, sent three inferior officials—referred to by the American envoys only as X, Y, and Z—to solicit a $250,000 bribe for Talleyrand, and a loan of $10 million to France, as prerequisites to any negotiation with the American representatives. The outraged Americans refused to comply, and several months of desultory negotiations proved fruitless. Marshall and Pinckney finally departed Paris to return home, while Gerry remained in Paris, deluded by the idea that his presence might prevent war.

For months during the winter of 1798 the United States received no news of these negotiations, and divisions deepened between those who wished to preserve peace with France and those who wished to adopt a warlike policy. Finally the dispatches from the envoys arrived, and President Adams published them in April 1798. Their publication astounded the nation, and the insults to the American envoys swung public opinion heavily behind the Federalist position. "Millions for defense, but not one cent for tribute" became the watchword of the day. John Marshall, upon his return from France, received an acclamation such as had been accorded to no other of his countrymen save Washington. Joseph

Hopkinson—who a few years later would appear before the United States Senate in defense of Samuel Chase—wrote the stirring hymn "Hail, Columbia," which was set to a popular march of the time.

Congress responded by authorizing ships of the United States Navy to capture French men-of-war; the navy was strengthened and its ships prepared for active duty. In June 1798 commercial intercourse with France was suspended. President Adams sent an emphatic message to Congress:

> I will never send another minister to France without assurances that he will be received, respected, and honored as the representative of a great, free, powerful and independent nation.[1]

The American Navy, assisted by merchant ships acting as privateers, began an undeclared naval war with France that would last for more than two years.

Many Federalists clamored for a declaration of war upon France, and many of the Republicans either joined in the anti-French feelings of the day or held their peace. John Adams realized that the outpouring of anti-French sentiment in the country was bringing heightened popularity to the Federalist party, yet in his considered judgment these provocations were not severe enough to warrant a declaration of war against France. His feelings were reciprocated on the other side of the Atlantic. France was fearful of becoming involved in a war with the United States at the same time that she was involved in a war with England and the other Continental powers. Talleyrand let it be known through the United States minister at The Hague that he would receive another American diplomatic representative with appropriate dignity and respect.

Without consulting his Cabinet, Adams in February 1799 sent to the Senate the nomination of William Vans Murray as minister to France. The other Federalist leaders were appalled, and pleaded and argued with Adams: Did he realize that he was burying the issue that had caused the surge in popularity of the Federalists? But the only modification he would make was to expand the representation into a commission. He named William R. Davie of North Carolina and Oliver Ellsworth of Connecticut—who, iron-

ically, had succeeded John Jay as Chief Justice of the Supreme
Court—along with Murray as a commission to negotiate differences with France. The envoys arrived in Paris in March 1800,
by which time Napoleon had taken over as First Consul. For months
the talks were deadlocked, but finally in September minimal
agreements were signed sufficient to avoid further hostilities. Like
his predecessor, John Jay, Oliver Ellsworth never returned to the
Supreme Court. In December 1800 he sent from Paris his letter
of resignation to John Adams, thereby enabling the latter to appoint John Marshall as Chief Justice.

During the uproar following the publication of the X,Y,Z correspondence in 1798, the country was swept by a dislike and fear
of France and of foreigners in general not unlike the reaction against
Russia and the Communists after the Second World War. Part of
this was justified, but part of it went to unnecessary extremes.
Congress enacted the Alien Act, which extended the required period of residence for citizenship from five to fourteen years, and
gave the president authority to expel suspicious foreigners. It also
enacted the Sedition Act, which made it a misdemeanor punishable by fine or imprisonment to speak maliciously of the president
or of Congress with the intent to defame them or to bring them
into contempt or disrepute.

The Jeffersonian Republicans were infuriated by the enactment
of the Sedition Act, and they secured the adoption first in Kentucky and then in Virginia of the Kentucky and Virginia resolutions. The legislatures of these states, by these resolutions, expressed
their view that the Alien and Sedition Acts were unconstitutional.
They declared that whenever Congress obviously exceeds its delegated authority, as in the enactment of these laws, each state has
"an equal right to judge for itself, as well of infractions as of the
mode and measure of redress." Here was not only the manifesta-
tion of Republican unhappiness at the repressive Sedition Act, but
the first rumbling of the extreme states' rights doctrine that would
eventually bear bitter fruit in the Civil War.

The Sedition Act was capable of being used as a weapon by
Federalist prosecutors to harass speakers or writers who opposed
the Adams administration, and the administration proceeded to
take advantage of it. Several celebrated trials of people charged
with violation of the Sedition Act took place in the last two years

of the Adams administration; one of them was the trial of James Callender in Richmond, Virginia, before Justice Chase in 1800.

As noted earlier, at this time the justices of the Supreme Court spent only a few weeks a year in Washington sitting as members of that Court. They spent the rest of their time riding circuit in the geographic areas to which they were assigned, sitting with a local federal district judge to try cases. Thus, although Chase was a justice of the Supreme Court of United States, none of the charges on which he was impeached pertained in any way to his discharge of that office. They were directed to his conduct as a trial judge while sitting on circuit.

The basis for the charge of sedition against James Callender, a pamphleteer and editor of Republican persuasion, was his book *The Prospect Before Us.* Whether it was "seditious" may have been fairly debatable, but it was surely unrivaled for turgidity. Callender in wearisome and repetitious detail accused President Adams of being a toady to English interests, and of wishing to install a monarchy in the United States. After a short trial in which there were heated exchanges between counsel for Callender and Justice Chase, Callender was convicted and sentenced to prison for a term of nine months.

Another act passed by Congress in 1798 brought the Federalist party into disfavor for quite a different reason. It was a federal property tax designed to finance the necessary expansion of the army and navy in the event of a possible war with France. Failure to pay the tax on the part of a property owner, of course, resulted in the property's being sold under execution, and in two Pennsylvania counties north of Philadelphia there broke out what has been called "Fries's Rebellion." With the benefit of hindsight, Fries's Rebellion does not seem to have been a great threat to the nation. Angry German farmers attempted to intimidate tax assessors, and John Fries organized a band of armed men who frightened a federal marshal into releasing prisoners held in Bethlehem, Pennsylvania. No shots were fired, there were no injuries, and the crowd soon dispersed.

But President Adams sent troops into the area to suppress the "rebellion," and Fries was arrested and bound over for trial. Had he committed a similar act in our day, he probably would have been charged with obstruction of justice; in that day, however, he was charged with treason, and tried before Justice Chase in Philadelphia in 1800. His counsel, like Callender's counsel, expressed outrage at some of Chase's rulings during the trial. Fries was convicted by the jury and sentenced to hang. Adams, to his great credit, and against the unanimous advice of his Cabinet, pardoned Fries in 1800.

Dissatisfaction with these two laws played a large part in the triumph of the Republican party in the election of 1800. In what some historians have referred to as "the second American Revolution," Thomas Jefferson was elected president and the Republicans gained control of both houses of Congress. But under our constitutional system, of course, they did not by virtue of winning that election gain control of the judiciary. This fact troubled Jefferson. He wrote, "The Federalists have retired into the judiciary as a stronghold . . . and from that battery all the works of Republicanism are to be beaten down and erased."

Jefferson's bitterness at the Federalists, and at the federal judiciary in particular, was occasioned in no small part by the actions of the lame-duck Congress that convened in February 1801. Although Jefferson and the Republicans had won both houses of Congress in the election of 1800, the new Congress would not come into existence until March 4, 1801, at which time Jefferson would succeed Adams as president. The lame-duck Congress was still controlled by the Federalists, and it proceeded to use its political power with considerable abandon.

Ever since the establishment of the federal judiciary, the justices of the Supreme Court had complained bitterly about the onerous circuit-riding duties to which they devoted most of the year. They were required to travel over bad roads by primitive conveyance from the seat of one court to another within their circuit. If they were delayed or became ill, the circuit-court session would have to be postponed, with attendant delay in the administration of justice. Then, sitting in Washington as the Supreme Court, they would have to decide appeals taken from their decisions and their associates' decisions in these lower courts. The turnover in the personnel of the Supreme Court during the first decade under the Constitution was great and did not enhance respect for the Court. John Adams, in his message to Congress in December 1799, urged that corrective steps be taken, but no legislation was enacted during Congress's regular session.

But then, in the lame-duck session of February 1801, Congress took action. It passed the Judiciary Act of 1801, which remedied most of the justifiable complaints about the existing system, and in a different setting it would have been regarded as a sound piece of legislation. The act created six new circuit courts, and sixteen new circuit judges, all of whom would be named by lame-duck president John Adams. The act also reduced the number of Supreme Court justices from six to five, so that the Republicans under Jefferson would have to await not one but two vacancies on the Court in order to appoint one of their own. Gouverneur Morris explained that the act was necessary because the Federalists were "about to experience a heavy gale of adverse wind; can they be blamed for casting many anchors to hold their ship through the storm?"[2]

John Adams proceeded to appoint tried and true Federalists to the sixteen new circuit judgeships, and to the new offices of justice of the peace, which were also created by the act. These appointees were dubbed by the Republicans the "Midnight Judges" because of the belief that Adams had stayed up until midnight making the appointments in the waning hours of his presidency. One of the recipients of the minor office of justice of peace for the District of Columbia was a man named James Marbury, but his commission was signed so late in the Adams administration that when Thomas Jefferson took office as president on March 4, 1801, it remained, undelivered, in the office of the secretary of state. Marbury's suit to compel the new secretary of state, James Madison, to deliver the commission to him was the basis for the celebrated decision of the Supreme Court in the case of *Marbury* v. *Madison*.[3]

It is not surprising that the Republicans cried "Foul!" at the enactment of the Judiciary Act of 1801. They regarded it, with considerable justification, as a piece of political chicanery. Thomas Jefferson felt a sense of personal pique. He and John Adams were both prominent among the "'Founding Fathers"; they had served together on the committee of the Continental Congress that drafted the Declaration of Independence that finally severed the thirteen colonies from England; they had worked together as American ministers to European countries between the time of the Treaty of Paris in 1783 and the adoption of the Constitution; they had served together in Washington's first administration. But the epi-

sode of the Midnight Judges seriously strained Jefferson's respect
for Adams. Three years later he would write to Abigail Adams—
with whom he remained friends throughout these trying times—
these words:

> I can say with truth that one act of Mr. Adams' life, and
> one only, ever gave me a moment's displeasure. I did
> consider his last appointments to office as personally un-
> kind. They were from among my most ardent political
> enemies, from whom no faithful cooperation could ever
> be expected, and laid me under the embarrassment of
> acting thro' men whose views were to defeat mine; or to
> encounter the odium of putting others in their places. It
> seemed but common justice to leave a successor free to
> act by instruments of his own Choice.[4]

Happily, Jefferson and Adams were both granted sufficient
longevity to patch up their quarrel, and by one of the great coin-
cidences of American history, both of these patriots died on July
4, 1826—the fiftieth anniversary of the Declaration of Independence. John Adams, with his last breath, exclaimed, "Thomas Jefferson still survives!" But he was wrong; Jefferson had died a few
minutes earlier at Monticello.

On March 4, 1801, Thomas Jefferson walked from his board-
inghouse near the Capitol in Washington to the Senate chamber,
where the presidential oath was admitted to him by his distant
cousin, newly appointed Chief Justice John Marshall. In his inaugural address he was conciliatory, saying:

> Every difference of opinion is not a difference of princi-
> ple. We have called by different names brethren of the
> same principle. We are all Republicans, we are all Fed-
> eralists.[5]

But for all his conciliatory words, Jefferson and his followers
were determined to change at least what they regarded as the excesses of the Federalists while in office. Chief among these excesses, the Republicans thought, was the Judiciary Act of 1801,
and they set about to repeal it. Article III of the Constitution

provided that federal judges should "hold their offices during good behavior," which suggested that there would be constitutional difficulties in removing these judges from office. In his annual message to Congress in December 1801, Jefferson, in a typically veiled reference to this difficulty, said:

> The judiciary system . . . and especially that portion of it recently erected will of course present itself to the contemplation of Congress.[6]

Jefferson accompanied this message with a statistical summary designed to show that there were more judges than were necessary to conduct the business of the federal courts. In January 1802 the Senate took up a bill repealing the Judiciary Act of 1801 and thereby abolishing the offices that act had created. Such a proposal would give the Republicans no patronage positions to fill, since the offices themselves would no longer exist. But it would rid the judiciary of the Federalist incumbents of the offices as well as of the offices themselves. The Senate recommitted the bill by a tie vote of 15 to 15 the first time around, with Aaron Burr using his casting vote to help the Federalist opposition. But the bill finally passed the Senate in February 1802 by a vote of 16 to 15. Later that month the House passed the same bill by a vote of 59 to 32, and the president duly signed it. The following year the Supreme Court—consisting entirely of Federalist appointees—upheld the constitutionality of the repealer.

Thus when Justice Samuel Chase, in May 1803, said in his charge to a grand jury of Baltimore, "The late alteration of the federal judiciary . . . and the recent change in our state constitution, by the establishing of universal suffrage . . . will . . . take away all security for property and personal liberty . . . and our Republican constitution will sink into a mobocracy, the worst of all popular governments," he figuratively waved a red flag at a bull. He denounced a major piece of legislation passed by the Republican administration, which had been thought necessary to correct the political excesses represented by the Judiciary Act of 1801. This new challenge was not the only grievance that the Republicans had against the conduct of Chase, and it could not help but remind them of their earlier grievances. Chase, the hanging judge, trying John Fries in Philadelphia; Chase, the prejudiced martinet, trying James Callender in Richmond; Chase, the political judge, forcing the Supreme Court to delay its August 1800 term while he campaigned in Maryland for the reelection of John Adams as president. The historian Henry Adams has summed up the matter in these words:

> If one judge of the United States should have known the peril in which the judiciary stood, it was Justice Samuel Chase of Maryland, who had done more than all the other judges to exasperate the democratic majority. His overbearing manners had twice driven from his court the most eminent counsel of the circuit; he had left the bench without a quorum in order that he might make political speeches for his party; and his contempt for the popular will was loudly expressed.[7]

Jefferson's letter to Nicholson suggesting that Chase ought to be impeached, written as soon as he learned of Chase's grand-jury charge, is scarcely surprising.

Historians have speculated as to whether Jefferson's elliptical suggestion to Nicholson that Chase be impeached might have been the opening volley in an attack that, if successful, would have led to the removal of other members of the Supreme Court. There is no doubt that some of the Republicans, such as Virginia Senator William Branch Giles, had this in mind. But whether Jefferson was of this view is a much more debatable question.

Jefferson had undoubtedly deeply resented the episode of the Midnight Judges; he saw it as an effort by the Federalists, defeated at the polls, to frustrate the popular verdict rendered in the election of 1800. The repeal of the Judiciary Act of 1801 was a political victory for the Republicans, and Samuel Chase's criticism of the repealer galled Jefferson. His reaction was to suggest Chase's impeachment. But the very circumstances in which he reacted—the provocative charge to the grand jury by Chase—suggests more a fit of pique on his part than the implementation of a carefully planned strategy to purge all the Federalist justices from the Supreme Court.

Thomas Jefferson was a party leader, and—unlike the Federalists—he wished very much to build an inclusive party rather than an exclusive one. He was president of the United States, and had numerous concerns other than his dislike of the federal judiciary with which to deal. He was quite capable of moving toward an objective with muffled oars, but he was also capable of changing the objective even as he rowed. For all of these reasons, judgment must at least be reserved as to how far Jefferson would have been willing to go in May 1803, first in his desire to remove Chase, and second in pursuit of a desire to remove other members of the Supreme Court.

Jefferson was the head of a party that, like most political parties, was anything but monolithic. John Randolph, who would lead for the House managers in the trial of Chase before the Senate, represented the "old Republican" element, and he viewed the election of 1800 as a call for radical action.

But this faction of the party by itself could not have delivered the victory the party received in the election of 1800. The more moderate Republicans saw no need for structural change in the government, and wished only to end what they regarded as Federalist excesses and abuse of power during the time that party had been in office. Indeed, they thought that by a wise administration of the national government many who were then Federalists could be attracted to the ranks of the Republicans. Albert Gallatin, whom Jefferson selected to be his secretary of the treasury, wrote to the president in that vein:

> It is so important for the permanent establishment of those Republican principles for which we have successfully contended, that they should rest on the broad basis of the people, and not on a fluctuating majority, that it would be better to displease many of our political friends than to give an opportunity to the irreconcilable enemies of a free government of inducing the mass of the federal citizens to make a common cause with them.[8]

Not only as party leader, but as president, Jefferson had to consider the different views within his own party, and his own desire to attract independents and moderate Federalists to its ranks. As president he also found, like many others after him, that the responsibilities of the office might change the views of the occupant. In March 1803—two months before Chase's charge to the grand jury—James Monroe had sailed to France as Jefferson's special envoy to assist the American minister in Paris, Robert R. Livingston, to purchase New Orleans from the French. In 1802 the Spanish authorities at the port of New Orleans had revoked the right of deposit previously accorded to American traders, whereby they might deposit their produce at New Orleans for transshipment without having to pay duty on it. This dismayed the settlers living beyond the Appalachians, who were heavily dependent upon shipment by way of the Mississippi River and its tributaries in order to get their produce to market. Actually, by the secret Treaty of San Ildefonso, signed in 1800, Spain had ceded the vast territory known as Louisiana to France, but possession had not changed at that time and the agreement was not publicized. It was only in 1802 that the U.S. representatives learned that in the long run they must deal with a newly powerful France, under Napoleon, rather than a much feebler Spain, with respect to the territory west of the Mississippi River.

At first the negotiations between Livingston and Monroe, for the United States, and the responsible French minister had dragged, but in late April the French ministry offered to sell not merely New Orleans, but the entire territory of Louisiana—an area comprising roughly all of the territory drained by the Mississippi River and lying west of it—to the United States for fifteen million dollars. Jefferson received word of the signing of the agreement at the end of June 1803 and broke the news in this country. The Republicans rejoiced, while the Federalists brooded, over this latest development.

As a matter of fact, Jefferson and his adherents were every bit as surprised as the Federalists by the purchase that Monroe and Livingston had made for the United States. Their instructions had been to seek New Orleans, and perhaps the area along the Gulf Coast known as the Spanish Floridas—almost all of this being *east* of the Mississippi—with the fallback position that this country would be willing to acquire only the city of New Orleans. But the envoys had purchased the city of New Orleans and a great empire *west* of the Mississippi, whose distant boundaries were only vaguely defined. The amount of money they had been authorized to pay was two million dollars; they had agreed to pay eight times that amount—fifteen million dollars. How would an administration that had proclaimed frugality as its watchword justify this expenditure to Congress?

The two political parties switched their traditional roles in the ensuing debate. Jefferson and the Republicans had proclaimed their doctrine of strict construction of the Constitution in the Virginia and Kentucky resolutions, and Jefferson and Madison had opposed the chartering of the Bank of the United States on the grounds that the Constitution had not specifically delegated to Congress the authority to charter a bank. But the Constitution likewise granted to Congress no specific authority to acquire additional territory. At first Jefferson himself drew up drafts of an amendment to the Constitution which would authorize the acquisition of Louisiana, but then word came from Livingston and Monroe that Napoleon was having seller's remorse about the transaction and would seize upon any reason to avoid it. Jefferson then urged his supporters in Congress to ratify the purchase "*sub silentio*" and "with as little debate as possible, and particularly so far as respects the constitutional difficulty." Thus Jefferson showed himself to be far more of a "pragmatist" than some of his earlier positions would have indicated.

The Federalists, on the other hand, urged the lack of constitutional authority in the Senate debates over ratification. On October 20, 1803, the Senate ratified the treaty acquiring Louisiana by a vote of 24 to 7, with all but one Federalist senator voting nay.

Thus Jefferson's desire to see the boundaries of this country pushed westward to the Rocky Mountains prevailed over his insistence on a strict construction of the Constitution. This most important accomplishment of his administration—and surely one of the most important accomplishments of any presidential administration in the history of this country—all but inexorably foreshadowed the idea of "manifest destiny," which would, within the next half century, make the United States extend from the Atlantic Ocean to the Pacific Ocean. The acquisition of this vast territory was no part of Jefferson's program for his administration, but it was the seizure of an opportunity of the moment.

Jefferson was like this; he was willing to subordinate some values that he believed in to accomplish ends that he believed in more. He was sufficiently offended by Samuel Chase's charge to the Baltimore grand jury to suggest to Joseph Nicholson that the House of Representatives commence impeachment proceedings. But how hard he would be willing to press the members of his own party in an effort to remove Chase, or whether if Chase was removed he would seek removal of other members of the Supreme Court, it was impossible to say at that time.

-4-

*T*he first day of the trial of Samuel Chase before the United States Senate—Monday, February 4, 1805—was given over entirely to Chase's reading aloud to the assembled senators his very detailed response to the charges brought against him. The House managers were then given time to file a reply to this response, and it was not until Saturday, February 9, that the first witnesses were called by the House managers. These witnesses would testify as to Chase's conduct of the trial of John Fries for treason in Philadelphia in 1800.

Philadelphia at that time was not only the capital of the United States, but it was the largest city in the country and the second-largest city in the English-speaking world. It had a population of 70,000; New York, 60,000; Boston, 25,000; Charleston, South Carolina, 18,000; and Baltimore, 13,000.

Philadelphia, unlike other major United States cities at the time, was built on William Penn's gridiron pattern and was the only city in the United States to have municipal street cleaners.

> Philadelphia, which served as the national capital until 1800, was generally agreed to be the cleanest, best-governed, healthiest, and most elegant of American cities. Neither London nor Paris, thought Jefferson, was quite so handsome as Philadelphia, and travelers rarely failed to remark its solid, prosperous atmosphere of sober well-being. It had the finest church in the nation (Anglican Christ Church), the largest public building (the State House), the most book shops and publishing houses, the

most banks, and the largest public market. It was the center of American medical and scientific study, and, with the possible exception of Boston, the nation's foremost educational center. Philadelphia had a planned street system (with even-numbered houses on one side, odd on the other), street-cleaning and watering services, excellent street lamps, a patrol and watch system, a good water supply with a steam pump, and a strong tradition of civic responsibility that derived from the days of Franklin. Its buildings, the traveler Charles Janson wrote in 1799, "are well built, chiefly of red brick, and in general three stories high. A great number of private houses have marble steps to the street door, and in other respects are finished in a style of elegance." Three-fifths of Philadelphia's streets were paved and had brick sidewalks with gutter and curb. High Street (later Market) was 100 feet wide, Broad Street 113 feet. The Philadelphia Market, an arcaded one-story building a half-mile long, was undoubtedly the finest in the world.[1]

The part of the charges against Chase that were based on his conduct at the Fries trial in Philadelphia were contained in the first of the Articles of Impeachment. They charged that he "did, in his judicial capacity, conduct himself in a manner highly arbitrary, oppressive, and unjust, viz.

1. In delivering an opinion, in writing, on the question of law, on the construction of which the defence of the accused materially depended, tending to prejudice the minds of the jury against the case of the said John Fries, the prisoner, before counsel had been heard in his defence:

2. In restricting the counsel for the said Fries from recurring to such English authority as they believed apposite, or from citing certain statutes of the United States, which they deemed illustrative of the positions, upon which they intended to rest the defence of their client:

3. In debarring the prisoner from his constitutional privilege of addressing the jury (through his counsel) on the

law, as well as on the facts, which was to determine his guilt, or innocence, and at the same time endeavoring to wrest from the jury their indisputable right to hear argument, and determine upon the question of law, as well as the question of fact, involved in the verdict which they were required to give. . . ."

Every trial is an effort—through the testimony of witnesses—to re-create at a later time events that have occurred in the past. The Chase trial was an effort to re-create the Fries trial, but the Fries trial in turn had been an effort to re-create the crucial events of Fries's Rebellion in 1798. There would be no testimony about Fries's Rebellion at Chase's trial—only testimony from several different witnesses about Chase's conduct of Fries's trial for that rebellion. But a brief account of Fries's rebellion is important as background for understanding this part of the charges against Chase.

After Congress enacted the Federal Property Tax in 1798 to raise money for the prosecution of the undeclared war against France, Pennsylvania, like other states, was divided into districts for the purpose of assessing and collecting the revenues. Assessors were appointed to appraise property and levy the tax in each of these districts. While this was not popular anywhere, opposition was extremely strong in Bucks and Northampton counties, which lay north of Philadelphia along the Delaware River. Many of the inhabitants of these counties violently resisted the efforts of the assessors and seized their assessment rolls.

The leader of this opposition was John Fries, a man of little education but considerable force of character. He had commanded a company of militia both during the Revolutionary War and also when the militia was called out to suppress the Whiskey Rebellion. In 1798 Fries was about fifty years old, and up until then had been a warm supporter of the Federalists and of the administration of John Adams.

When it became obvious that the local authorities could not enforce the assessment of the tax in this part of Pennsylvania, Judge Peters in the Federal District Court in Philadelphia issued warrants of arrest for some of the participants in the insurrection, and the marshal of the court arrested a number of persons and took them in his custody to Bethlehem, Pennsylvania. But then over one hundred armed insurgents proceeded to Bethlehem under the leadership of Fries and released the prisoners. No one was killed and no one was injured.

It was at this point that President John Adams issued his proclamation calling for the suppression of the rebellion. Fries was arrested and indicted for treason, which was then and is now a capital offense. He was tried and convicted the first time in Philadelphia in 1799 before Justice Paterson, a member of the Supreme Court of the United States, and Judge Peters. But the court granted him a new trial because of the possible bias against him of one of the jurors. Thus his trial before Justice Chase and Judge Peters in Philadelphia in 1800 was his second trial on this charge.

There was never really any dispute at either trial as to Fries's leading role in the rebellion. The principal question was one of law—whether his conduct had amounted to "treason" under the laws and Constitution of the United States. Thus the court's ruling on this question was especially important to Fries. Treason is the only crime defined in the United States Constitution, and the framers defined it strictly in order to make clear that they rejected some of the earlier English decisions in which men had been charged with treason for such things as imagining the death of the king. Article III, Section 3 provides:

> Treason against the United States, shall consist only in levying War against them, or in adhering to their Enemies, giving them Aid and Comfort. No Person shall be convicted of Treason unless on the Testimony of two Witnesses to the same overt Act, or on Confession in open Court.
>
> The Congress shall have power to declare the Punishment of Treason. . . .

Since the United States was not at war at the time of Fries's Rebellion, Fries could not be charged with "adhering to their Enemies," or "giving them Aid and Comfort." He could only be charged with levying war. At his first trial, Fries's lawyers had argued that if the armed rebellion had been directed only at one objectionable law it did not amount to levying war against the United States.

But the court had rejected this argument and ruled that any armed resistance to the enforcement of a federal statute could be treasonable.

The first two witnesses called by the House managers at the Senate trial were William Lewis and Alexander Dallas, the two lawyers who had represented Fries in the first trial and had undertaken to represent him at the second trial. William Lewis had been the lead counsel for Fries at both of his trials. Lewis was then about fifty years of age, and it is said that he was six feet in height as he stood, and would have been more but for the stoop of his shoulders. He was thin almost to the point of emaciation, with his most prominent feature being an extremely long nose. He had a deep, sonorous voice.

Horace Binney, writing half a century later, described Lewis's principal vice:

> He smoked cigars incessantly. He smoked at the fireplace in court. He smoked in the court library. He smoked in his office. He smoked in the street. He smoked in bed; and he would have smoked in church like Knockdunder, in the "Heart of Midlothian," if he had ever gone there. The smoking in bed was, in one instance, literally verified by myself and my venerable master, upon a winter journey to the Supreme Court at Washington, in the year 1809, when, in the days of coaching, we passed our first night at the Head of Elk; and I called Mr. Ingersoll's attention to it, after we had got into our respective beds in the same large room, and the last candle had been extinguished. The cigar was then seen firing up from Mr. Lewis' pillow, and disappearing in darkness like a revolving light on the coast.[2]

Lewis was a specialist in defending treason cases, of which there had been a great number in Philadelphia during and immediately after the American Revolution. He was a fierce guardian of the independence of the bar, and of the fullest right of defense on behalf of an accused criminal, so it is understandable that he was deeply offended by Chase's manner of proceeding at the Fries trial. He was interrogated by John Randolph for the House managers.

He stated that he was counsel for Fries at the second trial, and entered the courtroom on the morning of the day on which the trial was scheduled. Before the jurors in the case were called, Justice Chase said that he had been informed that at the previous trial of the case there had been a great waste of time in making long speeches on topics that had nothing to do with the business at hand, and in reading common-law cases. To prevent this in the future, Chase said, the court (consisting of himself and Judge Peters) had made up its mind as to the proper definition of treason, and had reduced its opinion to writing, in order that counsel might govern themselves accordingly.

Lewis's reaction had been immediate and dramatic. He said that he did not read a single line of the paper containing the opinion, but that "either waving my hand, or throwing the paper from me, I used this expression, 'I will never permit my hand to be tainted with a prejudged opinion in any case, much less in a capital one.' " Lewis then recounted that Justice Chase had said that the judges were the final authority on the law, and that if counsel thought they were wrong, counsel must address themselves to the court for that purpose, and not to the jury. Lewis then sent for his co-counsel, Alexander Dallas, and they both told Fries that they could render him better service by withdrawing from his defense than by continuing as his attorneys. Fries, understandably, was much taken aback at this advice, but he eventually acquiesced in it.

The following morning Justice Chase addressed Lewis and Dallas, and asked if they were ready to proceed with the Fries trial. Lewis responded that he and Dallas were no longer counsel for Fries, having withdrawn in protest over the court's action on the previous day. At this time both Justice Chase and Judge Peters urged counsel to remain in the case, and said they would remove any previous restriction that had been imposed on their conduct. But Lewis and Dallas remained adamant.

Lewis testified that he thought if Fries was convicted, he would be more likely to be pardoned by President Adams if he had been tried without counsel.

The managers next called Alexander J. Dallas. He was a prominent member of the Philadelphia bar, and would later serve in President James Madison's Cabinet as secretary of the treasury. He had risen to the top of his profession from humble beginnings in the British colony of Jamaica. He emigrated to the United States in 1783, and combined the practice of law with an active interest in Republican politics and sundry writings. From 1790 until 1800, he edited the reports of decisions of the United States Supreme Court, as well as of the federal court sitting in Pennsylvania and the Pennsylvania state courts. The physical appearance of Alexander Dallas is said to have been commanding. He was meticulous in dress, and kept the custom of powdering his hair after most other people had abandoned it.

After explaining how he was originally engaged to represent Fries, Dallas recounted his entrance to the courtroom on the day that Justice Chase had announced his written opinion on the subject of treason at the start of the second trial. Lewis accosted him upon his entrance into the courtroom, and explained what had previously happened. His account of the proceedings conformed closely to that of Lewis.

On the second day, Dallas said, both Chase and Peters announced that the opinion delivered the previous day had been withdrawn, and that counsel could proceed as they chose, Chase adding, "but it is at the hazard of your characters." This statement offended both Dallas and Lewis, and Lewis said to Chase, "You have withdrawn the papers; but can you eradicate from your own minds the opinion which you have formed, or the effect of your declaration on the attending jurors, a part of whom must try the prisoner?"

The Senate, after hearing the testimony of Lewis and Dallas, rose at four o'clock on Saturday afternoon, and convened again the following Monday at noon. The House managers called Edward Tilghman, an attorney who was present in the Philadelphia courtroom on the first day of the second Fries trial. He gave a more detailed description of William Lewis's reaction when Chase handed down the written opinion to the clerk:

> "The paper, as well as I can recollect, was then handed by Mr. Caldwell, the clerk of the court, to Mr. Lewis. Mr. Lewis cast his eyes on the outside of the paper, and looked down, as if he was considering what to say. He threw the paper from him, as it appeared to me, without reading it, and the moment he threw the paper down,

said, 'My hand shall never be stained by receiving a paper containing a prejudged opinion, or an opinion made
up without hearing counsel.' . . . When Mr. Lewis used
these expressions, his face was not turned to the court,
and he spoke with a considerable degree of warmth; the
court sat in the south part of the room, and Mr. Lewis
(I think) turned his face full to the westward, when he
used these expressions."

Tilghman also confirmed that on the second day both Chase
and Peters were very anxious that counsel should continue in the
defense of Fries, but they declined. On the third day of the trial
Justice Chase asked Fries if he wished other counsel, and he said
he did not. Chase then said that the court would be his counsel,
"And by the blessing of God, will serve you as effectually as your
counsel could have done." (In the event the court did not serve
Fries too well, because he was again convicted of treason and sentenced to hang. But William Lewis's prediction came to pass:
President Adams granted him a pardon.)

Robert Harper, one of Chase's attorneys, questioned Tilghman
as to whether Chase had stated that counsel must address themselves in making an argument on the law only to the court, whether
they might also argue to the jury. Tilghman replied that Chase
had not imposed any such restriction.

Later that day the House managers called William Rawle, who
rather than be sworn simply affirmed (as had William Lewis). Rawle
had been the United States attorney in Philadelphia and prosecuted Fries for treason at both his trials. He confirmed the substance of the testimony of the previous witnesses about the opinion
Chase had handed down from the bench at the beginning of the
second Fries trial—indeed, there was no real dispute about what
had happened. But Rawle added some facts to which he was privy
but to which the others were not.

Rawle testified that the court had risen before noon on the
morning of the first day of the Fries matter, and he had thereupon
gone home. He had been there only a few minutes when who
should appear at his door but Justice Chase and Judge Peters.
Peters then expressed great concern that Lewis and Dallas would
withdraw; Chase said he could not believe that they would do

this. Rawle agreed with Peters, saying that "the gentlemen of the Philadelphia bar were men of much independence and character, and that unless those papers were withdrawn, and the business conducted as usual at our bar, they would probably desist from conducting the defense." Chase regretted that the action of the court should have offended counsel, and said that he had not meant that anything he had done should prevent the lawyers from defending the case in the usual manner.

Peters then asked Rawle if he would go out and recover the "papers" (copies of the Chase opinion, which had been made by several of the lawyers present in the court at the time); Rawle agreed. He then went to the houses of two of the lawyers whom he had seen copying the papers, and asked them for the copies, which they readily gave him. These copies were returned to the clerk of the court.

Rawle then gave his own account of the proceedings in court the next morning:

> "The court asked if we were ready to proceed. Justice Chase said to the defense lawyers, 'You are not bound by the opinion delivered yesterday, you may contest it on both sides.' Mr. Lewis answered, 'I understood that the court had made up their minds, and as the prisoner's counsel have a right to make a full defense, and address the jury both on the law and the facts, it would place me in too degrading a situation, and therefore I will not proceed.' Judge Chase answered with apparent impatience—'You are at liberty to proceed as you think proper, address the jury and lay down the law as you think proper.' Mr. Lewis answered with considerable emphasis, 'I will never address the court on a criminal case on a question of law.' . . . Mr. Dallas then addressed the court. He contended that the rights of advocates had been encroached upon by the proceedings of the day before."

Rawle testified that he, like Lewis and Dallas, had never seen a court give an opinion on a legal question before counsel were heard in any criminal case he had tried. When he was later recalled as a witness by counsel for Chase, he stated his understanding that the restrictions as to the arguments of counsel applied to the prosecution as well as to the defense.

Robert Goodloe Harper, one of Chase's counsel, upon discovering that William Rawle had brought with him a copy of the opinion that Chase had handed down from the bench, offered it in evidence. The opinion said that the constitutional definition of treason was a "question of law," just like the question of what a particular statute meant, but the opinion went on to say:

> It is the duty of the court in this, and in all *criminal* cases, to state to the jury, their opinion of the law arising on the facts; but the jury are to decide on the present, and in all criminal cases, both the law and the facts, on their consideration of the whole case.

The court went on to state that it was of the opinion "that any . . . insurrection or rising to resist or to prevent by force or violence, the execution of any statute of the United States, for levying or collecting taxes, duties, imposts or excises; or for calling forth the militia to execute the laws of the Union, or for any other purpose . . . is a levying war against the United States, within the Constitution."

This was the essence of the testimony before the Senate as to Chase's conduct of the trial of John Fries in Philadelphia in 1800.

Chase himself did not testify in question-and-answer form at his trial before the Senate, but the statement he read to the Senate on the first day of the trial detailed his response to these charges. He said, first, that he believed himself bound by the authority of previous decisions of the same court on the point of law involved, the first of these decisions having been given by Justice Paterson of the Supreme Court of the United States and Judge Peters in the first trial of Fries, and the other having been given by Justice Iredell of the Supreme Court and Judge Paterson in the cases of Michell and Vigol. He said that he had given a copy of his opinion to Judge Peters, who had agreed with its substance. He was satisfied that the opinion was correct as to the law that it stated, but he made the point that its correctness should not be the subject of examination at an impeachment trial.

He also stated that there had been about one hundred civil cases to be disposed of at that session of the District Court in Philadelphia, and that there was a corresponding need for reasonable speed in moving the docket. Finally, he said that in his view the real reason that Lewis and Dallas had withdrawn from their representation of Fries was because they had seen that both the law and facts were against them, and that Fries would very likely be convicted; they sought to "excite odium" against the court by their withdrawal, and make it appear that Fries had been unjustly convicted in order to pave the way for a presidential pardon.

What are we to make of these charges against Chase, and his response? First, a preliminary word of caution, familiar to lawyers and judges but perhaps not to others. All we have available to us today is the transcript—the written notes made by a court reporter at the Senate trial—of what each witness said. While we may assume that the report is accurate, a mere record of questions and answers tells us nothing about what courts call the "demeanor" of the witness—the expression on his face, his attitude, his intonation, and similar things that the senators sitting in judgment were able to view firsthand. It is the difference between reading a letter from someone and talking to the person face-to-face; the words used in the conversation may be the same as the ones used in the letter, but because one is able to see the person with whom one is conversing, the conversation may give an entirely different impression from the letter.

Horace Binney, a half century later, wrote that he, too, had been present in the courtroom on the first day of the Fries trial in 1800. He stated that Lewis's conduct had the full sympathy of the bar. But he went on to say:

> The act of the Court was not regarded by the Bar as one of intended oppression of either the prisoner or his counsel, but as a great mistake, resulting, in part, from the character of the principal judge, a very learned and able man, but confident and rather imperious, and in part from his greater familiarity with the Maryland practice, where the judge used to respond, and perhaps still does, more exclusively, for the law, and the jury for the facts, . . . than was . . . the usage in Pennsylvania.[3]

What was being argued about here was an event that occurs in every trial: At the close of the evidence, the court "charges" the jury—instructs them—as to what the applicable law is. The written opinion that Chase handed to counsel on the first day of the trial was a statement of how he would charge the jury on the question of the law of treason. Looking at the matter from today's perspective, what Chase did was somewhat unusual, but by no means unknown. In my own practice of law in Arizona, extending over sixteen years in state and federal courts, every judge would decide questions of law and leave to the jury questions of fact. Most of the judge's rulings on questions of law would be contained in his charge to the jury given *after* all the evidence was in, but before the jury began its deliberations. It would have been most unusual during the time when I practiced for a lawyer to argue to the jury that the law was different from what the judge had said it was in his charge; indeed, it would have been so unusual that the lawyer would risk a reprimand from the judge.

The instructions the judge was to give the jury would be "settled" at some convenient point during trial. Each lawyer would submit to the judge proposed instructions—favoring his client, of course—for the judge to use in telling the jury what law was applicable to the case. Usually the judge would discuss these proposed instructions with counsel rather informally during a recess at the trial. If any lawyer deemed an instruction to be critical to his case, most judges—but by no means all—would hear a brief argument on the point. But some judges—particularly, it seemed to us, visiting federal judges from other states—would decide what instructions to give without counsel even being present. Judges, of course, were not limited to simply choosing between the instructions proposed by the lawyers, and might decide to give a standard instruction or to devise an instruction they felt suitable for the case.

The rules of procedure required that counsel be given an opportunity at some point to state "for the record" their objections to those portions of the charge they thought were erroneous, but this occurred after the judge had made up his mind and often after he had charged the jury.

Chase stoutly maintained, and Binney in his vignette indicates that the members of the Philadelphia bar agreed, that the charge

Chase gave the jury was a correct statement of the law. And Chase's position in the matter is also strengthened by his view that he was bound by previous decisions of the same court on the same point, rendered in two different cases with two different Supreme Court justices participating. By the standards of today, Chase's refusal to hear argument of counsel on the point could be considered hasty and ill-considered because it was a crucial point of law in a capital case, but it falls far short of any basis for impeachment even under the most liberal view of what might satisfy that standard.

One must go back in time for many generations of lawyers to understand fully the sympathy felt by the Philadelphia bar for the predicament of William Lewis and Alexander Dallas in the second trial of John Fries. To them, and to most lawyers of their time, the process by which a court reached a decision on a point of law was every bit as important as the ultimate correctness of the decision. A point of law was to be decided in only one way: Granted the decision would be by the judge, but it would be by the judge only after sitting and listening to opposing lawyers, both of whom had steeped themselves in knowledge of the precedents and each of whom hoped to persuade the judge by the force of his argument. They had studied up on the point of law in a way the judge had not. The idea that a judge should trust himself to think the matter through to a conclusion without the benefit of argument of counsel was as strange to the lawyers of that day as if the judge should attempt to decide a point of law without consulting the relevant statutes or precedents.

One can see a parallel development in the relationship of judges to lawyers from the beginning of the nineteenth century to the present time in the role played by oral arguments of lawyers before the Supreme Court of the United States. Originally there was no limit set on the time a lawyer might devote to arguing his case in that Court. Indeed, the Court had so little to do in its first few years that it would have had no good reason to place time limits on counsels' arguments.

In 1824 the Court heard arguments in the famous case of *Gibbons* v. *Ogden*,[4] in which it broadly construed the power granted by the Constitution to Congress to regulate "commerce among the several states." The oral argument in that case began at eleven o'clock in the morning, when Daniel Webster opened for Gibbons. He took two and one half hours; Thomas J. Oakley, counsel for Ogden, followed, and spoke for an hour on February 4 and for the entire Court day of February 5—a total of five hours. Thomas Emmet spent the whole of the third day, February 6, and two hours of February 7—a total of six hours—delivering his argument. And the arguments were finally closed on February 8 by William Wirt on behalf of Gibbons. The arguments consumed a total of twenty hours—five full Court days, four hours a day.

But as the Supreme Court's docket grew more crowded, this sort of expenditure of time even in a very important case proved to be a luxury. In the middle of the nineteenth century, the Court placed a limit of two hours on the time to be taken by counsel for each side. In the early part of the twentieth century, the Court limited the time for counsel on each side to one hour. By the middle of this century many cases were heard under the one-hour-per-side limitation, but the Court was also developing a "summary docket" to which it assigned cases it thought justified only one half hour of argument on each side. By a rule adopted in 1970, the one-half-hour time limitation was made standard procedure, with additional time for argument given only in cases of great importance and difficulty.

The Supreme Court of the United States has been far stricter in limiting the time for oral argument than have other courts of last resort that have inherited the Anglo-Saxon legal system. In England, the House of Lords—which is the court of final appeal there—still places no time limits on oral argument. The Supreme Court of Canada placed time limits on oral argument for the first time in 1988, and I remember, while visiting Canada on a legal exchange program in 1987, hearing a very able and respected member of the Canadian bar declare that it would be a sad day for the profession if such limits were to be imposed. The High Court of Australia, as of 1991, still allows unlimited oral argument in the cases it hears.

In the best of all worlds, the system would probably be best served by a bar thoroughly steeped in its obligation to the courts and limited only by self-discipline as to the amount of time a lawyer might take in arguing a point of law. But the position to which courts in this country have gradually come is that time is a commodity in very short supply, and if the courts are to decide the number of cases the public expects them to decide, the amount of time allowed for oral argument must be rationed.

In this sense, we can see that Samuel Chase was a much more modern judge than one might have expected. Because of the more than one hundred civil cases pending on the docket of the district court in Philadelphia at this time, Chase thought it imperative not to spend the court's time on arguments he regarded as all but useless. The arguments for and against this position are evident— to the lawyer and his client, the particular case in which they are involved is all-important, since someone's life, liberty, or property will depend on the outcome. But the court must necessarily view each particular case in the context of a larger docket: "Justice delayed is justice denied," and however important the case may be to the individual litigants, it must take its place along with a number of other cases that have an equal claim on the court's time.

While Chase had modern instincts about case management, he was also imperious and high-handed in his dealings with lawyers, not an appealing trait in a judge.

> Samuel Chase, of Maryland, one of the signers of the Declaration of Independence, a man of ripe legal learning, but of an arbitrary spirit, became an associate justice in 1796. From the beginning he was unpopular with the Philadelphia bar, owing to his despotic manner on the bench.
>
> In an important case before the court, says David Paul Brown in his "Forum," a learned gentleman by the name of Samuel Leake, from Trenton, was engaged. Mr. Leake was generally remarkable for the number of authorities to which he referred, and upon this occasion he had brought a considerable portion of his library into court, and was arranging the books upon the table at the time the judge took his seat, when the following colloquy took place:
>
> > Judge Chase "What have you got there, sir?"
> > Leake "My books, sir."
> > Judge Chase "What for?"
> > Leake "To cite my authorities."

Judge Chase "To whom?"
Leake "To your honor."
Judge Chase "I'll be d———d if you do."[5]

Viewing the matter as best we can from the perspective of the beginning of the nineteenth century, Chase's refusal to hear argument on the definition of treason in the second Fries trial was probably exceptional; he himself retreated on the second day from the position that he had first taken with respect to hearing argument on the proposed instruction. Whether it constituted a "high crime or misdemeanor" of the sort required for impeachment and conviction was of course another question. Judged even by the standards of 1800, it seems to me that it was at most an error of judgment, and surely not a ground for removal from office.

The second and third charges against Chase in connection with the Fries trial—that he refused to allow counsel to argue to the jury their own view of the law in the manner they wished to do— seems not to have been made out by the evidence presented to the Senate. The Chase opinion that was produced by William Rawle at the request of Robert Goodloe Harper stated that it was the duty of the court in a criminal case to state to the jury its opinion of the law, but that the jury was to decide both the law and the facts of the case. Chase's opinion would have made it much more difficult for counsel to persuade the jury that their view, rather than the court's, was the correct one, but it is very difficult to deduce from the testimony the Senate heard that Chase had actually forbidden the lawyers to argue their own view of the law to the jury.

-5-

The charges on which Chase was tried before the Senate were arranged in chronological order. First came the Fries trial in Philadelphia in April 1800, and next came a series of charges based on the trial of James Callender in Richmond in early June of that year. Callender was indicted by a federal grand jury for violating the Sedition Act.

In 1798 the Federalist-dominated Congress had passed this law, which made it a misdemeanor punishable by fine or imprisonment to speak or write against the president or Congress with the intent to defame them or bring them into contempt or disrepute. The act was based on the English common-law doctrines of seditious libel, but the American law was more lenient than the English in that it allowed proof by the defendant of the truth of the libel as a defense. The act also provided that "the jury which shall try the cases shall have a right to determine the law and the facts under the direction of the judge." The new law was denounced by the Republicans and by some Federalists as being violative of the First Amendment to the United States Constitution, which prohibited Congress from "abridging the freedom of speech, or of the press."

The federal grand jury in Richmond indicted Callender for statements made in his book *The Prospect Before Us*, published in that same year. The grand jury returned a two-count indictment against Callender, in which were listed twenty "charges" of portions of the book the grand jury found to be defamatory. The only one material for our purposes was the twelfth charge; it cited passages that said that President John Adams was a professed aristocrat, and that he had proved faithful and serviceable to the British interest.

Callender was not an admirable champion of freedom of the press. Julius Goebel, Jr., in his history of the beginning period of the Supreme Court of the United States, refers to Callender as "one of the reptilian adornments of contemporary journalism."[1] Jefferson's biographer Dumas Malone describes him as "one of the most notorious scandal-mongers and character assassins in American history."[2] Callender was born in Scotland in 1758, and it appears that he was forced to leave that country to avoid prosecution for the publication of a political pamphlet. He settled in Philadelphia and reported the proceedings of Congress for a Philadelphia newspaper; in 1796 we find him in Baltimore appealing to James Madison for appointment to the position of a schoolmaster. Later he published a work titled *History of 1796* with the financial assistance of others (including Alexander J. Dallas, counsel for John Fries at his trial). By 1800 he was living in Richmond, where *The Prospect Before Us* was published.

After being convicted for violation of the Sedition Act in a trial before Justice Chase and Judge Cyrus Griffin in the spring of 1800, Callender was sentenced to nine months' imprisonment and ordered to pay a fine of $200. When Jefferson became president in March 1801, he pardoned Callender and ordered the remission of his fine. Because of legal complications, it took time to return the money to Callender, and in the meantime he turned against Jefferson. Callender charged that Jefferson had taken one of his slaves, Sally Hemmings, as a mistress. In publicizing this charge, Callender included this parody on "Yankee Doodle" taken from a Boston newspaper:

> *Of all the damsels on the green,*
> *On mountain, or in valley,*
> *Alas so luscious ne'er was seen,*
> *As the Monticellian Sally.*
>
> *Yankee Doodle, who's the noodle?*
> *What wife were half so handy?*
> *To breed a flock of slaves for stock,*
> *A blackamoor's the dandy.*[3]

Callender died in July 1803; his body was found in three feet of water in the James River in Richmond. Officially his death was ruled accidental by reason of intoxication, but a Richmond newspaper expressed the view that it was actually suicide.

Richmond in the year 1800 had a population of 5,735 inhabitants. Incredibly by today's standards—where two newspapers in a metropolitan area such as Detroit find themselves obliged to share operating costs in order that both may survive financially—there were four newspapers in Richmond at this time. One of them was put out by James Callender, the defendant in the sedition trial.

Five of the eight Articles of Impeachment against Samuel Chase were devoted to his conduct while presiding at the trial of James Callender. Two of these five articles charged that Chase had failed to correctly apply Virginia law dealing with the method of proceeding against one charged with a misdemeanor. The most that can be said of these articles is that if proved, they showed that under Virginia law Callender should not have been tried at the term of court in which he was indicted, but at the next term. Chase had been appointed to the bench in 1796, but this was the first time he had sat and held court in Virginia, and an erroneous understanding of Virginia law under these circumstances could scarcely be thought of as grounds for impeachment. This is particularly so when his colleague on the bench, Judge Cyrus Griffin, who had been a practicing Virginia lawyer before his appointment, concurred with him.

The Articles of Impeachment also charged Chase with having improperly refused to grant Callender's attorneys a continuance—a postponement—until the following term of court in order that they might assemble witnesses and documents necessary for their defense. The affidavit filed by the attorneys indicated that witnesses would have to be summoned from as far away as New Hampshire to the north and South Carolina to the south, which in those days of travel by stagecoach would have been a considerable feat. Chase's answer, and in this he was supported by several neutral witnesses who testified at the impeachment trial, stated that he offered to continue the trial for several weeks, so long as it could be tried at that term of the court in Richmond. The granting of a continuance in a case has always been regarded as a matter in which the trial judge has a great deal of discretion, and it is difficult to fault Chase for his ruling on this point.

The House managers had done their cause no good when they lumped together charges such as these with the more serious charges contained in the other three articles.

The latter charges were these:

1. Chase, over the objection of defense counsel, ordered one John Basset to be seated as a juror even though Basset stated that he had made up his mind that the language used in Callender's book was defamatory of Adams.

2. Chase had refused to allow the testimony of Colonel John Taylor, a witness called by the defense, to be admitted in evidence.

3. Chase had required defense counsel to put their questions to Taylor in writing, for examination by the court, rather than allowing them to be asked orally.

4. Chase had repeatedly interrupted and harassed defense counsel in the presentation of their case.

Before turning to the testimony received by the Senate at Chase's impeachment trial on these points, it is worth noting that just as the trial of John Fries in Philadelphia had been held before Chase and District Judge Peters, the trial of James Callender in Richmond was held before Chase and District Judge Griffin. One of the points made by Chase in his defense to the charges based on each of these trials was that if he was guilty, surely Judge Peters, in the case of Fries, and Judge Griffin, in the case of Callender, were equally guilty. Judging from the testimony adduced, Chase was the sort of person whose personality, combined with his superior office, led him to dominate the proceedings. During the Callender trial he appears to have conferred on occasion, sotto voce, with Griffin, but the latter comes across as very much a junior partner.

The first witness called by the House managers was George Hay, who was the lead counsel for Callender at his trial. Hay was now forty years old; he had been thirty-five years of age at the time of Callender's trial. He had studied law and been admitted to the Virginia bar, and had also been a member of the Virginia House of Delegates. When Jefferson became president in 1801, he appointed Hay as the United States attorney for the District of

Virginia, in which position he had the unenviable task of conducting the prosecution of Aaron Burr for treason in 1807. He was not only a lawyer and legislator, but an active pamphleteer in the Republican cause. He resolved that if anyone in Virginia was prosecuted under the Sedition Act, he would offer his services for the defense.

When Hay was called as a witness on the afternoon of Monday, February 11, 1805, by the House managers, he announced that because of the five-year lapse between the time of the Callender trial and the time of his present testimony, he found it necessary to refer to a statement written out by himself and the other counsel for Callender. At this point Robert Goodloe Harper, counsel for Chase, objected on the grounds that the statement had not been prepared solely by Hay. Aaron Burr inquired of Hay whether the written notes had been prepared by him, and Hay responded that some parts had been made by him, but others by Phillip Nicholas and William Wirt, who associated with him in the defense.

The Senate impeachment court was thereby plunged into one of the mares' nests of the law of evidence, characterized by subtle distinctions between "refreshing one's recollection" and "past recollection recorded." It was brought out during this discussion that the notes had not been written by Hay himself, but by a clerk who had taken them from a printed statement. Burr finally put the question to the Senate as to whether Hay would be allowed to use the written notes, and the Senate by a vote of 18 to 16 decided that he would not. Hay sulked about this ruling during his entire testimony, remarking several times that he could be much more certain of what he was saying if only he were allowed to use the notes.

Hay testified that when John Basset was called as a juror he expressed unwillingness to serve because he had formed an opinion about the case through reading a newspaper. But according to Hay, Justice Chase asked him whether he had formed and delivered an opinion concerning the charges in the indictment. Basset answered this question in the negative, and Chase placed him on the jury.

John Basset himself testified that he had ridden into Richmond early in the morning on the day of the Callender trial and there saw David Randolph, the marshal of the court, standing on the corner of the street.

> Perceiving me, he came towards me; before I alighted from my horse, he informed me that I had been summoned as a grand juror, and that for not appearing, had been crossed, that it was my duty to go to the court and justify myself for my absence; that he summoned me on the petit jury for the trial of Callender, and that my serving in that capacity would be an apology for my previous absences.

Basset showed up at court that day, but the trial had been continued until Tuesday. He presented himself the next day, and when called to be a juror, he had said in substance that he had never seen the book called *The Prospect Before Us*, but had seen some extracts from it in a newspaper. He felt that if the extracts were correctly taken from the book, it appeared to him to be seditious.

Chase's answer to the charge dealing with his having seated Basset as a juror at the Callender trial was that notwithstanding the opinion Basset had formed, the book itself, rather than the newspaper extracts, was what was to be judged at trial. Additional questions to be decided by the jury were whether the charges might be proved to be true at the trial of the case, whether Callender was actually the author and publisher of the book, and whether he wrote it with the intent to defame the president.

Chase went on to say:

> It is the duty of courts before which criminal trials take place, to prevent jurors from being excused for light and insufficient causes. If this rule were not observed, it would follow, that as serving on such trials as a juror, is apt to be a very disagreeable business, especially to those best qualified for it, there would be a great difficulty, and often an impossibility, in finding proper juries. The law has therefore established a fixed and general rule on this subject, calculated not to gratify the wishes or the unreasonable scruples of jurors, but to secure to the party ac-

cused, as far as in the imperfection of human nature it can be secured, a fair and impartial trial. . . .

It is impossible for any man in society to avoid having, and extremely difficult for him to avoid expressing, an opinion, as to the criminality or innocence of those acts, which for the most part are the subjects of indictments for offenses of a public nature; such as treason, sedition, and libels against the government. Such acts always engage public attention, and become the subject of public conversation; and if to have formed or expressed an opinion, as to the general nature of those acts, were a sufficient ground of challenge to a juror, when alleged against him, or of excuse from serving when alleged by himself, it would be in the power of almost every offender, to prevent a jury from being impannelled to try him, and of almost every man, to exempt himself from the unpleasant task of serving on such juries.

In 1800, as in the present day, jurors who were impartial as between the government and the criminal defendant had been thought essential to afford a fair trial. Chase in his defense appears to have been anticipating the modern problem of pretrial publicity, which comes not only from newspapers, but from television and radio as well. The Supreme Court of the United States has had to address this question numerous times, and in one recent case[4] has had to deal particularly with the question of the effect of pretrial publicity on potential jurors.

The *Murphy* case arose out of the conviction in Florida of "Murph the Surf" for the robbery of a home in Miami Beach, Florida. There had been extensive media coverage of several different criminal trials in which Murphy was a defendant, and he claimed that the jurors at his robbery trial had been influenced by the pretrial publicity. The Supreme Court in this case said that the mere existence of any preconceived notion as to the guilt or innocence of an accused was not enough to disqualify a person from jury service; it was sufficient if the prospective juror could lay aside his impression or opinion and render a verdict based on the evidence presented in court.

Based on the present-day standard laid down in the *Murphy* case, it would seem that Basset's opinion, based on a newspaper account, that there were passages in the book that were covered by the Sedition Act would not by itself have disqualified him as a juror. But once he had expressed that opinion, either the attorneys, the court, or both would have made further inquiry as to whether he thought he could fairly decide the case on the basis of the evidence presented at trial. Justice Chase's seating of Basset as a juror without this sort of further inquiry would seem to have been wrong by present-day standards.

Two of the other charges against Chase for his conduct of the Callender trial related to the testimony of Colonel John Taylor, who was called as a witness by the defense. Taylor—generally known as John Taylor of Caroline because of the county in which his plantations were located—was a longtime advocate of "strict construction" of the Constitution and a strong partisan of Jefferson. He had authored the famous Virginia Resolution by which the Virginia Assembly had denounced the Alien and Sedition Acts. He believed in states' rights, local democracy, and an essentially agrarian society.

Hay and Nicholas had not had an opportunity to confer with Taylor about his testimony, and so they were uncertain how to answer when Chase asked them what they proposed to prove by Taylor as a witness. The attorneys answered as best they could, to the effect that Taylor's testimony would "justify"—that is, prove the truth of—one of the twenty charges of libel in the indictment. Chase then told them to reduce the questions to writing. Hay and Nicholas objected, and Hay at the impeachment trial said that never before in his practice had such a requirement been imposed upon him. Chief Justice John Marshall, who also testified as a witness at the trial before the Senate, had been in the courtroom in Richmond during the Callender trial. He, too, said that this was the only time during his practice of law that he had ever heard a judge require that questions be reduced to writing.

Counsel reluctantly complied, and expressed the view that they did not wish to be limited to the three questions which they now presented in writing. Those questions were:

1. Did you ever hear Mr. Adams express any sentiments favorable to monarchy or aristocracy, and what were they?

2. Did you ever hear Mr. Adams, whilst Vice President, express his disapprobation of the funding system?

3. Do you know whether Mr. Adams did not in the year 1794, vote against the sequestration of British debts, and the suspension of intercourse with Great Britain?

Chase, after examining the questions, ruled that Taylor's evidence was inadmissible because it did not justify the entire twelfth charge. The charge was that the president was a professed aristocrat, and had proved faithful and serviceable to the British interests. Since Taylor's evidence would not prove the truth of all of this charge, it could not be admitted at all.

Chase, having raised this objection on his own, at this point nonetheless requested the U.S. attorney to waive any objection to the testimony, but the U.S. attorney stated that he did not feel he could do so.

Chase's insistence that questions on direct examination be submitted to the court in writing before they were propounded to the witness was, in the view of every witness who testified on that point at the impeachment trial, extraordinary. There was no doubt it was embarrassing to the lawyers, but how much it actually impeded the presentation of the defense seems debatable. For a judge to impose such a requirement in connection with the *cross-*examination of a witness would be far more damaging; on cross-examination, an alert lawyer will frequently use the witness's answer to the preceding question as the basis for his next question. Cross-examination is something that cannot usefully be prepared in advance by a detailed outline. Ordinarily, with *direct* examination it is different; there are a certain number of points a lawyer wishes to bring out with a particular witness, and the process of doing so is usually rather methodical. Chase's ruling here was more hurtful to defense counsel than it might have been because they had not previously had an opportunity to "horse shed" the witness: that is, in the legal parlance of an earlier day, to take the witness aside into the "horse shed" outside the courthouse and find out exactly what he would say in answer to particular questions.

Raoul Berger, in his work *Impeachment: The Constitutional Problems*, takes the view that Chase's ruling excluding Colonel Taylor's proposed testimony was egregiously wrong.[5] Julius Goebel, at least by implication, defends Chase's ruling.[6] The principle upon which Chase based his ruling, that in defending against a charge of libel, the defendant must "justify"—show the truth of—the entire charge was not disputed. But to require that the testimony of each witness show the truth of the entire charge is a highly unusual application of the traditional rules of evidence. Callender had said that Adams was an aristocrat, and that he was a toady to the British interests. The questions propounded to Taylor at the least could have proved that Adams was an aristocrat, and might marginally have brought out that on particular occasions he took a position favorable to Great Britain. While a trial judge has the authority to exclude evidence that is only marginally relevant and that is highly prejudicial in some other respect, that would not seem to have been the case here.

The Articles of Impeachment also charged that Chase had at times ridiculed defense counsel, and had interrupted them in their presentation of their case. Chase did on occasion make fun of defense counsel, and "play to the galleries." Colonel John Taylor, who was not allowed to testify at the Callender trial, got in his innings when he was called as a witness at the impeachment trial before the Senate. On cross-examination by Robert Goodloe Harper, the following colloquy occurred:

> Q. You have said, you considered the interruptions of the court as highly calculated to abash the counsel; did you mean thereby to give your opinion that they were so intended, or that such was their tendency?

> A. I thought they were so intended, and they had their full effect. They were followed by a great deal of mirth in the audience. The audience laughed, but the counsel never laughed at all.

Koko, the Lord High Executioner in Gilbert and Sullivan's opera *The Mikado*, places on his list of potential victims "that *Nisi Prius* nuisance, who just now is rather rife, The Judicial humorist." No one unfamiliar with the courtroom practice of law can fully realize the tremendous advantage that a judge has over the lawyers who appear before him, and the corresponding obligation upon the judge to refrain from ridiculing or making light of the lawyers. But Samuel Chase was either unaware of any such obligation or unwilling to acknowledge it.

At the Callender trial Chase was both the "Judicial humorist," and the imperious law professor teaching truant law students the law. George Hay urged upon the court the proposition that the jury had a right to determine every question necessary to the ultimate question of guilty or not guilty. Chase asked him whether he contended that this proposition was true in civil cases as well as in criminal cases—a question that might well be put by a law professor to a student who was reciting, but had no bearing on the criminal case that was then being tried. Hay answered, quite sensibly, that although he thought it was true in both civil and criminal cases, he thought he need only prove it was true in criminal cases.

Again, when William Wirt was urging another proposition on behalf of the defendant, he said the conclusion that followed was perfectly syllogistical. At this point Chase bowed to him "in a manner," Hay said, "which he could not describe," and said " 'a *non-sequitur*, Sir.' " And when Hay argued that under the law of Virginia the jury rather than the court should assess the fine, and that Virginia law governed the federal court in this case, Chase told him he was mistaken, and went on to say that the point he urged was "a wild notion."

The charge that Chase repeatedly interrupted the lawyers in the process of presenting their case is much more debatable. The lawyers insisted that they were arguing to Chase about their right to urge upon the jury that it decide that the Sedition Act violated the First Amendment to the United States Constitution. Chase's position was that they were in fact arguing the point to the jury, after he had ruled that this was a question to be decided by the court, and not by the jury. It is difficult to tell from the various versions of the matter given at the Senate impeachment trial, or indeed from a transcript of the Callender trial, who was right. Hay and Nicholas insisted that the judge so harassed them with his interruptions that ultimately they—like the lawyers for Fries in Philadelphia—picked up their papers, abandoned the case, and walked out of court. John Marshall was asked about the subject by John Randolph:

Q. Did the interruptions take place on the part of the court only when the counsel pressed the point of the unconstitutionality of the Sedition Law?

A. I believe that it was only at those times, but I do not recollect precisely.

George Hay was recalled as a witness by the managers after a number of other witnesses had testified, and on cross-examination gave this testimony in answer to questions from Harper:

Q. I understood you to say that it was your intention to argue the point. What point did you mean?

A. I meant to contend against the constitutionality of the second section of the Sedition Law.

Q. Did you not mean to argue it before the public, although you knew it would be unavailing if addressed to the Court? Did you mean by that argument to acquit the traverser, or to produce a political effect out of doors?

A. I meant to address my arguments to the Court. If they should work the acquittal of the traverser, or operate anywise in his favor, it was a thing to be desired; if they should affect also the public mind, that too was a desirable circumstance.

If Chase had refused to allow counsel to argue in the court a legal question, the situation would have been similar to that presented in the Fries trial. But if he instead was insisting that they abide by a ruling he had already made—that the question of the constitutionality of the Sedition Act could not be argued to the jury, and was to be decided by the court—a much different situation is presented. It is by no means unknown for a judge to admonish counsel for pursuing a line of questioning to a witness that the judge has already ruled to be out of bounds. While it is more unusual for a judge to interrupt counsel's closing argument to a jury with such an admonition, Chase's admonition did not come during closing argument, but at a time during the trial itself. Knowing what we already know of Chase, it would not be at all surprising if his overbearing nature led him to interrupt when he should not have done so. But knowing also of George Hay's attitude toward the matter, it would not be surprising to have had a more temperate judge than Chase conclude that Hay was in effect arguing to the jury a question the court had ruled he should not argue to the jury.

The testimony most damaging to Chase with respect to the Callender trial had nothing to do with his conduct of the trial, but with incidents that occurred before he ever reached Richmond to try the case. Because these incidents were not referred to in the Articles of Impeachment, Chase's answer, which he read to the senators, does not address them. Presumably he could have testified about them as a witness in his own behalf at the impeachment trial, but he chose not to do so.

John Mason testified that he had attended the session of the federal court in Annapolis in the spring of the year 1800 where Justice Chase was presiding, and immediately after the adjournment of the court, Mason, Chase, and Judge Winchester found themselves together in the courtroom and engaged in what Mason described as a "jocular" conversation. Chase asked Mason his opinion of the book *The Prospect Before Us*. Mason responded that he had not seen it, and that from what he had heard of it he never wished to see it. Chase replied that Luther Martin had sent a copy of it to him, with the libelous parts underscored, and that he planned to take it to Richmond with him as a proper subject for prosecution. He added that before he left Richmond he would teach the people to distinguish between the liberty and licentiousness of the press.

The next day James Triplett testified that he traveled on the same stagecoach as Justice Chase from Annapolis to Richmond in 1800. At that time this journey—a distance of 150 miles—took several days. Chase handed Triplett a book and asked him if he had read it. Chase also asked Triplett if he had ever seen Callender, and he replied that he had not. Someone else apparently related an account of Callender's having been arrested under a Virginia vagrancy statute, and Chase replied, "It is a pity you have not hanged the rascal." Triplett later stayed in the same house as Justice Chase in Richmond, and while there Chase told him that the grand jury had made a presentment against Callender and that the marshal had gone to find him in Petersburg.

This testimony, revealing as it did the rather clear bias of Chase against Callender, was something of an embarrassment for his attorneys when they made their closing arguments to the Senate. Robert Goodloe Harper treated the matter thus in his closing argument:

> [Justice Chase], in the course of some loose and thoughtless conversation, from which it would have been more prudent to abstain, applied some harsh epithets to "The Prospect Before Us," and its reputed author; and expressed an apprehension that he would escape punishment. But does it follow that because a judge remarkable for hasty and strong expressions, has applied some harsh and angry epithets to a person believed to be an atrocious offender, he will not do him justice, when he comes on trial?

This is scarcely a satisfying justification of why Chase presided at Callender's trial after he had made these statements about him and about *The Prospect Before Us*. By way of shedding some light on the matter, it is worth noting that at common law a judge was required to disqualify himself for *interest* in a case—that is, reason to think that he might gain or lose economically by a ruling in the case—but there was no provision for disqualification for *bias* in favor of or against a party.[7] A leading contemporary authority on the subject puts the matter this way:

> In short, English common law practice at the time of the establishment of the American court system was simple in the extreme. Judges disqualified for financial interests. No other disqualifications were permitted, and bias, today the most controversial ground for disqualification, was rejected entirely.[8]

Not until 1911—more than a century after the Callender trial—was any provision made by law for a federal judge to disqualify himself on account of bias.

One would like to know more about the practice at the time of the Callender trial, and to learn whether, even if there was no requirement that a judge disqualify himself by reason of bias, a judge might voluntarily have done so and made arrangements for another judge to sit in his place. But even if no such provision existed, and it was inevitable that Chase preside at Callender's trial, surely he should have refrained from making the statements attributed to him.

For many years historians who treated the Chase impeachment trial took the general view that while Chase was overbearing in his manner and harsh in his rulings on the bench, the impeachment charges against him were trumped up by his political opponents, and he deserved to be acquitted.[9] But in 1973 Raoul Berger published *Impeachment: The Constitutional Problem,* in which he took the position that the Senate should have convicted Chase and removed him from office. Berger focused principally on the charges based on Chase's conduct in the Callender trial, and to a lesser degree on his conduct of the Fries trial. He concluded that the evidence showed his "evident disposition to play the hanging judge," and his "oppressive misuse of power."[10] Berger contends that Chase's statements preliminary to the trial, his exclusion of John Taylor's testimony, his seating of John Basset as a juror, and his harassment of defense counsel in this case were sufficiently egregious to justify conviction.

There can be no question but that the evidence adduced at the trial before the Senate showed that Chase was impatient, overbearing, and at times arrogant, but this falls short of showing that Chase was actually the malevolent figure that Berger makes him out to be. Chase, after proving to his own satisfaction that the testimony of Colonel Taylor was inadmissible, nonetheless requested the United States attorney to waive any objection to it. The Sedition Act authorized the court to impose a fine of up to $2,000 and a prison sentence of up to two years, upon one convicted under it. Chase gave Callender the relatively light sentence of nine months in jail and a $200 fine. During the Fries trial, he went with Judge Peters to the home of William Rawle, the United States attorney—itself an *ex parte* contact with the attorney for one of the parties which would probably violate the canons of ethics today—in order to try to figure out a way to keep the attorneys for Fries from withdrawing from the case. When Callender's attorneys were so offended by Chase's ruling that they withdrew from his defense, Chase urged them to continue and assured them that he would cease interrupting them.

Adams in his *History* states that Chase's conduct drove the ablest lawyers in the circuit from his courtroom in two cases—that of Fries and that of Callender—but this statement, too, must be understood in perspective. There is good reason to think, on the basis of the evidence presented to the Senate, that Fries's attorneys withdrew at least in part to increase the chances of a presidential pardon for him if he were convicted. There is also reason to think that Callender's attorneys were every bit as interested in making a political statement by their defense as they were in obtaining the acquittal of Callender.

A milder view of Chase is also supported by others who either observed or studied his conduct of the trial of John Fries. Horace Binney, who was present in the courtroom in Philadelphia at the time of the Fries trial, stated, "Chase's conduct of the trial was not regarded by the bar as one of intended oppression of either the prisoner or his counsel, but as a great mistake." Stephen Presser, who has studied at length the proceedings in the courts of Pennsylvania at this time, says:

> . . . [T]hough Chase's personal characteristics were largely responsible for the political storm he created, Chase was still not an American Jeffreys. He was not the unrestrained ogre or "hanging judge" that some still make him out to be.[11]

Finally, neither the Fries trial nor the Callender trial seems to have resulted in a miscarriage of justice under the law as it was understood at that time. There was no dispute about Fries's leading part in the "rebellion," and if Chase was correct about the law of treason—a point on which two of his Supreme Court colleagues and two district judges agreed with him—it was perfectly proper for the jury to find him guilty. Likewise, once the court had rejected the challenge to the Sedition Act as being violative of the First Amendment to the Constitution, and Callender had attempted to "justify" only one of the twenty charges named in the indictment, it was perfectly proper for the jury to find him guilty. In 1964 the Supreme Court of the United States opined that the Sedition Act *did* violate the First Amendment.[12] Samuel Chase would probably not have agreed with the opinion, but it is not fair to tax him with failing to understand the steady enlargement of the First Amendment in the 164 years following the Callender trial.

-6-

Still another count in the charges against Samuel Chase was based on his handling of a grand jury in New Castle, Delaware, where he held court in late June 1800. Article VII charged that at this session of the court Chase:

> Did descend from the dignity of a judge and stooped to the level of an informer, by refusing to discharge the grand jury, although entreated by several of the said jurors so to do; and after the said grand jury had regularly declared, through their foreman, that they had found no bills of indictment, nor had any presentments to make, by observing to the said grand jury, that he, the said Samuel Chase, understood "that a highly seditious temper had manifested itself in the state of Delaware, among a certain class of people, particularly in New Castle County, and more especially in the town of Wilmington, where lived a most seditious printer, unrestrained by any principle of virtue, and regardless of social order—that the name of this printer was—but checking himself, as if sensible of the indecorum which he was committing, added, "that it might be assuming too much to mention the name of this person, but it becomes your duty, Gentlemen, to inquire diligently into this matter." . . . The said Samuel Chase did, moreover, authoritatively enjoin on the District Attorney of the United States the necessity of procuring a file of the papers to which he

alluded. . . . And, by a strict examination of them, to find some passage which might furnish the ground-work of a prosecution against the printer of the said paper. . . .

The basic outline of what happened on these two days in late June while Chase was holding Court in Delaware was not disputed; some of the details were. The grand jury appeared at the opening of court on the first day, retired to the room set aside for them, and after about an hour returned to tell the judge that they had no indictments or presentments to make. Chase then told them that he had been informed that there was a seditious newspaper conducted in the state, which made a practice of libeling the government. He asked the grand jury whether they had given any attention to this matter, and the jurors answered that they had not. Chase told them that his charge had included offenses under the Sedition Act, and that it was their duty to inquire into such matters.

At this point several of the jurors asked to be released, because it was the time of a hay harvest in Delaware and they were needed on their farms. But Chase declined to release them. He turned to the district attorney and asked if the latter could obtain a file of these papers. Someone else volunteered to do so, and the United States attorney agreed to review them. Chase then told the grand jurors that they must attend again on the following morning at ten o'clock.

The next morning the jurors returned to court with the United States attorney, and Chase inquired whether anything had been found in the papers of a seditious nature. The attorney replied that nothing had been found in the papers that would be a proper subject for prosecution unless it was a piece that attacked Chase. Chase replied that they should take no notice of that, and thereupon dismissed the grand jury.

George Read, the United States attorney in 1800, was the first witness called by the managers in connection with this charge, and he supported the claim that Chase had commented that a "highly seditious temper had manifested itself in the state of Delaware, among a certain class of people, especially in New Castle County, and more especially in the town of Wilmington." But

Gunning Bedford, who was the district judge who sat with Chase in Delaware, said that Chase had made no such statement. He related a conversation between himself and Chase after court:

> On my way to Judge Chase's lodgings, I said to him, "My friend, I believe you know not where you are; the people of this county are very much opposed to the Sedition Law, and will not be pleased with what you have said." Judge Chase clapped his hand upon my shoulders and replied, "My dear Bedford, no matter where we are, or among whom we are, we must do our duty."

Bedford stated that he did not think he would have made this comment to Chase after the court session if Chase had made the statement with which he was charged during court. Nicholas Van Dyke, Archibald Hamilton, and John Hall, other witnesses who had been present in court that day, stated that they could not recollect Chase's making any such statement. George Read alone, then, thought that Chase used the particular language set forth in the charge, while the other witnesses disagreed with him.

The language of the charge against Chase gave the impression that the jurors had been badgered to return an indictment, and more or less begged him to release them from this onerous duty. But both Read, the United States attorney, and James Lee, one of the grand jurors, confirmed that the jurors' desire to be released stemmed from their eagerness to get back to their farms.

So long as the Sedition Act was on the books, the grand jurors were obligated to look into possible criminal violations of that law as well as into violations of the very few other federal criminal statutes that were in existence at this time. Chase was obviously very much concerned with violations of the Sedition Act, and another judge might have left it to the United States attorney and to the grand jurors to decide whether any violations had taken place without calling their attention to the printer in question. But the oppressive environment in the courtroom portrayed by the language of the charge was belied by all of the witnesses, including Read. Chase held the grand jurors over for a second day in order to look into a possible violation of federal law at a time when they wished very much to be back on their farms harvesting hay. This was another article that the House managers showed poor judgment in incorporating in their Articles of Impeachment.

The last of the articles of impeachment was based on Chase's charge to the grand jury in Baltimore in May 1803. Article VII charged:

> The said Samuel Chase, disregarding the duties and dignity of his judicial character, did, at a circuit court, for the District of Maryland, held in Baltimore, in the month of May, 1803, pervert his official right and duty to address the grand jury then and there assembled, on the matters coming within the province of the said jury, for the purpose of delivering to the said grand jury an intemperate and inflammatory political harangue, with intent to excite the fears and resentment of the grand jury, and of the good people of Maryland against their state government, and constitution, a conduct highly censurable in any, but peculiarly indecent and unbecoming in a judge of the Supreme Court of the United States. . . . And . . . that the said Samuel Chase . . . did, in a manner highly unwarrantable, endeavor to excite the odium of the said grand jury, and of the good people of Maryland, against the government of the United States, by delivering opinions which . . . were at that time and as delivered by him, highly indecent, extra-judicial, intending to prostitute the high judicial character with which he was invested, to the low purpose of an electioneering partizan.

There was some dispute as to what Chase actually said, but in his response he stated that he had read the charge from a written paper, and on this point he appears to have the better of the argument. The critical language in the charge was this:

> You know, gentlemen, that our state and national institutions were framed too secure to every member of the society *equal* liberty and *equal* rights; but the late alteration of the federal judiciary, by the abolition of the office of the sixteen circuit judges, and the *recent* change in our

state constitution by the establishing of *universal* suffrage, *and* the further alteration that is contemplated in
our state judiciary, (if adopted) will in my judgment take
away *all security for property and personal liberty*. The independence of the national judiciary is already shaken to
its foundation; and the virtue of the people alone can
restore it. The independence of the judges of this state
will be entirely destroyed, if the bill for abolishing the
two supreme courts, should be ratified by the next general assembly. The change of the state constitution by
allowing universal suffrage, will in my opinion certainly
and rapidly destroy all protection to property, and all
security to personal liberty; and our Republican constitution will sink into a *mobocracy*, the worst of all possible
governments.

Chase in his answer to the charge also indicated that he re-
pented giving it. He said:

Admitting these opinions to have been incorrect and un-
founded, this respondent denies that there was any law
which forbids him to express them, in a charge to grand
jury; and he contends that there can be no offence, without the breach of some law.

Chase also stated in his answer:

It has been the practice in this country, ever since the
beginning of the Revolution, which separated us from
Great Britain, for the judges to express from the bench,
by way of charge to the grand jury, and to enforce to
the utmost of their ability, such political opinions as they
thought correct and useful. There have been instances in
which the legislative bodies of this country, have recommended this practice to the judges; and it was adopted
by the judges of the Supreme Court of the United States,
as soon as the present judicial system was established.

There is no doubt that Chase was correct in his answer to this article when he stated that it had been the practice in the federal courts from the beginning to give a general charge to the grand jury when a session of the court opened at a particular city. The function of the general charge was to instruct the grand jury as to the provisions of federal criminal law, so that the jurors would know what sort of conduct to inquire into with a view to bringing in indictments. The state courts had usually proceeded in this way, and it was quite natural for the newly created federal courts to follow suit.

But during the very first few years, the only significant federal criminal offenses designated by Congress pertained to customs or shipping. Discussion of these would necessarily be brief, and there was a natural tendency on the part of the judge to "pad" the charge with other material. Since the Supreme Court justices were viewed as representatives of the new federal government by the inhabitants of the cities in which they held court, the most obvious source of additional material for a charge would be an explanation of the structure of the new government. The justices understandably tended to view this new government with an approving eye.

During the first administration of George Washington—when party differences were only beginning to make their appearance— these grand-jury charges tended to arouse no particular ire on the part of anyone. But as the party of Jefferson and Madison moved into avowed opposition to the policies followed by the administration of John Adams, some grand-jury charges took on a more partisan flavor.

A newspaper in Portsmouth, New Hampshire, described the charge of Justice William Paterson of the Supreme Court of the United States as follows:

> After the jury were impaneled the Judge delivered a most elegant and appropriate charge. The *Law* was laid down in a masterly manner: *Politics* were set in their true light by holding up the Jacobins as the disorganizers of our happy country, and the only instruments of introducing discontent and dissatisfaction among the well-meaning part of the Community. *Religion & Morality* were pleasingly inculcated and enforced as being necessary to good gov-

ernment, good order, and good law; for "when the righ-
teous are in authority, the people rejoice."[1]

In the same year Justice Iredell delivered a charge to a grand
jury which a sympathetic newspaper described as follows:

> After some general reflections of the relative situation be-
> tween the United States and France, the learned judge
> went into a defense of the Alien and Sedition laws, and
> proved them, it is believed, to the satisfaction of every
> unprejudiced mind to be perfectly consistent with the
> principles of the Constitution and to be founded on the
> wisest maxims of policy. The Judge concluded with call-
> ing the attention of the Grand Jury to the present situa-
> tion of the country and with remarks on the mild and
> virtuous administration of the government."[2]

Thus, what had started out as charges praising the government
created by the new Constitution had in a short time evolved into
charges praising the policies of a particular administration.

Julius Goebel describes the evolution in these words:

> The introduction of this routine at the first term of the
> several Circuit Courts appears to have occasioned no public
> surprise over the fact that the new court should be con-
> ducted no differently than those of the states. The open-
> ing formalities, the calling over and swearing of the grand
> jury and the delivery of a general charge, seemingly an
> innocuous ceremony, excited no remark except as to the
> literary quality of the Justices' compositions. With the
> passage of time this attitude of amiable acceptance was
> to become one of angry criticism, because the judges'
> charges came to reflect an increasing sense of apostolic
> mission.[3]

In one sense, Chase's charge to the Baltimore grand jury seems
no more egregiously partisan than do the charges of Iredell and
Paterson described above. It would be unthinkable today for a
federal judge to opine to a grand jury, as Iredell did, his view that

a controversial act of Congress was not only constitutional but embodied sound policy as well. And Chase's charge was no more partisan than Paterson's, with its fulsome praise of the Adams policies and criticism of the opponents of those policies.

But there are at least two important differences that set Chase's charge apart. First, the charges by Paterson and Iredell were given at a time when the Federalists controlled both houses of Congress, and there was therefore no realistic threat of impeachment; Chase's was given after the Jeffersonians had taken control of Congress in the "second American Revolution" of 1800. Second Chase's charge dealt not only with the repeal by Congress of the Midnight Judges Act of 1801, but with matters pertaining to Maryland state government. To Jeffersonians who were strict constructionists and believed fiercely in a limited role for the federal government, Chase's comments about Maryland politics were particularly offensive; Article VIII had expressly differentiated between Chase's comments about changes in the Maryland laws and his comments about the congressional repeal of the Judiciary Act of 1801. These differences between Chase's charge and the others are perhaps more political than logical, but impeachment as provided for in the Constitution can never be wholly divorced from politics.

It is also worth noting that the impeachment article based on the grand-jury charge was probably the easiest for those of the senators who were not lawyers to understand and evaluate. Charges based on the Fries trial and the Callender trial generally dealt with points of trial practice and procedure with which laymen were not familiar. But the question of whether a judge should let his political views play a part in his charge to a grand jury was not one that was governed by ancient legal precedents or by statements in Blackstone's *Commentaries*. The federal government was scarcely fifteen years old; one person's opinion on the subject should presumably be as good as another's.

The article of impeachment based on Chase's charge to the Baltimore grand jury was the last of the series, and chronologically it was quite logical that it should appear in this position. The trial of John Fries in Philadelphia, the trial of James Callender in Richmond, and the proceedings before the grand jury in Delaware had all taken place in 1800. Chase's charge to the grand jury in Baltimore took place in May 1803. But there is nonetheless an irony in its having been placed last in the articles, because it was Chase's grand-jury charge that originally provoked Jefferson to write to his political lieutenants in the House of Representatives suggesting that Chase be impeached.

The testimony on both sides of the case finished on the morning of Wednesday, February 20, 1805. Closing arguments began that same day, continued on Thursday, Friday, Saturday, and Monday, and concluded on Tuesday, February 26.

Peter Early of Georgia led off for the managers, speaking for about an hour on all of the charges except the ones based on the failure to follow Virginia law during the trial of James Callender. Much of his discussion was factual and legal; occasionally he lapsed into florid rhetoric:

> [W]hen in that review we behold an American citizen summoned to the bar of justice to undergo a trial in which his life is at stake; when we behold this judge, contrary to all precedent and in violation of every feeling of humanity, pre-occupying the only ground upon which the case of the accused was defensible, and closing upon him this only possible avenue to safety, truly I feel that my feeble powers of language are not competent to a description of the scene; it must be left to the strong expression of silence. For this transaction then in the name of the American people we denounce Judge Chase. We denounce him for invading their most valuable privilege, *the trial by jury*. We denounce him for taking into his own unhallowed hands, the disposal of the life of an American citizen; and we invoke the justice of the nation to expiate by the proper punishment this most unholy sin.

Next came George Campbell of Tennessee, who spoke for about an hour and a half. He too dwelt on the denial of the right to jury trial in the Fries case, though he mistakenly located the source of that right in the Eighth Amendment to the Constitution, rather than the Sixth Amendment. He, too, on occasion pulled out the rhetorical stops:

Here let us pause a moment, and behold the unfortu-
nate, and, in the language of his able counsel, poor Fries,
trembling before his condemning judge; stript of the aid
of counsel, his only and forlorn hope; the fatal fiat of his
condemnation pronounced in the solemn language of a
written opinion; and this friendless, unprotected, and
unheard, about to be consigned to the hand of the re-
lentless executioner! Let us view this spectacle, and then
let me ask, if this can be considered an impartial administration of justice.

According to the two Federalist senators who contempora-
neously recorded their views in diaries, both Early and Campbell
spoke so poorly and so tediously that they emptied the Senate
chamber not only of spectators but of their colleagues from the
House of Representatives.[4]

Next came Congressman Clark, who spoke for about five minutes on the charges contained in Articles V and VI dealing with
the claimed violations of Virginia law at the Callender trial. He
said what could be said for these articles, which was not much.

Joseph Hopkinson of Philadelphia then opened for the defense.
He, too, appealed to emotion, telling the senators, "We appear for
an ancient and infirm man, whose better days had been worn out
in the service of that country which now degrades him; and who
has nothing to promise you for an honorable acquittal but the
approbation of your own consciences." He spoke of the importance of the case to Chase "to the full amount of his good name
and reputation, and of that little portion of that happiness, the
small residue of his life may afford."

He went on to argue that the charges against Chase did not
amount to an "impeachable" offense under the Constitution. The
Constitution spoke of "treason, bribery, or other high crimes or
misdemeanors." The charges against Chase obviously did not par-
take of treason or bribery, so they must come under the head of
"high crimes or misdemeanors." But, Hopkinson argued, to be a
high crime or misdemeanor the charge must be an indictable offense under the criminal law, and the managers had made out no
claim that the charges against Chase were such. This very important legal question would be debated back and forth between the

House managers and counsel for Chase during these closing arguments, but neither side was entirely consistent in its position. Chase's defenders argued that the terms "high crimes or misdemeanors" were words of art, that is, they had a very particular meaning: A crime was a serious criminal offense, and a misdemeanor was a lesser criminal offense. Unless the managers could show that Chase's acts were criminally punishable under some existing law, they could not form the basis for conviction. This view was supported by so great an English authority as Blackstone. The managers responded that under English law, from which the impeachment provisions of the Constitution were borrowed, they were indeed words of art, but were not necessarily limited to offenses punishable by the criminal law but extended to malfeasance or misconduct in office. This debate would be renewed at the impeachment trial of President Andrew Johnson in 1868.

Hopkinson spoke for two hours on the Fries case alone; he was followed by Phillip Barton Key who spoke for about an hour on the principal part of the Callender charges. Charles Lee followed him and, in a true act of supererogation, devoted an hour defending against the charges contained in Article V and Article VI based on the violations of Virginia law in the Callender trial.

On Saturday, February 23, Luther Martin rose in the Senate chamber to deliver his oration on behalf of Chase. The Senate galleries could not contain the throng that had turned out to hear the "impudent Federalist bulldog." It is not easy to divine, nearly two centuries later, exactly what was the key to his success as an advocate. It obviously was not his pleasing appearance or manner; his biographers describe him thus:

> Of only medium height, with thinning hair and features distinguished only by the ravages of alcohol, a voice far from melodious and a sputtering, saliva-spraying delivery, he was a far less impressive figure than the scintillating Hopkinson and Pinkney or the suave Harper and Wirt.[5]

These same biographers offer these reasons for his success in his chosen profession:

He could be coarse, ungrammatical, and unnecessarily prolix, but he had a phenomenal memory for precedents, a firm grasp of almost every field of the law, and an ability to show the reasons for, and the reasonableness of, the law as he expounded it. Added to these attributes was, as Plumer noted, his broad and disarming sense of humor—a trait uncommon among lawyers—and a gift for perfectly timing his most devastating arguments.[6]

Martin began as might have been expected:

Did I only appear in defense of a friend, with whom I have been in habits of intimacy for nearly thirty years, I should feel less anxiety on the present occasion, though that circumstance would be a sufficient inducement; but I am, at this time, actuated by superior motives. I consider this cause not only of importance to the respondent and his accusers, but to my fellow citizens in general (whose eyes are now fixed upon us), and to their posterity, for the decision at this time will establish a most important precedent as to future cases of impeachment.

He then proceeded to damn the House of Representatives with faint praise, saying that his discussion would occupy more time than he could wish, but "as the charges are brought forward by such high authority as the House of Representatives of the United States, it becomes necessary to bestow upon them more attention than they would deserve, were they from a less respectable source." We see the able and wily Martin at his best a moment later when he looks over the assembled senators and says:

I see two honorable members of this court [Messrs. Dayton and Baldwin], who were with me in the convention, in 1787, who as well as myself, perfectly know why this power [the power to try impeachments] was invested in the Senate. It was, because among all our speculated systems, it was thought this power could nowhere be more properly placed, or where it would be less likely to be abused. A sentiment, Sir, in which I perfectly concur;

and I have no doubt, but the event of this trial will shew
that we could not have better disposed of that power.

By five o'clock on Saturday afternoon, Martin had spoken for
more than five hours. He asked, and was granted, permission to
finish his argument on Monday. He spoke for nearly two hours
on that day, sometimes analyzing, sometimes expostulating, sometimes ridiculing the arguments of the managers. In his conclusion
he offered the senators a way of voting for acquittal without necessarily reflecting on the House of Representatives. He pointed
out that the Articles of Impeachment had necessarily been drawn
on the basis of *ex parte* statements of potential witnesses for the
prosecution. But the Senate had heard these witnesses cross-
examined, and had heard testimony of other witnesses brought
forward by the defense. He said, presumably tongue in cheek:

> But these charges have been patiently discussed—a mass
> of evidence has been produced here, which they had not,
> and after this full investigation, the honorable members
> who impeached him, and who have regularly attended
> his trial, I doubt not, are perfectly satisfied that he ought
> to be acquitted, and will rejoice at that acquittal.

Martin was followed by Robert Goodloe Harper, whose speech
for the defense was both learned and verbose. Then came Joseph
Nicholson of Maryland for the managers, who gave by far the
best arguments for their position. Caesar Rodney of Delaware,
who followed him, suffered by comparison. Then came John Randolph, who had been the moving force in the House of Representatives behind the impeachment. During his speech he remarked
that he had lost his notes, and apologized for his indisposition.
Randolph's biographer says this of his performance:

> But, apart from his normal state of health, poor at its
> best, Randolph brought to this . . . speech in the Chase
> case pretty much everything that he had to bring to such
> a case; fresh, crisp ideas, happy images, blistering invec-
> tive, quick strokes of instinctive intelligence, and pol-
> ished declamation. But law and legal methods of statement

and reasoning, in other words the things most essential to the proper presentation of his case, he did not bring, because he did not have them to bring.[7]

Randolph's peroration was impressive:

We have performed our duty, we have bound the criminal and dragged him to your altar. The nation expects from you that award which the evidence and the law requires. It remains for you to say whether he [Judge Chase] shall again become the scourge of an exasperated people, or whether he shall stand as a landmark and a beacon to the present generation and a warning to the future that no talents, however great, no age, however venerable, no character, however sacred, no connection, however influential, shall save that man from the justice of his country who prostitutes the best gifts of Nature and of God and the power, with which he is invested for the general good, to the low purposes of an electioneering partisan.

The closing arguments concluded on Tuesday, February 26, and at that time the Senate decided to convene at noon on Friday, to vote on the Articles of Impeachment. On that day, Aaron Burr opened the proceedings with his usual injunction that "the Sergeants-at-Arms will face the spectators and seize and commit to prison the first person who makes the smallest noise or disturbance." Again the galleries were packed. The Senate had decided that on each article the president of the Senate should call on each member of the Senate to vote individually, and that upon being so called, the member should rise in his place and answer "guilty" or "not guilty." Henry Adams, in the second volume of his *History of the United States of America*, describes the proceedings in the Senate that day as follows:

The Senate chamber was crowded with spectators when Vice-President Burr took the chair and directed the Secretary to read the first Article of Impeachment. Every member of the Senate answered to his name. Tracey of

Connecticut, prostrated by recent illness, was brought
on a couch and supported to his seat, where his pale,
face added to the serious effect of the scene. The first
article, which concerned the trial of Fries, was that on
which Randolph had founded impeachment, and on which
the Managers had thrown perhaps the greatest weight.
As the role was called, Senator Bradley of Vermont, first
of the Republican members, startled the audience by
saying "Not Guilty." Gaillard of South Carolina, and,
to the astonishment of everyone, Giles, the most ardent
of impeachers, repeated the same verdict. These three
defections decided the results, but they were only the
beginning. Jackson of Georgia, another hot impeacher,
came next; then Dr. Mitchell, Samuel Smith of Maryland, and in quick succession all the three Smiths of New
York, Ohio, and Vermont. A majority of the Senate declared against the Article, expectation complete.[8]

The vote on the Fries article was 16 in favor of conviction, 18
in favor of acquittal. The vote on the second article—based on
Chase's seating of John Basset as a juror at the Callender trial—
was 10 guilty, 24 not guilty. On the third article—dealing with
the exclusion of the testimony of Colonel John Taylor at Callender's trial—the supporters of conviction rallied their forces and
obtained 18 votes in favor of conviction to 16 for acquittal. This
was a majority, but the Constitution required an extraordinary
majority of two thirds.

On the fourth article, which dealt with the other charges relating to the Callender trial, the vote was the same as on the third.
The two articles based on Chase's claimed failure to follow Virginia law during the Callender trial were overwhelming victories
for Chase and his counsel: On the first of these articles all thirty-
four senators voted not guilty, and on the second four voted guilty
and thirty not guilty. On Article VII, dealing with the proceedings before the grand jury in New Castle, Delaware, ten senators
voted guilty and twenty-four not guilty. Finally the Senate came
to the charges contained in Article VIII—based on Chase's charge
to the Baltimore grand jury in 1803—and here the prosecution
mustered its largest vote. Nineteen senators voted guilty, and fif-

teen voted not guilty. But even this number fell 4 votes short of the two-thirds majority required.

When Senator Wright of Maryland, who was the last senator to be called upon, responded "Guilty" on that article, it was clear that Chase had prevailed. Aaron Burr rose, recited the counts on each article, and then said:

> Hence it appears that there is not a constitutional majority of votes binding Samuel Chase, Esquire, guilty, on any one Article. It, therefore, becomes my duty to declare that Samuel Chase, Esquire, stands acquitted of all the Articles exhibited by the House of Representatives against him.

The transcript of the proceedings of the Chase impeachment trial then concludes: "Whereupon, the Court adjourned without day."

-7-

*T*he managers made no secret of their profound disappointment with the judgment of the Senate. No sooner had the House members returned to their own chamber after having witnessed the vote than, in the words of John Quincy Adams, "the leading managers vented their spleen against the decision with all their virulence."[1] John Randolph offered a resolution to amend the Constitution to provide that federal judges should be removable upon a joint address of the two houses of Congress to the president. Joseph Nicholson, not to be outdone, offered another resolution to amend the Constitution to provide that members of the Senate should be subject to recall at any time by their respective legislatures. Since the lame-duck session of Congress was about to expire, both of these resolutions were postponed until the convening of Congress the following December. Neither of them was ever heard of again.

As Adams returned home from the Senate chamber after the vote on March 1, he caught up with and walked with Senator William Cocke of Tennessee. Cocke had voted Chase guilty on every article but the fifth. According to Adams:

> He told me that he had always been very sorry that the impeachment was brought forward, and though, when compelled to vote, his judgement had been as unfavorable to Mr. Chase as that of any member of the Court, he was heartily glad of his acquittal, which it appeared

to him would have a tendency to mitigate the irritation
of party spirit.[2]

Federalist newspapers such as the *Columbian Centinel* and the
Charleston Courier hailed the acquittal with approval. The Republican *Richmond Enquirer* lamented that Chase had been spared
"through the mercy of our Constitution. . . . To impartial persons who resort to a much higher authority—to the merits of the
prosecution itself—he must stand condemned, if not of the highest
crimes and misdemeanors, at least of judicial tyranny of no ordinary standard."[3]

When Congress adjourned on March 3, 1805, John Quincy
Adams confided the following observation to his diary:

> . . . [T]his was a party prosecution, and is issued in the
> unexpected and total disappointment of those by whom
> it was brought forward. It has exhibited the Senate of
> the United States fulfilling the most important purpose
> of its institution, by putting a check upon the impetuous
> violence of the House of Representatives. It has proved
> that a sense of justice is yet strong enough to overpower
> the furies of factions; but it has, at the same time, shown
> the wisdom and necessity of that provision in the Con-
> stitution which requires the concurrence of two-thirds
> for conviction upon impeachments. The attack upon Mr.
> Chase was a systematic attempt upon the independence
> and powers of the Judicial Department, and at the same
> time an attempt to prostrate the authority of the Na-
> tional Government before those of the individual States.[4]

Why was Chase acquitted? And what were the long-term consequences of his acquittal to the independence of the federal judiciary and to the independence of the Supreme Court as an
institution? The second of these questions, from the perspective
of nearly two hundred years, is much easier to answer than the
first, and it will be dealt with in the next chapter.

Several of the historians who have written on the subject have
taken the view espoused by John Quincy Adams: The impeachment was a partisan effort by the Republicans to "get" Chase, and

the six Republicans who refused to vote for conviction were simply rising above party politics and doing their duty as impartial judges. But the case presented by the managers against Samuel Chase was not devoid of substance, and his thoroughly partisan attitude during parts of the proceedings against John Callender in Richmond was obviously censurable. It is not self-evident that the nine Federalist senators, who adamantly voted Chase not guilty on every article, were motivated solely by patriotic duty, while the twenty-five Republican senators, who distributed their votes on a far more discriminating basis among the eight articles, were political janissaries.

No senator made any comment on the floor of the Senate explaining his votes on any of the Articles of Impeachment. We know much less about the members of the Senate in 1805 than we know about the members of that body today. And in 1805 there were no media interviewers waiting in the halls of the Capitol to pose the inevitable questions of why and wherefore.

Nine out of thirty-four senators were Federalists and each of these nine voted "Not Guilty" on each of the Articles of Impeachment. On the eighth article—based on Chase's charge to the Baltimore grand jury, where the impeachment forces mustered the most votes—nineteen senators, all Republicans, voted "Guilty." But simple arithmetic shows that on this same vote six Republican senators voted "Not Guilty." The key to Chase's acquittal is obviously to be found in the views entertained by the six Republicans who, so to speak, deserted their party.

One of them, Senator Bradley of Vermont, expressed the view during the trial that the managers were not proving their case against Chase. The only other one of the six of whose comment we have any record was Dr. Samuel Mitchill of New York. He served in the House of Representatives before serving in the Senate, and during the twelve years in which he lived in Washington, he wrote almost daily letters to his wife when she was not with him. He was a man of considerable erudition, referred to by Thomas Jefferson as the "Congressional Dictionary," and known among his colleagues as the "stalking Library."

His newsy letters tell of attending the horse races in the "Territory of Columbia" with other members of the House of Representatives, and of the hardships of travel from New York to

Washington. In 1804 he wrote his wife that he had refused to sign a petition circulating in the Senate requesting the governor of New Jersey to quash the proceedings against Aaron Burr growing out of his killing of Alexander Hamilton in the summer of 1804. He told his wife:

> This refusal required some resolution, for I was warmly beset, and by Republican influence too, to become an applicant in favor of Colonel Burr. I conceived, however, that as I had hitherto kept clear of the quarrels which had raged among my political acquaintances, it would be better for me to persist in doing so. And I believed that my first act as a Senator [he had been sworn in as a senator only the week before] ought to be something more to the purpose for which I was appointed than this. But Messrs. Giles, Sumter, Wright, and others had put their names to it.

In December 1804 Mitchill wrote:

> On Friday the Managers on the part of the House of Representatives, seven in number, exhibited their Articles of Impeachment at full length and in due form against Samuel Chase, one of the Associate Judges of the Supreme Court of the United States, for high crimes and misdemeanors. This is a great accusation; it excites much curiosity and feeling hereabout, and on this very important trial it has become my lot to sit as one of the judges.

On the day of the vote in the Senate on the charges against Chase, Mitchill reported to his wife:

> This day at noon the Senate met in their judicial capacity to give judgment on the cause of Samuel Chase, one of the Justices of the Supreme Court of the United States, lately tried on an impeachment. He was found *not guilty*. The votes of the Senators who find him guilty being a constitutional minority, and the rest pronouncing him not guilty. Two-thirds being necessary to convict a judge of

high crimes and misdemeanors, the accused is acquitted of the whole eight articles, and all the charges therein contained.

Thus this tedious and important trial is brought to an end. All this mighty effort has ended in nothing. On this occasion myself and my colleague Smith acted with the Federalists. But we did so on full conviction that the evidence, our oaths, the Constitution, and our conscience required us to act as we have done. I suppose we shall be libeled and abused at a great rate for our judgment given this day.[5]

One possible explanation for the defection of the minority of the Republican senators on the key votes where the impeachers mustered a majority is the personality and character of John Randolph. When Jefferson in May 1803 decided to ask his lieutenants in the House of Representatives to consider impeaching Chase, he wrote not to Randolph but to Joseph Nicholson. The matter devolved into Randolph's hands because Nicholson thought it best that he not initiate it himself. More than a year had elapsed between the time that Randolph took charge of the impeachment proceedings in the House, and the vote on the Articles of Impeachment against Chase in the Senate. During that year, Randolph's action in the House in connection with the settlement of the Yazoo Fraud claims had antagonized a considerable number of the members of his own party.

In 1795 members of the Georgia legislature had been bribed by land speculators to give them a grant of more than thirty-five million acres of Indian lands in what was then the Yazoo Territory. This land lay to the west of Georgia and eventually would become the states of Alabama and Mississippi. A new legislature, elected the following year by voters who had learned of the fraud, enacted a law rescinding the sale. Years later the Supreme Court, in the case of *Fletcher* v. *Peck*,[6] would opine that the new legislature had no power to rescind the grant made by its corrupt predecessors. But in 1804 this question was still subject to dispute, and states' rights advocates like Randolph vigorously insisted that the rescinding act of the second legislature was valid. Before that act became effective, however, much of the land had been sold by the original purchasers to Northern speculators who themselves had no knowledge of the fraud involved, and who in turn sold it to parties even more distant from the original transaction.

The federal government became involved because of its dispute with Georgia over the ownership of the land in the Yazoo Territory. In 1802 Georgia ceded these lands to the federal government, but in exchange, that government agreed to satisfy the claims of the innocent purchasers of the Yazoo lands. President Jefferson appointed a special commission for this purpose, which included three members of his Cabinet: James Madison, Albert Gallatin, and Levi Lincoln. The commission decided that the parties had no strictly legal claim, but offered a settlement whereby the government would grant five million acres of land in satisfaction of the claims of bona fide purchasers. In February 1804—at the very time that the House was considering whether to impeach Samuel Chase—the commission presented its report for adoption by Congress.

At this juncture John Randolph introduced a series of resolutions denouncing the compromise recommended by the presidential commission. The gist of these resolutions, based both on states' rights and morality—was to forbid the appropriation of money to carry out the recommended settlement. His resolutions created sharp division among the Republicans, and he succeed in having the House postpone action on the commission's recommendations until the following session. When the House again took up the matter in January 1805—only a month before the trial of Chase was to begin in the Senate—Randolph attacked the commission's proposal with extraordinary vehemence. In the words of Henry Adams:

> Hitherto as a leader he had been at times arrogant; but from this moment he began the long series of personal assauts which made him famous, as though he were the bully of a race course, dispensed from regarding ordinary rules of the ring, and ready at any sudden impulse to spring at his enemies, gouging, biting, tearing, and rending his victims with the ferocity of a rough-and-tumble fight. The spectacle is revolting, but terrific; and

until these tactics lost their force by repetition, few men had the nerve and quickness to resist them with success.[7]

He attacked Gideon Granger, Jefferson's postmaster general, by name, and Madison, Gallatin, and Lincoln in only a slightly more veiled manner. Gideon Granger may have deserved the obloquy that Randolph heaped upon him. Notwithstanding his official position, he headed up the lobby maintained in Washington by the New England-Mississippi Company, which was composed of purchasers of Yazoo lands who lived in New England and the middle states. He even went so far as to appear upon the floor of the House of Representatives to solicit votes for legislation favorable to the purchasers. But there is no reason to think that Madison, Gallatin, and Lincoln had done other than propose a compromise—albeit one with some political overtones—of a difficult and complicated dispute. Randolph's sympathetic biographer, while praising Randolph's philippics as oratory, notes the effect of their acerbity:

> . . . [T]he conduct of Randolph in this instance was magnificent; but it was not Political Leadership. Under the circumstances, the fiery invective that he exhaled against the Yazoo conspirators and the Committee on Claims could not fail to scorch the garments and to irritate the skin of the President, Madison, and Gallatin, as well as some of the leading Democratic members of the House from the Middle States and New England. . . .[8]

The House approved the compromise recommended by the commission by the narrow margin of 63 to 58, Randolph carrying with him even the two sons-in-law of President Jefferson.

Some of this antagonism on the part of other Republicans against Randolph was bound to carry over into the impeachment trial. John Quincy Adams noted in his diary in December 1804 that Representative John Jackson of Virginia—the brother-in-law of James Madison—spoke disparagingly of Randolph.[9] And while Adams walked with Senator Cocke of Tennessee after the vote in the Senate, Cocke also expressed his hostility to Randolph. Adams also noted in his diary that after the Senate vote on the impeachment charges, Madison himself expressed amusement at the discomfiture of the House managers over the result.[10] Republican senators might view with considerably less enthusiasm the case against Chase when the managers were led by John Randolph than they would have viewed the same case if the managers had been led by a less mercurial and erratic champion.

There is no reason to think that Thomas Jefferson ever changed his mind about the desirability of impeaching and convicting Samuel Chase, but it seems possible that his ardor may have cooled between the time he wrote the letter to Nicholson and the time that Chase was actually tried. Part of this cooling might have been due to having a number of other things to deal with as president, and part might have been due to his increasing estrangement from Randolph. James Madison seems to have been at least indifferent to the proceedings from the outset, and may have been unsympathetic to them. He was a much more detached, calm and collected individual than Jefferson, and much more of a friend to the idea of an independent judiciary than was his mentor. But other than the remark referred to by Adams in his diary, there is simply no evidence of Madison's having done anything in connection with the impeachment proceedings.

Finally, one should not rule out statesmanship of a high order as the motivating factor in the case of some Republican senators who voted to acquit. The Federalist senators, who to a man voted "Not Guilty," were convinced that the impeachment proceedings were a partisan attack by the Republicans on the independence of the federal judiciary—the branch of government that was in the hands of Federalist appointees. To them the choice probably appeared easy, no matter how damning the evidence against Chase might be. To those Republicans voting to convict, the independence of the judiciary did not loom as large as the necessity to remove a judge who could be viewed at worst as a bullying partisan, and a Federalist partisan at that. Neither of these motives was ignoble. But perhaps to some Republicans the demonstrated misconduct of Chase in the Callender case would have been grounds for removal only if it could have been accomplished consistently with the maintenance of an independent judiciary; thinking that it could not be, they accepted Chase's continuance in office as the lesser of two evils.

–8–

*T*he acquittal of Samuel Chase by the Senate had a profound effect on the American judiciary. First, it assured the independence of federal judges from congressional oversight of the decisions they made in the cases that came before them. Second, by assuring that impeachment would not be used in the future as a method to remove members of the Supreme Court for their judicial opinions, it helped to safeguard the independence of that body.

It should be remembered that all of the charges brought by the House of Representatives against Samuel Chase were based on his claimed misconduct while sitting on circuit as a trial judge, and not while sitting as a Supreme Court justice. This fact illustrates the greater vulnerability to attack through impeachment of a trial judge than a judge of a collegiate court such as the Supreme Court of the United States. In a collegiate court, the decision of a case is determined by a majority of several judges, and it is all but impossible to single out one in the majority and to say that he, rather than another, was responsible for the result.

The trial judge of today, by contrast, sits alone. In Chase's day, as we have seen, the circuit justice sat with a local district judge; and one of Chase's defenses was that if he were to be impeached so also should Judge Peters for the events at the Fries trial, and Judge Griffin for the events at the Callender trial. But the records of these proceedings show, particularly with respect to Judge Griffin, that Chase's authority and temperament were so dominant that for all practical purposes he might have been sitting alone.

A trial judge is likewise subject to a body of law of which he is not the final arbiter. Decisions from other courts can be pointed to, if his decision is challenged, to show that a particular ruling was wrong. In the case of a court of "last resort" such as the United States Supreme Court, on the other hand, what it says is the law *is* the law. People may violently disagree with a particular decision, but it is very difficult to show that it is "contrary to law." Samuel Chase had joined in Chief Justice John Marshall's opinion in the celebrated case of *Marbury* v. *Madison*[1] only a few months before his charge to the Baltimore grand jury led Thomas Jefferson to suggest that he should be impeached. Portions of the *Marbury* ruling—which had held that the federal courts could declare an act of Congress invalid, and said in passing that the Supreme Court could, where appropriate, issue a writ of mandamus to Secretary of State James Madison—were undoubtedly as obnoxious to some Republicans as anything Chase was charged with doing in the Articles of Impeachment. But no effort was made to impeach him on this basis, and the reasons are rather obvious. Chase, along with four colleagues, simply joined in an opinion prepared by John Marshall. There was no basis to single out Chase in preference to his four colleagues, and less reason to single out any of them other than John Marshall, who authored the opinion in the case. So although Chase was a justice of the Supreme Court, the efforts to remove him by impeachment were addressed entirely to his actions as a trial judge on circuit.

The first notable test of judicial independence after the Chase acquittal occurred two years later at the trial of Aaron Burr for treason in Richmond. Burr's term as vice-president expired in a matter of days after the Senate acquitted Chase. On the day following the vote in the Senate, Burr bade farewell to the senators in a speech that, according to Senator Mitchill, moved some of them to tears. He then disappeared from public life and from the eastern seaboard, headed for what was then the southwest—the valleys of the Ohio and Mississippi rivers. For the next two years he journeyed back and forth across this territory for purposes he did not disclose. There was a movement afoot on the part of some who lived in the area south of the Ohio River between the Appalachians and the Mississippi River to secede from the United States. There was a movement on the part of others to harass, and perhaps to make war against, Spain, which even after the Louisiana Purchase continued to own what is now Texas. In May 1805 Burr had stopped at Blennerhassett Island in the Ohio River (a few miles below present-day Parkersburg, West Virginia), where Harman Blennerhassett and his wife had established a considerable estate. In October 1806 he returned to the island and discussed with Blennerhassett some sort of an expedition to lands west of the Mississippi River. Blennerhassett's later writings for an Ohio newspaper praised the idea of separating the states west of the Appalachians from the United States.

At about this time Thomas Jefferson issued a proclamation warning Americans in this part of the nation against a conspiracy to cause the states beyond the Appalachians—Tennessee, Kentucky, perhaps Ohio—to secede from the Union, or to mount an armed expedition against Spain. Pressed by Congress for information as to the leadership of the conspiracy, Jefferson in January 1807 declared that Aaron Burr was the leader, and that "his guilt was placed beyond question."

Burr was then at a place in Mississippi territory near Baton Rouge, Louisiana. He sought to flee in disguise, but was apprehended by United States marshals and taken on an overland journey of many weeks by horseback to Richmond.

Burr arrived in Richmond in the later part of March 1807, his military guard delivered him to the civil authorities, and he was confined in the Eagle Tavern. Chief Justice John Marshall arraigned him in one of the rooms of the hotel, and ruled on the basis of the very sketchy evidence available to him at that time that Burr could be held to answer a high misdemeanor, but could not be held to answer the capital offense of treason. He admitted Burr to bail, much to Jefferson's displeasure, and ordered Burr to appear at the next session of the circuit court in Richmond in late May.

On May 22, 1807, the proceedings against Burr opened in the House of Delegates in the state capitol, designed at Jefferson's own suggestion as a copy of the famed Maison Carrée at Nîmes, France. The cast of characters assembled there would have been familiar to anyone who had attended the Senate trial of Samuel Chase. Aaron Burr, who presided at the Chase trial, was of course now the defendant. John Marshall, who appeared at the Chase trial, was now the presiding judge. Luther Martin, who had defended Chase, came to the assistance of Burr as defense counsel. George Hay, one of the principal witnesses against Chase in connection with the Callender trial, was the United States attorney for Virginia who would prosecute Burr. He was assisted by William Wirt, the junior counsel for the defense in the Callender case. The foreman of the grand jury was none other than John Randolph, the leader of the House managers at the Chase trial. Thrown in for good measure were future celebrities such as Andrew Jackson and Washington Irving, who attended as spectators.

From the beginning of the proceedings, Thomas Jefferson took an inordinate interest in obtaining the conviction of Burr, and alternately importuned Hay and badgered him with suggestions. It was thus particularly important to Burr that the judge who tried him not be overawed by the chief executive's zeal for conviction.

During the course of the proceedings, Burr's lawyers insisted that they be furnished certain executive documents in the possession of Thomas Jefferson in order to conduct their defense. Hay and Wirt, urged on by Jefferson, insisted that a court had no right to require the attendance of the president at a trial, or even to subpoena documents from him. But Marshall ruled to the contrary, holding that the court did have the authority to require Jefferson to produce the documents in question.

The grand jury indicted Burr for treason, based on the plans he allegedly made at Blennerhassett Island to cause the secession of the southwestern states. Sifting through the evidence offered by the government at Burr's trial, Marshall ruled in effect that the government had not sufficiently proved the crime of treason as it was required to be proved under the Constitution. As noted earlier, the United States Constitution contains very specific limitations on the method by which the government can charge and convict for treason: Treason consists only of levying war against the United States or adhering to its enemies. Since the United States was not at war at this time, the government had to show that Burr had "levied war" against the United States. The Constitution also contained an additional evidentiary safeguard: For conviction of treason, there must be two witnesses to the same "overt act" of the defendant. The government's witnesses, Marshall ruled, had not met this latter test.

The jury acquitted Burr on the charge of treason, returning this very strange form of verdict:

> We of the jury say that Aaron Burr is not proved to be guilty under this indictment by any evidence submitted to us. We therefore find him not guilty.

Marshall then ruled that the evidence was sufficient to hold Burr to answer on a charge of organizing an expedition against Spain. But that was only a misdemeanor, and the charge had to be brought against him in Ohio, which it never was.

When Marshall ruled adversely to the government on a preliminary motion, Jefferson wrote to Senator Giles that "the nation will judge both the offenders and judges for themselves. If a member of the Executive or Legislature does wrong, the day is never far distant when the people will remove him. They will see then & amend the error in our Constitution which makes any branch independent of the nation."[2] In his annual message to Congress that year, Jefferson made a thinly veiled threat against Marshall:

> I shall think it my duty to lay before you the proceedings, and the evidence publicly exhibited on the arraignment of the principal offenders before the circuit court of Virginia. You will be enabled to judge whether the defect was in the testimony, in the law, or in the administration of the law, and wherever it shall be found, the legislature alone can apply or originate the remedy. . . .

Marshall had refused to yield to pressure from the Republican president in his conduct of the Burr trial. Would he have acted with equal independence had Samuel Chase been convicted by the Senate two years before? One can only speculate as to the answer to this question, but the willingness to give up the doctrine of judicial review expressed in his letter to Chase (see page 126) suggests that he was a sufficiently political animal to allow an institution to be bent in order that it might not break. Happily, the acquittal of Chase prevented him from having to consider any such possibility.

The history of removals of federal judges by impeachment and conviction after the Chase acquittal and the Burr trial is testimony to the complete independence of federal judges from removal because of their judicial decisions. From that time until the present writing, thirteen federal judges have been impeached, and six have been removed from office; none of the charges was based on their judicial decisions.

The first of these convictions occurred during the Civil War, when West H. Humphreys, a federal judge in Tennessee, accepted an appointment as a judge of the Confederate States of America without resigning his appointment under the government of the United States. When the House of Representatives learned of this fact, it first authorized an inquiry, and then by voice vote impeached him. Humphreys could not be personally served with the charges, and he neither appeared at his Senate trial nor defended himself. The Senate in June 1862 unanimously removed him from office.

In the early part of this century Congress created a new federal court called the United States Commerce Court, which had a life of less than twenty years. In 1912 the House of Representatives impeached one of the judges of that court, Robert W. Archbald, on charges that boiled down to personally profiting from his office in a variety of improper ways. The trial in the Senate was a lengthy one, and in January 1913 Archbald was convicted on five of the thirteen articles and removed from office.

In June 1933 the House resolved to investigate Halsted L. Ritter, a United States district judge for the Southern District of Florida. A delay of nearly three years ensued, but in March 1936 the House impeached Ritter and charged him with various improprieties, including corruption, practicing law while serving as a judge, and preparing and filing false income-tax returns. In April of that year the Senate convicted him on one of the seven articles by exactly the two-thirds margin required by the Constitution: Fifty-six voted guilty, and twenty-eight not guilty.

In October 1986 Harry E. Claiborne, a judge of the United States District Court for Nevada, was convicted by the Senate of three articles growing out of conduct that led to an earlier criminal conviction for tax evasion. The Senate, however, refused to convict on another article which would have prevented any inquiry by the Senate into the merits of the earlier criminal conviction.

Three years later, the Senate convicted two more federal judges and removed them from office. The first was Alcee Hastings, a judge of the United States District Court for the Southern District of Florida. Hastings had been earlier charged with the federal criminal offense of soliciting a bribe; unlike Claiborne's case, the jury had acquitted Hastings. But the House impeached him for having taken a bribe; the Senate heard evidence and convicted him by a vote of 69 to 26.

Less than a month later the Senate convicted United States District Judge Walter Nixon, of the Southern District of Mississippi, of having lied to a federal grand jury about discussions he had with a United States attorney concerning a drug-smuggling case that involved the son of a friend. Nixon, too, had been found guilty of a criminal offense, and his refusal to resign from the bench after conviction was the reason the House proceeded with impeachment.

This is not to suggest that there were only six miscreants among the thousands of federal judges who have held that office for two centuries. Some resigned the office rather than face the threat of impeachment and conviction. One who did this—Martin Manton—found, however, that even the resignation did not avail him to avoid his just deserts. He ultimately paid an even higher price for his misconduct than removal from office when he was found guilty of the crime of obstructing justice and sentenced to prison.

Martin Manton was born in Brooklyn, New York, in 1880. He worked nights and during summer vacations to put himself through Columbia University Law School. He graduated with a law degree at the age of twenty-one, passed the state bar examination, and began practicing in his native Brooklyn. A few years later he made his debut in local Democratic politics, and joined the law firm of one of the prominent Tammany leaders in New York City. In 1916 Woodrow Wilson appointed him a district judge for the Southern District of New York, and two years later Wilson elevated him to the Court of Appeals for the Second Circuit.

In the depths of the Great Depression Manton was the senior judge of the Court of Appeals—what would now be called the chief judge—and was noted for his opinions in the field of patent law, the articles he contributed to learned legal journals, and his ability as a speaker on public occasions. What was not known, but

was soon to be revealed, was the extent of Manton's financial dealings during the time he was a judge. In 1931 a New York bank,
the Bank of the United States, failed. In its inventory of assets it
showed Manton as having borrowed $39,000 from it on an unse-
cured personal loan, and having endorsed notes for the additional
sums of $70,000 and $69,000, respectively. Manton's response when
these facts were made public was that the personal note had been
paid at maturity, and the two endorsed notes would be paid when
due. He explained that the endorsed notes were for loans made to
two real-estate companies in which he held stock but was not an
officer. *The New York Times* noted at the time that Judge Manton
was reputed to be one of the wealthiest judges on the federal bench.

A far different picture was painted when Manton testified before the liquidator of the Bank of the United States three years
later and acknowledged that he had been insolvent for the past
three years. Values of the real estate owned by holding companies
he controlled had plummeted with the onset of the Depression
and were now heavily encumbered; as a last resort he had borrowed on his life-insurance policies. Manton testified that count-
ing his obligations as guarantor or endorser on notes defaulted by
corporations in which he held an interest, he had debts in the
amount of $736,000. His assets, on the other hand, totaled $6,000.
Many eyebrows in New York and elsewhere were raised when
this information became public, but it was not an impeachable
offense for a judge to become insolvent.

In January 1939 the New York County district attorney, Thomas
E. Dewey, wrote to the chairman of the Judiciary Committee of
the United States House of Representatives, indicating that in half
a dozen cases in which Manton had sat as a judge he had taken
what had amounted to bribes. When this letter became public it
did more than merely raise eyebrows, and the day after it was
reported in the press, Manton announced that he would shortly
issue a statement that would "satisfy the public that there was
nothing wrong or immoral" about his judicial conduct. But instead of issuing such a statement, Manton on the same day tendered his resignation as a judge to President Franklin D. Roosevelt.
Manton explained that the resignation was inspired solely by his
wish to avoid becoming the central figure in a controversy that
would weaken public confidence in the administration of justice.

The chairman of the Judiciary Committee of the United States House of Representatives, Hatton Sumners, was asked whether or not Manton would be impeached. Sumners replied, "Why kick at the place where the fellow used to be?" Momentarily it appeared that Manton would succeed in avoiding any more of the limelight.

Dewey was a prosecutor for the state of New York, and not for the United States. If there were to be criminal charges pursued, it was much more logical for the United States attorney to prosecute than for Dewey to do so. But he let it be known that if the federal government would not charge Manton, he would, under state criminal statues. United States Attorney John T. Cahill presented evidence to a federal grand jury in the Southern District of New York, and Manton was indicted for conspiracy and obstruction of justice. The indictment listed eight separate instances in which Manton had accepted bribes and loans in the total amount of $186,000 from parties having lawsuits in the court over which he presided. This, it should be noted, was at a time when the annual salary of a United States circuit judge was $12,500.

The gist of the criminal charges against Manton were that on several different occasions on which appeals were pending before his court, and he was sitting on the three-judge panel that would hear the appeal, he had solicited outright bribes, or bribes thinly disguised as loans, from one of the litigants in the case. Most of the cases involved charges of patent infringements, an area of the law in which Manton was regarded as especially knowledgeable.

Manton pleaded not guilty, although several of those indicted with him pleaded guilty and testified against him. Manton testified about the various properties in his financial empire, explaining that his chief tangible assets

> [C]onsisted of two large hotels, eight apartment houses, fourteen two-family houses, two hundred six acres of undeveloped land on Long Island, a carpet-cleaning establishment, a paper products company, and a laundry concern. In the latter three companies he held stock in his own name. The real estate company, however, was owned by several holding companies in which he held interests of varying degrees.[3]

Manton also was asked on cross-examination how he explained the fact that in only one year after the date on which he testified he was insolvent in 1934, he completely turned his fortunes around and went from nearly three quarters of million dollars in debt to a net worth of about three quarters of a million dollars. Manton's explanations were disingenuous, and the jury convicted him notwithstanding the fact that all four of his colleagues on the circuit court—Harrie B. Chase, Augustus N. Hand, Learned B. Hand, and Thomas W. Swann—testified as character witnesses in his defense.

None of Manton's colleagues on the Court of Appeals for the Second Circuit could participate as judges when his appeal from his conviction came to that court. The Chief Justice of the United States, Charles Evans Hughes, appointed a special panel of judges to hear the case. Charles Clark, who had been appointed to that Court of Appeals after Manton had resigned, was one of the judges; the other two were Harlan Fiske Stone, associate justice of the Supreme Court assigned to the Second Circuit, and George Sutherland, a recently retired justice of the Supreme Court. Justice Sutherland wrote the opinion for the appellate court affirming Manton's conviction, and one senses in reading it how much it must have pained the author to write it. Manton chose to add a final desperate twist to his tragic fate by contending that he had never sought any of the bribes until he had already made up his mind on the merits of the case; he then sought bribes from the party in whose favor he had already decided to rule on the basis of the law. Justice Sutherland delivered a stinging rebuke to this contention:

> . . . [W]e may assume for present purposes that all of the cases in which Manton's action is alleged to have been corruptly secured were in fact rightly decided. But the unlawfulness of the conspiracy here in question is in no degree dependent upon the indefensibility of the decisions which were rendered in consummating it. Judicial action, whether just or unjust, right or wrong, is not for sale; and if the rule shall ever be accepted that the correctness of judicial action taken *for a price* removes the stain of corruption and exonerates the judge, the event

will mark the first step toward the abandonment of that
imperative requisite of even-handed justice proclaimed by
Chief Justice Marshall more than a century ago, that the
judge must be "perfectly and completely independent with
nothing to influence or control him but God and his conscience."[4]

The case of Martin Manton was notable because it was unique.
He had willfully abandoned in exchange for money the complete
independence that the Chase acquittal had conferred upon the federal judiciary in this country: a freedom on the part of a judge to
decide the case before him without regard to either public opinion
or the oversight of either the executive or legislative branches of
government. This is an attribute of our judicial system that is
shared by only a few other countries even among those who pride
themselves upon having written constitutions and safeguards for
judicial independence. The disadvantage of such a system, of course,
is that overbearing and even partisan judges, once appointed, remain on the bench to try cases. But in the times since Chase was
tried, an elaborate system of appellate review in federal criminal
cases has been put into effect which goes far towards ameliorating
the consequences of erroneous or partisan rulings by a trial judge.

In Chase's day, the right of appeal in federal criminal cases was
very limited, and remained so throughout the nineteenth century.
It was necessary for a defendant to obtain a certificate of division
between the circuit justice and the district judge in order to appeal
his conviction to the Supreme Court of the United States. On an
important question of law these judges would sometimes "agree to
disagree," but unless that happened the dominant role of the circuit justice tended to eclipse the views of the district judge.

But today, any final judgment of conviction entered by a district court in a criminal case is appealable as a matter of right to a
federal court of appeals. These courts, created by Congress in 1891,
consist of panels of three judges which sit in geographical divisions throughout the country. The result of allowing appeals as a
matter of course in criminal cases has been the development of a
body of decisional law, from the Supreme Court and from the
courts of appeals, which governs in considerable detail the actions
of trial judges. No longer is it necessary to resort primarily to

Blackstone's *Commentaries* to determine whether the action of a trial
judge was in accordance with law, and today a judge who denies
a criminal defendant the right to present vital evidence on his behalf will very likely be reversed on appeal.

Finally, it should be noted, one of the lesser consequences of
the proceedings against Chase was that Supreme Court justices
sitting on circuit stopped including political harangues in their
charges to grand juries.

The Supreme Court as an institution also benefited from the
Chase acquittal. As pointed out earlier, it is much more difficult
to prove the sort of gross error that might constitute grounds for
impeachment against a judge of a collegiate court of last resort
than it is against a trial judge. If the former has voted with the
majority, the view of the majority *is* the law until it is changed by
the court, by statute, or by constitutional amendment. If the judge
in question has expressed views in dissent that outraged members
of Congress, it is very unlikely that the matter will be pursued by
that body since dissenting views are not the law. Only if one were
to adopt the view advanced by Senator Giles could a good case
for removal be made against a member of the Supreme Court.
Giles, according to John Quincy Adams, had shortly before the
Chase trial tried to persuade Senator Israel Smith of New York:

> [O]f certain principles, upon which not only Mr. Chase,
> but all the other judges of the Supreme Court, excepting
> the one last appointed, must be impeached and removed
> . . . and if the Judges of the Supreme Court should dare,
> as they had done, to declare an Act of Congress uncon-
> stitutional, or to send a mandamus to the Secretary of
> State, as they had done, it was the undoubted right of
> the House of Representatives to impeach them and of
> the Senate to remove them, for giving such opinions,
> however honest or sincere they may have been in enter-
> taining them. Impeachment was not a criminal prosecu-
> tion. . . . And a removal by impeachment was nothing
> more than a declaration by Congress to this effect: you
> hold dangerous opinions, and if you are suffered to carry
> them into effect, you will work the destruction of the

Union. We want your offices for the purpose of giving
them to men who will fill them better.[5]

But the Articles of Impeachment against Chase had been framed
on no such theory: Each of them charged a departure from existing law in the various rulings that he made at trial. Even had
Chase been convicted by the Senate, the result would not have
been a convincing precedent for attempting to remove other members of the Supreme Court. Having said this, it must be added
that so astute a jurist as John Marshall was very troubled during
the proceedings against Chase as to what their impact might be
on the Supreme Court.

Writing to Samuel Chase in January 1804, at the time that the
House voted the Articles of Impeachment against the latter Marshall observed:

> Admitting it to be true . . . that on legal principles Colo.
> Taylor's testimony was admissible, it certainly consti-
> tutes a very extraordinary ground for an impeachment.
> According to the antient doctrine a jury finding a verdict
> against the law of the case was liable to an attaint; & the
> amount of the present doctrine seems to be that a Judge
> giving a legal opinion of the legislature is liable to im-
> peachment.
>
> As, for convenience & humanity the old doctrine of
> attaint has yielded to the silent, moderate but not less
> operative influence of new trials, I think the modern doc-
> trine of impeachment should yield to an appellate juris-
> diction in the legislature. A reversal of those legal opinions
> deemed unsound by the legislature would certainly bet-
> ter comport with the mildness of our character than a
> removal of the Judge who has rendered them unknown-
> ing of his fault.[6]

Here was the author of *Marbury* v. *Madison* himself offering (if
only in private to a colleague) to allow Congress to overturn constitutional decisions of which it disapproved in exchange for abandonment of impeachment as a weapon against the judges who might
make such rulings. There was obviously talk among the more rad-

ical Republicans of using impeachment for just that purpose, and it just as obviously frightened Marshall. If it seems difficult to understand why, nearly two centuries later, some insight into Marshall's point of view can be gained by trying to put ourselves in his place.

Though the impeachment of Chase was framed in terms of specified departures from the law, which could with some license be arguably described as "high crimes or misdemeanors," in the preceding year the Senate had convicted and removed from office Judge John Pickering of New Hampshire. Pickering was described in the language of those days as both "hopelessly insane" and as an "incurable drunkard." As might be expected these characteristics adversely affected his conduct on the bench:

> In this condition he had refused to hear witnesses for the Government in the case of the ship Eliza, seized for the violation of the revenue laws. He peremptorily ordered the vessel returned to its captain, and finally declined to allow an appeal from his decree. All of this had been done with ravings, cursings, and crazed incoherences.[7]

No one disputed that Pickering had been rendered wholly incompetent to perform any judicial duties, but what was to be done with him? The only method of removal provided by the Constitution was impeachment and conviction for "treason, bribery, or other high crimes and misdemeanors," and it was difficult to bring Pickering's afflictions under any of these four headings. Nonetheless, the Republicans, with Jefferson's full approval, decided to move against him, and in March 1803 the House voted Articles of Impeachment. The trial in the Senate began in March 1804. Pickering himself did not appear, but his son presented a petition admitting the insanity of his father, and requesting the Senate to hear evidence on this point. At common law, of course, if insanity was proved it was very doubtful that a defendant could be convicted of crimes and misdemeanors. The Senate agreed to hear evidence of insanity by way of mitigation, and the House managers were so displeased that they temporarily withdrew.

But the trial proceeded, and in March 1804 Pickering was convicted of high crimes and misdemeanors by a party-line vote, and removed from office. Three Republican senators, however, left the Senate chamber in order to avoid voting—one of them, Senator Stephen Bradley of Vermont, would later vote to acquit Chase.

The conviction of Pickering suggested that the Republicans were quite willing to use impeachment as a method of removal of a judge from office simply because it was desirable to remove him, without paying any nice attention to the constitutional requirement that the removal be based on "high crimes and misdemeanors." Shortly before the House impeached Pickering, the Pennsylvania House of Representatives had impeached Alexander Addison, a state court judge. The Pennsylvania Senate, controlled by the Republicans, had convicted him and removed him from the bench. Thus impeachment was "in the air" at the time of the Chase trial, and it had been effectively used against both a federal judge and a state court judge shortly before Chase's trial.

Today we think of the Supreme Court as the well-established and thoroughly independent head of the judicial branch of the federal government. While many people inevitably disagree with many of its decisions, the thought of changing its membership by means other than those contemplated by the Constitution would be firmly rejected by public opinion. But the Supreme Court had not achieved any such status at the time of the Chase impeachment; on the contrary, it had gotten off to a very slow start.

The first session of the Supreme Court, called for February 1, 1790, in New York City, was not auspicious. Although the Court consisted of six members—Chief Justice John Jay and five associated justices—only three of them made it to Court on that day. The court adjourned until the following day, when the necessary quorum was present and proceeded to admit attorneys.

In 1794 President George Washington appointed Chief Justice John Jay as a special envoy to England to try to settle some of the disputes between the two countries that had existed since the end of the Revolutionary War. Jay promptly sailed for England in the spring of 1794, and did not return to the United States until the summer of 1795. There is no indication that he was greatly missed on the Supreme Court. When he returned he discovered that he had been elected governor of New York in absentia, and resigned his position as Chief Justice to assume what he apparently thought was a more prestigious office.

President Washington, after having his nomination of John Rutledge turned down by the Senate, appointed Oliver Ellsworth to succeed Jay. But President Adams, who succeeded Washington, managed to find a foreign mission for Ellsworth: He was appointed an envoy to France to try to settle disputes between the United States and that country. He fell ill in France, and in December 1800 sent his letter of resignation as Chief Justice to President Adams.

Adams offered the Chief Justiceship again to John Jay, but Jay turned it down, writing to Adams:

> . . . The efforts repeatedly made to place the Judicial Department on a proper footing have proved fruitless. I left the Bench perfectly convinced that under a system so defective, it would not obtain the energy, weight or dignity which are essential to its affording due support to the National Government, nor acquire the public confidence in the respect which, as the last resort of the Justice of the nation, it should possess.[8]

The seat of the national government was moved from Philadelphia to the newly created District of Columbia in late 1800. But less than two weeks before the commencement of the Supreme Court's February 1801 term, the District Commissioners realized that no space at all had been provided for the Supreme Court in the new capital. The Commissioners wrote to Congress:

> As no house has been provided for the Judiciary of the United States, we hope the Supreme Court may be accommodated with a room in the Capitol to hold its sessions until further provisions shall be made. . . .[9]

Congress responded to this suggestion by designating a committee room on the ground floor of the Capitol building as a courtroom. It was a small and undignified chamber—twenty-four feet wide, thirty feet long—but there the Supreme Court of the United States sat for seven years until more spacious quarters were provided.

Alexander Hamilton in "Federalist Paper No. 78" referred to

the judiciary as the "least dangerous branch," and certainly anyone looking at the stature of the Supreme Court in January 1801
would have agreed with him. The Court had been in existence
more than ten years, but had docketed only 115 cases; its first
Chief Justice had been absent in England for more than a year
before resigning; its third Chief Justice had been absent in France
for more than a year before resigning. The Senate had refused to
confirm its second Chief Justice, John Rutledge of South Carolina.
In that very month—January 1801—John Adams appointed John
Marshall as Chief Justice. Marshall during his thirty-four-year tenure
in that office would dramatically raise the stature of the Court,
but as of the time of the Chase impeachment he had just begun
this monumental labor. The Court had exerted its newly proclaimed authority to declare acts of Congress unconstitutional in
the case of *Marbury* v. *Madison*, decided in February 1803, but it
was still far short of establishing the prestige and authority that it
would have at the conclusion of Marshall's tenure. Whether public
opinion would rally to its defense if the Republicans succeeded in
convicting Chase, and reached out to impeach other members of
the Court, was by no means clear.

The acquittal of Chase, therefore, was significant in that it seemed
to draw a line as the proper use of the congressional power to
impeach and remove a judge from office. Jefferson himself freely
acknowledged this fact shortly after the Chase acquittal, saying
that impeachment was a "scarecrow" which would not be used
again. The Senate's action prevented the Republicans from further exploring and expanding the possible use of impeachment to
remove from office judges whose views they considered to be unwise or out of keeping with the times.

The nature of the tripartite system of federal government established by the Constitution is such that the various branches are
frequently in conflict with one another, the judiciary as well as
the legislative and the executive. The Supreme Court is no exception; Robert H. Jackson, shortly before he himself became a member of the Court, described its role in these words:

> Yet in spite of its apparently vulnerable position, this
> Court has repeatedly overruled and thwarted both the
> Congress and the Executive. It has been in angry colli-

sion with the most dynamic and popular Presidents in our history. Jefferson retaliated with impeachment; Jackson denied its authority; Lincoln disobeyed a writ of the Chief Justice; Theodore Roosevelt, after his Presidency, proposed recall of judicial decisions; Wilson tried to liberalize its membership; and Franklin D. Roosevelt proposed to "reorganize" it. It is surprising that it should not only survive but, with no might except the moral force of its judgments, should attain actual supremacy as a source of constitutional dogma.[10]

As indicated by this observation of Jackson, these confrontations by no means ceased with the acquittal of Chase, as two examples will illustrate. Following the Civil War, the Radical Republicans in Congress sufficiently increased their numbers in the election of 1866 so as to enable them to enact laws providing for the "reconstruction" of the seceded states by dividing them into military districts. The commanding generals of these districts were authorized to remove state officials, and to commit recalcitrant citizens for trial before military commissions rather than civil juries. The commanding general of the military district embracing Mississippi ordered one William H. McCardle, the editor of a newspaper in Vicksburg, to be held for trial before a military commission on charges that his vituperative editorials incited insurrection, disorder, and violence, that they libeled some of the figures in the military government, and that they "impeded reconstruction." McCardle sought a writ of habeas corpus in the federal circuit court in Mississippi, claiming that his arrest and detention were in contravention of the Constitution and laws of the United States.

A short time before, the Supreme Court had decided the case of *Ex Parte Milligan*, which held that Congress could not constitutionally provide for the trial of civilians by military courts so long as the civil courts were open and functioning. Congressional leaders feared that the Supreme Court, on the basis of this decision, would hold large portions of the Reconstruction Acts invalid. They were anxious to avoid such a holding by any conceivable means. McCardle's case was heard in the United States circuit court in Jackson, Mississippi, in November 1867, and that court ruled against his constitutional claims. The law as it existed gave McCardle a right of appeal to the Supreme Court, which he promptly took. The Supreme Court thought the case sufficiently significant that it granted a motion to advance the case on its calendar and set arguments for the first week of March 1868. The case was argued for several days because of its importance, and submitted to the Court for decision on March 9.

Congress, meanwhile, decided to use the power granted it by Article III of the United States Constitution, which stated that the Supreme Court should, generally speaking, have appellate jurisdiction of all cases in the federal courts "with such Exceptions, and under such Regulations as the Congress shall make." Congress took the bull by the horns and simply repealed the statute giving the Supreme Court the right to hear appeals from the circuit courts in habeas corpus cases. The repealer bill was vetoed by President Andrew Johnson, but both houses of Congress overrode the veto and the bill became law on March 27. Ten days later the Supreme Court adjourned and ordered that the McCardle case be put over until the next term. A year later, the Court heard argument on the question posed by the act of Congress depriving it of jurisdiction in the case, and the following month Chief Justice Salmon P. Chase delivered a unanimous opinion holding that Congress had acted within its power to take away McCardle's right of appeal to the Supreme Court.

Congress had accomplished its purpose of preventing a possibly hostile Court from using the power of judicial review to invalidate a piece of legislation that was of vital concern to those who controlled the legislative body. But there was no threat of impeachment; Congress simply employed another one of the constitutional checks and balances at its command.

Almost seventy years later, a major confrontation between the executive branch and the Supreme Court took place. President Franklin D. Roosevelt had been returned for his second term by a landslide majority in the election of 1936. He had repeatedly been frustrated during his first term by Supreme Court decisions that had declared unconstitutional various portions of the New Deal legislation he had pushed through Congress. On one decision day—thereafter known to New Dealers as "Black Monday"—the Supreme Court had held two such laws unconstitutional, and for good measure had decided that Roosevelt did not have the authority to remove a member of the Federal Trade Commission with whose philosophy he disagreed.

The president and the Democratic party had made no issue of the Court during the 1936 election, but in February 1937 Roosevelt sent to Congress a proposal to "reorganize" the Supreme Court. This reorganization was to be accomplished by allowing the president to appoint to the Court, for each justice who was over seventy years of age and did not elect to retire, an additional justice, up to a total number of six. Six of the nine members of the Court at that time were over seventy years of age, and if none of them chose to retire, the bill would immediately authorize the president to appoint six additional justices so that the membership of the Court would then total fifteen. At that time the Court was sharply divided between those whose judicial philosophy was unsympathetic to New Deal measures, on the one hand, and those who felt that such measures were permissible under the Constitution, on the other. The six new justices to be appointed under the president's bill would clearly tip the balance in favor of the New Deal.

Roosevelt felt strongly about the Court's serving as a roadblock to the enactment of economic and social legislation which the vast majority of the people in the country had indicated by their votes that they wished to have enacted. His party had a four-to-one majority in the House of Representatives, and an even larger majority in the Senate. While it first appeared that this degree of control of both houses of Congress by his party would assure the bill of passage, public opposition gradually increased and the bill finally died in the Senate in the summer of 1937. Once again there had been a confrontation between the Supreme Court and one of the other branches of government, and once again the other branch—this time the executive—challenged the Court. But just as in the days of the *McCardle* case after the Civil War, there was no thought of impeachment as a weapon to remove members of the Court because of their judicial philosophy.

Neither the Chase acquittal nor any other single event could possibly remove the potential for conflict between the federal judiciary and the other branches of the federal government. That sort of conflict is contemplated by the Constitution, and it would require a rewriting of that document to avoid the occasional confrontations that have taken place. But the Chase acquittal has come to stand for the proposition that impeachment is not a proper weapon for Congress (abetted, perhaps, by the executive as in the case of Chase) to employ in these confrontations. No matter how angry or frustrated either of the other branches may be by the action of the Supreme Court, removal of individual members of the Court because of their judicial philosophy is not permissible. The other branches must make use of other powers granted them by the Constitution in their effort to bring the Court to book.

Alexander Hamilton

Thomas Jefferson

Aaron Burr

Samuel Chase

Luther Martin

John Randolph of Roanoke

Andrew Johnson

Benjamin Wade

Salmon Chase

Charles Sumner

William Fessenden

Edwin M. Stanton

The House Managers

-9-

More than half a century after the trial of Samuel Chase, a head-on collision between the executive and legislative branches of the federal government occurred. It, too, would result in impeachment by the House of Representatives, and trial in the Senate. But this time the defendant was Andrew Johnson, president of the United States. The struggle between Johnson and the Radical Republicans in Congress had gradually intensified after he succeeded Abraham Lincoln as president when the latter was assassinated in April 1865. It came to a head over the weekend of Washington's Birthday in 1868. The national press reflected the frenetic excitement of that weekend in its dispatches from the nation's capital. On Saturday, February 22, the *Philadelphia Inquirer* carried the following leader on its front page:

JOHNSON VS. STANTON.

"A. J." Resumes Active Hostilities

DEPOSES THE SECRETARY OF WAR

Gen. Lorenzo Thomas as His Successor

A DECIDED SENSATION IN THE SENATE

Committee of Senators Visit Secretary Stanton

THEY REQUEST HIM TO REMAIN IN OFFICE

Mr. Stanton Decides to Hold On

HE WILL REMAIN IN HIS OFFICE DAY AND NIGHT

And Yield Only to Force

Proceedings of the Senate in Executive Session

JOHNSON'S ACTION DISAPPROVED

His Communication Returned to Him

HOW THE HOUSE RECEIVED THE NEWS

A Resolution of Impeachment Offered

IT IS TO BE ACTED UPON TO-DAY

Violation of the Tenure of Office Act

WARRANT FOR ADJUTANT-GENERAL THOMAS

[SPECIAL DESPATCHES TO THE INQUIRER.]
WASHINGTON, Feb. 21.

The rest of the story filled in the details. On Friday, February 21, Andrew Johnson, with no previous notice to Congress, sent to the Senate a message announcing that he had removed Edwin M. Stanton as secretary of war, and designated Adjutant General Lorenzo Thomas as acting secretary. Stanton had been the stalking horse for the Radicals in Johnson's Cabinet, remaining there long after he had ceased to agree with the policies of the administration. Upon receiving word of Johnson's action, Stanton refused to surrender physical possession of his office, and groups of his congressional supporters urged him to stand fast. The Senate remained in session into the early evening on Friday, passing by a vote of 29 to 6 a resolution declaring that the president had no authority to remove Stanton. The House of Representatives had a tumultuous session in which it decided to sit on the following day, Saturday, to consider a resolution impeaching Andrew Johnson for high crimes and misdemeanors.

The Sunday editon of *The New York Times* reported the actions in the House of Representatives on Saturday:

WASHINGTON.

Further Particulars of the War Department Troubles.

Secretary Stanton Causes the Arrest of Adjutant-General Thomas.

Thomas Held to Bail and Stanton Still in Office.

Impeachment Resolutions Presented in the House.

Speeches by Messrs. Stevens, Brooks, Bingham, Farnsworth, Beck, Logan and Others.

The Debate to be Continued and a Vote Taken To-morrow.

Special Dispatches to the New-York Times.
WASHINGTON, Saturday, Feb. 22.

PROCEEDINGS IN CONGRESS.

The proceedings at the other end of the avenue, however, were of a very grave and serious character. The knowledge that the Reconstruction Committee would probably report to-day, brought a great throng of people to the Capitol. The galleries of the House were full long before 12 o'clock ; still they kept coming, and before 1 the lobbies and the cloak-rooms overflowed with ladies, and' in an hour more every available seat on the floor, except those of members, were surrendered to their wives and daughters.

The Senate simply met and adjourned, the Republican members in informal caucus having decided not to transact any business.

The House met and proceeded with the transaction of the business before it. The Reconstruction Committee met at 10:30 at the rooms of Mr. STEVENS, and proceeded at once to discuss the matter before them. It was but a few moments ere it was discovered that the seven Republican members of the Committtee were unanimous in the opinion that Mr. JOHNSON'S action of yesterday was such a palpable violation of the law that they could no longer refuse to take action upon it. After some further discussion it was agreed, seven to two, (BROOKS and BECK, Democrats, being the negatives,) that the Committee report in favor of the impeachment of the President. The Committee

then adjourned for one hour, to enable a report
to be prepared, and to obtain certified copies of
certain papers necessary to the report.

The determination of the Committee was
soon known, and created intense excitement,
though generally anticipated. The fact that all
the so-called Conservative members of the Committee were now favorable to immediate impeachment carried great weight, and the passage of the resolution when it got into the House
seemed a foregone conclusion.

The House met at 12 and the regular
business was proceeded with, but amid
much confusion, as the attention of all
was concentrated on the War Department question and the expected report in favor of impeachment. Mr. ELDRIDGE, of Wisconsin, attempted to get the House to hear WASHINGTON's
Farewell Address and then adjourn. The House
was willing to hear the address, but was not
willing to adjourn. Besides, the Speaker decided Mr. ELDRIDGE to be out of order, from
which he appealed, and his motion was laid on
the table almost unanimously.

At 2 P. M. the Reconstruction Committee
made their appearance in the hall, and a buzz of
excitement ran through the galleries and the
House. Mr. STEVENS took his seat, looking better than usual, and the House, which was in

Committee of the Whole, shortly rose, and then, amid profound silence and the most eager and painful interest, Mr. STEVENS rose in his seat.

At this juncture the Speaker took the precaution to add to the dignity and solemnity of the proceedings by announcing that there must be neither applause nor dissent, from either floor or galleries, and that a disregard of the rules of the House would be followed by the prompt ejectment of the offenders. This had an admirable effect, and Mr. STEVENS announced, with few preliminary remarks, the report of the Committee, as follows, which was then read by the Clerk :

In addition to the papers referred to, the Committee find that the President, on the 21st day of February, 1868, signed and ordered a commission or letter of authority to one LORENZO THOMAS, directing and authorizing said THOMAS to act as Secretary of War, *ad interim*, and to take possession of the books, records, papers and other public property in the War Department, of which the following is a copy:

EXECUTIVE MANSION,
WASHINGEON, D. C., Feb. 21, 1868.
SIR: The Honorable EDWIN M. STANTON having been removed from office as Secretary of the Department of War, you are hereby authorized and empowered to act as Secretary of War *ad interim*, and will immediately enter upon the discharge of the duties pertaining to that office. Mr. STANTON has been instructed to transfer to you all records, books, papers and other public property intrusted to his charge. Respectfully yours,
(Signed)   ANDREW JOHNSON.
To Brevet Major-Gen. LORENZO THOMAS, Adjutant-General U. S. A.
(Official copy.)—Respectfully furnished to Hon. EDWIN M. STANTON.
(Signed)   L. THOMAS,
Secretary of War *ad interim*.

Upon the evidence collected by the Committee, which is hereafter presented, and in virtue of the powers with which they have been invested by the House, they are of the opinion that ANDREW JOHNSON, President of the United States, be impeached of high crimes and misdemeanors. They, therefore, recommend to the House the adoption of the accompanying resolution:

THADDEUS STEVENS,	C. T. HURLBURD,
GEORGE A. BOUTWELL,	JOHN F. FARNSWORTH,
JOHN A. BINGHAM,	H. E. PAINE.
F. C. BEAMAN,	

Resolved, That ANDREW JOHNSON, President of the United States, be impeached of high crimes and misdemeanors.

The Tuesday edition of the New York *World* described the proceedings in the House of Representatives on Monday:

WASHINGTON.

Impeachment of the President of the United States.

Vote of the House of Representatives: 126 to 47.

THE DEBATE IN THE HOUSE.

The Scene in the House During the Speaking and Voting.

Message of the President to the Senate.

Events at the White House and War Department,

&c.,   &c.,   &c.

WASHINGTON, February 24.

President Andrew Johnson and the Republican-controlled Congress had increasingly diverged from one another on the issue of how the Confederate states should be treated following the surrender of General Robert E. Lee to General U. S. Grant at Appomattox in the spring of 1865. Now, three years later, Johnson had precipitated a showdown when he removed Edwin M. Stanton from the latter's position as secretary of war. Congress struck back forthwith: The House impeached Johnson because in its view his dismissal of Stanton violated the recently passed Tenure of Office Act. This act provided in essence that all federal officials whose appointment required Senate confirmation could not be removed by the president without its consent. In the spring Johnson would be tried before the Senate. Thus the events of the Washington's Birthday weekend in 1868 brought to a head a great political crisis in the affairs of the nation. But neither the cause of the crisis, nor the manner of its resolution, can be understood without understanding the history of the Republican party. And to understand that requires in turn a brief examination of the American attitude toward Negro slavery over a period of two and a half centuries.

In August 1619—twelve years after the founding of the first permanent English settlement in North America at Jamestown, Virginia—a ship described as a "Dutch Man of Warre" brought twenty African slaves to the Virginia colony. The captain offered to exchange the slaves for food, and the colonists agreed. The institution of slavery was not recognized in England, but English law did recognize a class of "indentured servants" who were pledged to masters for a term of years; after serving that term, they obtained their freedom. At first the newly arrived Africans were treated like indentured servants, but in less than half a century Virginia legally recognized the institution of slavery. The slaves furnished valuable labor for the colony's tobacco plantations. During the seventeenth century slavery was also established in Maryland and Carolina, and in the eighteenth century it was established in Georgia.

Slavery in North America was not limited to the southern colonies, but the number of slaves in the northern colonies was far smaller than in the South. Northern colonists were more devoted to industry and commerce, and their agriculture was conducted on relatively small farms rather than large plantations. But New

England ship captains did a brisk business carrying cargoes of slaves from West Africa to the West Indies and to the ports of the southern colonies.

During the colonial period each colony was legally subordinate to the king and Parliament in England but was completely independent of every other colony. When the colonists revolted against England in 1775, it became necessary for the thirteen colonies to devise means for taking common action. They chose a loose federation administered by a body called the Continental Congress.

On July 4, 1776, the colonies declared their independence from England in a memorable instrument authored by Thomas Jefferson. The Declaration of Independence commenced with the familiar recital of the wrongs done to the colonists by King George III. One of the recitals that Jefferson placed in his original draft of the Declaration condemned the king for countenancing slavery:

> He has waged cruel war against human nature itself, violating its most sacred rights of life and liberty in the person of a distant people who never offended him, captivating and carrying them into slavery in another hemisphere, or to incur miserable death in their transportation thither. . . .

On June 28, 1776, the drafting committee reported Jefferson's version to the Continental Congress, but its consideration was postponed until the Congress actually adopted a resolution declaring the independence of the colonies. That occurred on July 2, and Congress then took up the draft of the Declaration of Independence. The delegates debated, and in places added to, subtracted from, or modified the language Jefferson proposed. Certain "southern gentlemen" from South Carolina and Georgia objected to the paragraph condemning the king for his encouragement of slavery, and in deference to their views the Congress deleted the paragraph. Thus began a series of political compromises in which the Americans felt obliged to weigh the dislike many of them had for slavery against their desire to form, and later to preserve, a union of the English-speaking colonies.

By the Treaty of Paris, which formally ended the Revolutionary War in 1783, England ceded to the United States all of her territory east of the Mississippi River. Many of the states had made claims to land beyond the Appalachians, but following the treaty they ceded to the federal government their claims to territory north of the Ohio River.

The Articles of Confederation, adopted in 1781, had established a Congress as the governing body of the new nation; but while it was stronger than the Continental Congress, it was still too weak to effectively govern the young country. This defect led to a call for a constitutional convention, which gathered in Philadelphia in May 1787. In July of that year—while the Constitutional Convention was sitting in Philadelphia—Congress in New York adopted the Northwest Ordinance to govern the territory lying beyond the Appalachians and north of the Ohio River. This ordinance would provide a framework for the governance of these territories for many years after the Constitution created the new federal government, and would be a model for later laws governing more distant territories. The ordinance provided: "There shall be neither slavery nor involuntary servitude in said territory."

Meanwhile, at Independence Hall in Philadelphia, the delegates to the Constitutional Convention took a much more ambiguous position on slavery. The Committee of Detail of the Convention, which proved to be a good deal more than that, reported to the parent body in early August a draft of the document that was ultimately signed by the framers in September. In that draft Congress was given the power to regulate commerce among the several states and with foreign nations, and the method for apportioning seats in the House of Representatives was established. The Southern states did not want the new federal Congress to have authority to regulate the slave trade, but they wanted slaves to be counted as part of the population that would determine the allotment of seats in the House of Representatives. No one, North or South, thought that Congress was to have any power over the domestic institution of slavery as it existed in the various states.

Some Northern delegates denounced the slave trade and slavery itself—Roger Sherman of Connecticut said he thought the latter was "iniquitous"—but were willing to compromise to satisfy the demands of the Southern states. Gouverneur Morris of New York was less accommodating:

[He] declared slavery to be a "nefarious institution, the curse of heaven on the states where it prevailed." Travel through the whole continent! declaimed Morris angrily. Compare the free regions, their "rich and noble cultivation . . . with the misery and poverty which overspreads the barren waste of Virginia, Maryland and the other states having slaves." Must the North then send its militia to defend the South against such an institution, should the need arise and slaves rebel against their masters? "Wretched Africans!" exclaimed Morris. "The vassalage of the poor has ever been the favorite offspring of aristocracy!"[1]

Most influential Southern delegates were adamant. John Rutledge and the two Pinckneys from South Carolina insisted that their state would not join any Union that left Congress free to regulate the slave trade. Many Northern delegates swallowed their dislike of the institution and a series of compromises was reached.

The word *slavery* is never mentioned in the text of the Constitution, but three separate provisions gave it grudging recognition. Article I, dealing with the legislative power of the federal government, provided that representatives should be apportioned among the states "according to their respective Numbers, which shall be determined by adding to the whole Number of free Persons, including those bound to Service for a Term of Years, and excluding Indians not taxed, three-fifths of all other Persons." The effect of this apportionment formula was to give to the slave states a considerable advantage in the House of Representatives, since the population of "other Persons"—slaves—was heavily concentrated there. Article I, Section 9, placed limitations on the power of Congress, and the first of these dealt with the slave trade:

The Migration or Importation of such Persons as any of the states now existing shall think proper to admit, shall not be prohibited by the Congress prior to the Year 1808. . . .

As a partial concession to the broad authority to regulate commerce, which had been granted to Congress earlier in the article, the limitation contained a proviso that Congress could impose a tax or duty on slaves imported, but that such tax could not exceed ten dollars per "Person."

Finally, Article IV provided:

> No Person held to Service or Labour in one State, under the Laws thereof, escaping into another, shall, in Consequence of any Law or Regulation therein, be discharged from such Service or Labour, but shall be delivered up on Claim of the Party to whom such Service or Labour may be due.

It was this latter provision particularly, and the stringent law enacted by Congress to implement it, that would inflame the North in the decade before the Civil War.

In 1790, the first census taken by the government organized under the new Constitution showed that the population of the nation was slightly less than four million people. Nearly one fifth of these were Negroes. Almost nine tenths of the Negroes lived in the five states below the Mason-Dixon line: Maryland, Virginia, North Carolina, South Carolina, and Georgia. These five states had a combined population of 1.793 million; of that number slightly more than a third were slaves, and less than 2 percent were free Negroes. Virginia had the highest ratio of Negroes to total population: 304,000 to 747,000.

At this time the South was in the throes of an agricultural depression, brought on by exhaustion of its overused soil and a saturated market for the produce of its fields: tobacco, in the upper part of the Atlantic South, and rice and indigo in the lower part. In England the Industrial Revolution had produced among its other wonders machinery for spinning and weaving cotton fiber into cloth, and the climate of much of these Southern states was suitable for raising cotton.

But the great obstacle to the successful cultivation and marketing of cotton was the difficulty of removing the seeds from the boll; done by hand it was a labor-intensive task that added greatly to the cost of production. Shortly after the Revolutionary War, planters along the Atlantic Coast of Georgia and South Carolina began to grow long-staple cotton from which it was not necessary to remove the seeds. But this kind of cotton could be grown only along the coast. In 1793 a Connecticut schoolteacher, Eli Whitney, journeyed south in search of employment and invented the cotton gin, which used machinery to remove the seeds from short-staple cotton. Southern agriculture as a result was revolutionized, since it now became profitable to grow cotton not only in the sea-island areas along the coast but in the upland areas as well. All that was needed was land and labor, and the slaves would supply the labor. The institution of slavery thereby acquired a new vitality in the Southern states.

In December 1806, in his annual message to Congress, President Thomas Jefferson noted the approach of January 1, 1808, the date after which Congress might prohibit the slave trade consistently with the Constitution. After considerable debate Congress enacted a law prohibiting the importation of slaves into the United States, and prohibiting coastwise trade in slaves if carried on in small vessels. Thus was hesitantly taken the first small step toward the curbing of slavery.

But at about the same time Indiana settlers, many of whom had come from Virginia, repeatedly petitioned Congress to repeal that portion of the Northwest Ordinance that prohibited slavery in the territory of Indiana, which at that time also included the present-day state of Illinois. Congress refused to do so. In 1809 Illinois was split off into a separate territory, but the efforts to legalize slavery continued. The Illinois Constitutional Convention of 1818 saw a vigorous debate over a provision that would allow slavery, and the defeat of that measure occurred partly because its proponents feared that its adoption might jeopardize statehood. The advocates of slavery, then, were not confined to the South.

During the first three decades after the adoption of the Constitution, the South gradually lost out to the North in terms of population. The census of 1820 showed the free states with a population of 5.152 million while the slave states had 4.485 million. These population figures translated into 105 members in the House of Representatives for the Northern states, compared to 81 members for the Southern states. To the extent that sectional differences arose between the North and the South, it would be particularly important to the South to maintain a rough equality between slave states and free states in order to assure equal representation in the

United States Senate. Of the thirteen original states, six were "slave" and seven were "free." Beginning with Vermont in 1791, and continuing with Ohio, Indiana, and Illinois, four new free states had been added to the Union by 1820. During this same period of time, five new slave states had been added: Kentucky, Tennessee, Louisiana, Mississippi, and Alabama.

In February 1819 a bill admitting Missouri to the Union as a state was being debated in the House of Representatives. Congressman James Tallmadge of New York offered an amendment prohibiting the further introduction of slaves into Missouri, and requiring the manumission at age twenty-five of all children born thereafter to slave parents. The amendment carried in the House, but the amended bill was defeated in the Senate.

After Congress adjourned, state legislatures, mass meetings, and newspaper editors took up the question, and there ensued the first national debate on the extension of slavery. When Congress again addressed the matter in January 1820, it enacted the famous "Missouri Compromise." Missouri was admitted as a slave-holding state, and Maine was admitted as a free state, maintaining the equal ratio. Slavery would be thereafter prohibited in the territories of the United States north of the line comprising the southern boundary of Missouri. The "slavery question" was put to rest for a generation, and both North and South went back to the business of making a living and developing the new nation. But in the words of one noted historian:

> But for a moment the veil had been lifted, and some saw the bloody prospect ahead. "This momentous question, like a fire bell in the night, awakened and filled me with terror." wrote Jefferson. "I considered it at once as the Knell of the Union." And John Quincy Adams recorded in his diary, "I take it for granted that the present question is a mere preamble—a title-page to a great, tragic volume."[2]

Sectional divisions between the North and the South occurred not merely over the institution of slavery but on the question of tariffs as well. Tariffs—customs duties imposed on goods imported into the United States—were the principal source of income for the federal government in the first century of its existence. But the issue that came to increasingly divide the manufacturing sections of the nation from the agriculture sections was whether customs duties should be imposed at a level sufficient only to produce the necessary revenue to operate the government, or whether they should be imposed at a higher level in order to protect infant American industries from foreign competition. Hamilton in his Report of Manufactures in 1791 had urged the imposition of protective tariffs to protect American industry, but Congress at that time could not be persuaded.

As manufacturing came to play an increasing role in the economy of the Northeast, however, pressure for tariff protection for these manufacturers increased. Henry Clay from Kentucky and John C. Calhoun from South Carolina advanced a program called the "American system," which combined a protective tariff for manufacturers with federal financial support for internal improvements such as roads and canals. In 1816 Congress enacted a protective tariff for the first time. The results pleased domestic manufacturers, who were thereby given an advantage over competing manufactured goods imported from abroad, but displeased the agricultural areas, which sold their products abroad but had to pay increased prices for manufactured goods. Southern planters, in particular, saw not only the protective tariff but the program of "internal improvements" as devices for taxing the South for the benefit of the North.

In 1828 Congress enacted what would later be known as the "tariff of abominations," which raised duties on imported goods even higher than they had been under the tariff of 1816. By this time John C. Calhoun had become disenchanted with the "American system," and his home state of South Carolina began to speak of seceding from the Union. The North and the South both sought to attract the votes of what was then called the "West" (but what would now be called the Midwest) for their respective positions. The western states were interested in encouraging the sale of public lands, so that people from the eastern seaboard might be encouraged to migrate and settle there. In January 1830 a Senate debate, which had begun on the subject of public land, expanded to include the theory of the Constitution and the right of states to secede from the Union. Daniel Webster of Massachusetts delivered his famous reply to Senator Robert Y. Hayne of South Carolina, a reply that contained a peroration that would be soon known throughout the country:

> I have not allowed myself, Sir, to look beyond the Union, to see what might lie hidden in the dark recess behind. I have not cooly weighed the chances of preserving liberty when the bonds that unite us together shall be broken asunder. I have not accustomed myself to hang over the precipice of disunion, to see whether with my short sight, I can fathom the depth of the abyss below; nor could I regard him as a safe counselor in the affairs of this government, whose thought should be mainly bent on considering, not how the Union may be best preserved, but how tolerable might be the condition of the people when it should be broken up and destroyed. . . . When my eyes shall be turned to behold for the last time the sun in heaven, may I not see him shining on the broken and dishonored fragments of a once-glorious Union; on states dissevered, discordant, belligerent; on a land rent with civil feuds, or drenched, it may be, in fraternal blood! Let their last feeble and lingering glance rather behold the gorgeous ensign of the Republic, now known and honored throughout the earth, still full high advanced, its arms and trophies streaming in their original lustre . . . bearing for its motto . . . that . . . sentiment, dear to every true American heart,—Liberty *and* Union, now and forever, one and inseparable!

Two years later another tariff was enacted, which still further inflamed the South Carolinians, and in November 1832 a convention summoned by the legislature of that state declared the tariff enacted by Congress to be null and void, and forbade federal officers to collect customs duties within the state after February 1, 1833. President Andrew Jackson responded by issuing his "Nullification Proclamation" in which he said:

> Each State having parted with so many powers as to constitute, jointly with the other States, a single nation,

cannot possess any right to secede, because such a secession does not break a league but destroys the unity of a nation.

South Carolina attracted little support from other Southern states, and Congress combined firmness with conciliation. In March 1833 it passed and the president signed both a force bill, authorizing the president to use the army and navy to collect customs duties if judicial process was obstructed, and a compromise tariff, providing for a gradual decrease in the tariff schedules over a period of ten years. The South Carolina Convention then reconvened and repealed the nullification ordinance. But a chord of the extreme states' rights theme, which would lead to secession a generation later, had been sounded.

An obvious disadvantage of slavery, even in the eyes of its supporters, was the possibility of a slave revolt. Whites in the slave-holding states lived in fear of such an uprising and this fear was realized in 1831 in Virginia. Nat Turner, who had been taught to read and write and acted as a lay preacher for other slaves, led a revolt:

> After months of planning, Turner launched his revolt on Sunday, August 21st. Turner and six other slaves, each armed with a hatchet and an ax, began the revolt by attacking Turner's master, Joseph Travis. The entire family including the mistress, two boys, and a baby were killed. Turner led his band from plantation to plantation, picking up insurrectionists and murdering every white family. Within twenty-four hours, fifty-nine whites were killed.
>
> The white population of Virginia reacted. As many as three thousand armed men rushed to defeat Turner. By Tuesday, his revolt was ended and Turner was in hiding. For the next two months, until Turner was captured, Virginia was a blood bath, with innocent as well as guilty slaves being murdered, while the countryside rang with rumors of other plots and new marches by Turner. Only the capture, trial, and execution of Turner brought a semblance of normalcy.[3]

Many Southerners laid the blame for Nat Turner's uprising at the doorstep of William Lloyd Garrison, the Boston publisher of a new newspaper named *The Liberator*. He was one of a new breed at the extreme end of the spectrum of antislavery opinion in the United States; he denounced the Constitution as "a covenant with death and an agreement with hell" because of its compromises on the issue of slavery, and proceeded to publicly burn a copy of the document. He believed in outright abolition of the institution of slavery wherever it existed, and favored the separation of the North from the South. To him and his cohorts the preservation of the Union was not worth the price of tolerating slavery. But at this time his views represented only a tiny fraction of those in the North who thought slavery was wrong; most of them were entirely reconciled to its continuation where it already existed.

In 1835 American abolitionists began sending petitions to Congress to abolish slavery and the slave trade in the District of Columbia—where everybody agreed that Congress did have authority to regulate that trade. But to Southerners, the District of Columbia as the national capital had a symbolic significance, and they saw no reason for Northern, rather than Southern, views to prevail on this question. These petitions received no attention once they were submitted, but the Southerners demanded a more stringent rule. They succeeded in 1836 in having the House vote a "gag resolution," which provided that all petitions or papers "relating in any way" to slavery should be laid on the table.

The First Amendment to the United States Constitution provides that "Congress shall make no law . . . abridging . . . the right of the people . . . to petition the Government for a redress of grievances." John Quincy Adams, who had been a senator at the time of the impeachment trial of Samuel Chase, and thereafter served a term as president of the United States, was at this time a member of the House of Representatives. Considerably advanced in years, he was not an abolitionist, but he thought that the "gag rule" was a violation of the right to petition guaranteed by the Constitution, and he fought it tooth and nail. Finally, in 1844, Northern opinion succeeded in repealing the "gag rule" in the House of Representatives.

The political metamorphosis through which John Quincy Adams had gone from the time he was a senator during the Chase impeachment proceedings to the time of his fight against the gag rule forty years later illustrates the changes that had occurred in political alignments during that period. At the time of the Chase trial, Adams had been a Federalist. But the Federalist party even then was dying everywhere except in New England, and he shortly joined the bandwagon of Jefferson and his Republicans. James Madison succeeded Thomas Jefferson as president in 1809, and during his second administration Congress enacted a protective tariff and chartered a Second Bank of the United States. Legislation more congenial to old-time Federalists, or more antithetical to agrarian Republicans such as John Randolph, could scarcely be imagined. The Republican party's policy of inclusiveness had led to the abandonment of its earlier insistence on strict construction of the Constitution and states' rights.

The administration of President James Monroe, the third member of the "Virginia Dynasty," who also served two terms as president, was known as the "era of good feelings" because there was so little partisan dispute at the national level. In the election of 1820 Monroe carried every single state, and was denied a unanimous vote in the Electoral College only because one elector thought it was not fitting that any later president should receive the same electoral accolade as had George Washington.

But the entrance of Andrew Jackson into national politics in the election of 1824 revived partisan animosity, and although in that year he lost the presidency to John Quincy Adams, he turned the tables in 1828. Thus was ushered in the era of "Jacksonian Democracy." Jackson introduced the spoils system into American politics, glorified the "common man," and bitterly fought the Second Bank of the United States. He was in many ways a strong believer in states' rights; he vetoed an act of Congress known as the "Maysville Road Bill" because he did not believe that federal funds should be spent for constructing or improving roads or canals in the interior of the United States. In taking these positions he antagonized such Senate greats as Daniel Webster, Henry Clay, and their adherents, who favored the "American system" of protective tariffs and internal improvements. By the election of 1836 these opponents of Andrew Jackson had come to call themselves Whigs, and for the next twenty years the American political scene would be primarily a contest between the followers of Andrew

Jackson, who would call themselves Democrats, and the Whigs. John Quincy Adams continued his political evolution and became a Whig.

Worldwide, the movement to abolish not merely the slave trade but the institution of slavery itself was making rapid progress. In 1833 the English Parliament enacted a law freeing all slaves in the British colonies but providing that their owners be compensated. France did the same thing for French possessions in 1848. In a period of about forty years, beginning with Argentina in 1813 and ending with Peru in 1854, all of the Latin American republics save one abolished slavery. At the end of that period, slavery was a legal institution in the Western Hemisphere only in Brazil, in the Spanish and Dutch West Indies, and in the United States.

In 1836 Texas, which had been settled almost entirely by Americans from slaveholding states, declared its independence from Mexico. For the next few years it repeatedly sought annexation to the United States; but Northerners saw annexation as providing the possibility of not merely one but several additional slave states being admitted to the Union, and they opposed it. Arkansas and Michigan had recently been admitted, keeping the number of slave states and free states equal at thirteen each. But the future without Texas looked unpromising for the South: Florida was the only organized territory that recognized slavery, while three free territories in the North—Iowa, Wisconsin, and Minnesota—were sure to be requesting admission in the near future. Efforts to annex Texas by treaty were defeated in the Senate because ratification by that body required a two-thirds vote. But in 1845 Congress by joint resolution—which required only a majority in each house— annexed Texas to the Union.

Less than a week after the annexation of Texas, James K. Polk was inaugurated as the eleventh president of the United States. Polk had been the first "dark horse" presidential candidate in history, and was one of three Tennesseeans to occupy the presidency within a space of forty years. Polk's administration was Manifest Destiny writ large. During his single term of office the United States secured its title to the Oregon Territory in the Pacific Northwest and, by defeating Mexico in the Mexican War, acquired the Mexican Cession—an area of more than half a million square miles, from which the present-day states of California, Nevada, Utah, major parts of Arizona and New Mexico, and smaller parts of Colorado and Wyoming were carved. The Mexican War was popular in the states of the Mississippi Valley, but it was thoroughly unpopular in New England, where antislavery sentiment was becoming more prominent. The abolitionists looked upon the Mexican War—which had been started, with virtually no provocation from Mexico, by President Polk—as a device by which the Southern states could acquire more territory for slavery.

The question of how to administer the vast new domain acquired from Mexico would start a new round in the debate over slavery. Before the war had even ended, Congressman David Wilmot of Pennsylvania sought to amend a bill appropriating money for a secret fund to bribe the Mexicans into ceding California by adding a proviso that any territory acquired as a result of the Mexican War should be subject to the same prohibition against slavery as that contained in the Northwest Ordinance. The amendment was defeated, but the debate continued. Northerners opposed to slavery took the position that, while Congress could not disturb that institution where it existed, it could use its plenary authority to legislate for territories to prohibit its introduction into the newly acquired area. Freedom should be national, and slavery sectional. The Southerners who favored the extension of slavery, on the other hand, took the position that they were as entitled to settle the new territories as Northerners were, and that just as Northerners, they were entitled to take with them into the new territories their property—even if that property consisted of slaves.

In the presidential election of 1848 a significant third party appeared for the first time: the Free Soil party. Northern antislavery elements dissatisfied with both the Democratic and Whig nominees for president met in Buffalo and nominated former president Martin Van Buren on a platform of "free soil, free speech, free labor, and free men." The Free Soilers did not carry the electoral votes of a single state, but polled 300,000 popular votes—more than 10 percent of the total vote cast. The Free Soil party elected nine members to the House of Representatives, including George W. Julian of Indiana and Joshua Giddings of Ohio. These Free Soil members of Congress constituted an advance guard of Northerners who were no longer willing to temporize over the extension of slavery.

The Free Soilers also acquired the balance of power in the Ohio legislature in the 1848 election, and that legislature would shortly elect Salmon P. Chase to the United States Senate. The New York legislature would at the same time elect William H. Seward to the Senate. Both would be strong voices in that body for the antislavery views of the North.

The election of 1850 would result in two more Free Soilers being sent to the Senate. The Massachusetts legislature, after extended manipulation and bargaining, elected Charles Sumner, a devoted and outspoken abolitionist. The Ohio legislature elected Benjamin F. Wade. While Sumner was an orator and a scholar, Wade was a self-educated lawyer, who had risen from positions of rough manual labor to that of state legislator. Sumner would be one of Andrew Jackson's leading opponents in 1868; Ben Wade would be president *pro tempore* of the Senate at that time, and as such he would succeed to the presidency if the Senate convicted Johnson in his impeachment trial.

George Julian describes his first meeting with his fellow Free Soilers in the new Congress in these words:

> With the exception of two Indiana members, I had no personal acquaintance in either branch of Congress, and, on entering the old Hall of Representatives, my first thought was to find the Free Soil members, whose political fortunes and experience had been so similar to my own. The seat of Mr. Giddings was pointed out to me in the northwest corner of the Hall, where I found the stalwart champion of free speech busy with his pen. He received me with evident cordiality, and at once sent a page for the other Free Soil members. Soon the "immortal nine," as we were often sportively styled, were all together. . . . I was delighted with all my bretheren, at once entered fully into their plans and counsels.[4]

It was this Congress that would deal with the territorial problems that arose from the Mexican Cession. In January 1850 Henry Clay of Kentucky introduced in the Senate resolutions that would provide for the immediate admission of California as a free state, organization of territorial governments in New Mexico and Utah without mention of slavery, a new and more stringent fugitive-slave law, and abolition of the domestic slave trade in the District of Columbia. This was the last session at which the "great triumvirate" consisting of Clay, John Calhoun of South Carolina, and Daniel Webster of Massachusetts would be together in that body. Calhoun opposed these measures, but he was too ill to read his own speech; within a month he would be dead. Next spoke Daniel Webster, nearing seventy years of age and still devoted to the Union. This time he pleaded with his fellow Northerners to compromise and accept the harsh fugitive-slave law as a price for preserving the Union. Seward, the freshman senator from New York, opposed the compromise. He conceded that Congress had the constitutional authority to establish slavery in the territories, but went on to say that "there is a higher law than the Constitution which regulates our authority over the domain." This statement would haunt Seward when the Republican party met to nominate a presidential candidate ten years later. Stephen A. Douglas, a young senator from Illinois, known as the "little Giant," supported Clay's and Webster's efforts to obtain a compromise.

The measures passed Congress in the summer of 1850 after extended debate, and President Millard Fillmore signed them into law. They were known as the Compromise of 1850, the second great compromise designed to patch up sectional differences between the North and South in order to save the Union.

> Wild jubilation marked the closing scenes of the contest in Washington. On the day that the House passed the California and Utah bills, a general celebration began. Bonfires, processions, serenades, speeches, suppers, drinking, and cannon-salutes filled the next twenty-four hours. At nightfall the principal buildings were illuminated. Exhilarated crowds gathered, shouting "The Union is saved!"[5]

Similar celebrations were held in cities throughout the country. In New York a giant meeting was held at Castle Garden, called by a group of conservative Whig and Democratic merchants not only to celebrate the passage of the Compromise but to show disapproval of abolitionist sentiment. Millard Fillmore's annual message to Congress spoke of the provisions of the Compromise as "a final settlement" of the slavery question. Stephen Douglas told the

Senate in its short session in the winter of 1850–1851 that he had "determined never to make another speech on the slavery question. . . ." A round robin was circulated in Congress declaring that its many signatories would never support for president, Congress, or a state legislature any person not known to be a supporter of the Compromise and an opponent of any renewal of slavery agitation. The final seal of approval seemed to have been put on the Compromise of 1850 when both the major parties—the Whigs and the Democrats—endorsed it in their platforms for the 1852 presidential election. The Democrats elected their candidate, Franklin Pierce of New Hampshire, by a wide margin of electoral votes, although by a smaller margin of popular votes. Pierce was a "doughface"—an antislavery epithet for a Northern man who had Southern sympathies.

New England was the center of abolitionist sentiment, and it did not like the Compromise; the lower South was the home of the southern "fire-eaters" and it did not like the Compromise; but the rest of the country seemed quite content to let sleeping dogs lie. But already the sleeping dogs were beginning to rouse themselves. In March 1852 Harriet Beecher Stowe published her novel *Uncle Tom's Cabin*, which graphically depicted the sufferings of the slaves. At the end of the year 1852, 300,000 copies had been sold, and it was ultimately translated into half the languages of the world. Read about the fireside in Northern homes, the book spread abolitionist sentiments; read by the upper classes in England, it would influence the position Britain took with respect to the North and South during the Civil War.

The most difficult part of the Compromise of 1850 for Northerners to live with was the Fugitive Slave Law. Whether or not slaves could be taken by their masters from the South into such faraway places as New Mexico or Utah was a rather theoretical question; but when a slave catcher sent by a Southern master to recapture a runaway slave appeared in a state such as Massachusetts, the effect of the Compromise was brought home with a vengeance. An action could be instituted in court simply by the filing of a sworn affidavit, and no right of jury trial was accorded to the putative slave. The abbreviated hearing required was not before a judge but before a court commissioner who was empowered to remand the fugitive to the agent of the master without any appeal or stay. In 1854 Anthony Burns, a fugitive slave, was detained in the courthouse in Boston for examination. When he was identified by his master and ordered returned, it required a battalion of United States artillery and platoons of marines to carry out the order, escorting the slave through streets lined with outraged citizens. The Fugitive Slave Law was a dead letter in Massachusetts after this spectacle.

Henry Clay and Daniel Webster both died in 1852, and the Senate which they and John C. Calhoun had dominated for so long was open to a new generation of leaders. Prominent among them was Stephen A. Douglas of Illinois, who would in short order upset the temporary respite from quarreling over the extension of slavery which had followed the Compromise of 1850. In 1854 he introduced in the Senate his Kansas-Nebraska Bill, which embodied his doctrine of "popular sovereignty." The settlers in the new territory should decide for themselves whether or not they would have slavery, and the provisions of the Missouri Compromise that would have forbidden slavery in these territories would be repealed. President Pierce brought the weight of the administration to bear in favor of the bill, and after fierce debate it passed both houses of Congress and was signed into law in May 1854.

But the "Northwest"—Michigan, Wisconsin, Minnesota, and Iowa—was especially aroused against the measure. Douglas himself had said, after having toured the North after Congress adjourned in August, that he could have traveled from Boston to Chicago by the light of fires kindled to burn him in effigy. In February 1854 a meeting was held in a schoolhouse in Ripon, Wisconsin, to oppose the extension of slavery, and to recommend that a new party be formed to do it. This gathering led to a state convention in Madison in July which adopted the name "Republican" for the new party. A week earlier a state convention in Jackson, Michigan, had adopted the same name for its new party. The Whig party had become moribund after the election of 1852 because its Northern and Southern wings had been unable to settle their differences about the question of slavery. Many Northern Democrats were upset by the passage of the Kansas-Nebraska Act, and they along with Northern Whigs were grist for the Republican mill. Many antislavery people were at first reluctant to join a brand-new party, and so fielded "anti-Nebraska" or "Fusion" tickets in the election of 1854. The result was that although the Democrats lost the congressional elections of that year, those who defeated them marched under a number of different banners. Another new party, the American Party or "Know-Nothings," polled a large number of votes by virtue of its anti-immigrant and anti-Catholic position.

Meanwhile, both Northerners and Southerners were sending immigrants to settle Kansas, and violence quickly broke out. Charles Sumner delivered a lengthy oration in the Senate in May 1856, titled "The Crime against Kansas," in which he maligned Senator Andrew Butler of South Carolina. Three days later a South Carolina congressman, a distant cousin of Butler, attacked Sumner with a stick while he was sitting helplessly at his desk in the Senate chamber, and beat him senseless. The sectional pot was rapidly coming to a boil.

A few days after the beating of Sumner, the Republican party held a national nominating convention in Philadelphia. It turned for its nominee not to any of the Northern politicians who had been standing up in defense of "free soil" principles, but to John C. Frémont. Frémont, known as "the pathfinder" because of his many expeditions in the Far West, was viewed as having enough of what we would today call charisma to attract the attention of the average voter. He was opposed by James Buchanan, a time-serving Democrat who had been absent as minister to England during the furor over the Kansas-Nebraska Bill. In the election of 1865 Buchanan carried every slave state except Maryland, together with the Northern states of Pennsylvania, Illinois, and Indiana. He polled over 1.8 million votes to Frémont's 1.34 million. Former president Millard Fillmore, running on a third-party ticket, received 874,000 votes. But the victory was one from which the Democrats could draw little comfort. The Republican party was not a national party, but a Northern antislavery party; in its very first presidential election, it had made a remarkably good showing against the long-established national Democratic party. By the time of the impeachment trial of Andrew Johnson twelve years later, the Republican party would dominate the Senate and hold in its hands the fate of Andrew Johnson in the same way that the Jeffersonian Republicans in the Senate in 1805 had held in their hands the fate of Samuel Chase.

-10-

James Buchanan was inaugurated as president on March 4, 1857, and in his inaugural address he dealt with the question of the authority of Congress to prohibit slavery in the territories in these words:

> [It is] a judicial question, which legitimately belongs to the Supreme Court of the United States, before whom it is now pending, and will, it is understood, be speedily and finally settled. To their decision, in common with all good citizens, I shall cheerfully submit, whatever this may be. . . .[1]

The *New-York Tribune*, a leading antislavery newspaper edited by Horace Greeley, editorially responded the next day:

> You may "cheerfully submit"—of course you will to whatever the five slaveholders and two or three dough-faces on the bench of the Supreme Court may be ready to utter on this subject; but not one man who really desires the triumph of freedom over slavery in the territories will do so. We may be constrained to obey as law whatever that tribunal shall put forth; but, happily, this is a country in which the people make both laws and judges, and they will try their strength on the issues here presented.

Actually Buchanan knew far more than he should have about the Supreme Court's forthcoming decision in the case of *Dred Scott* v. *Sandford*.[2] The lawsuit had begun as a "test case" in St. Louis, nominally brought by a slave who contended that he had been emancipated when he was taken by his master to reside in the territory of Minnesota where slavery was prohibited. After the case was argued in the Supreme Court, the majority of the justices at conference had settled on a narrow ground of decision that made it unnecessary to rule on the extent of the congressional authority to prohibit slavery in the territories. But two members of the Court disagreed with the holding on the narrower point and planned to write a dissent upholding the authority of Congress to prohibit slavery in the territories. This development gave pause to some of the members of the majority, and they decided that they, too, should reach the question of congressional authority and hold it to be lacking. One of them, Justice John Catron of Tennessee, who continued to dabble in Democratic politics even after his appointment as an associate justice by President Andrew Jackson, asked Buchanan to urge his fellow Pennsylvanian, Justice Robert Grier, to agree with this position. Buchanan apparently acceded to this request, and in his correspondence with Grier was made fully aware of how the Court would decide this question.

Two days after the inauguration, the Supreme Court handed down its opinion in the *Dred Scott* case. The majority opined that Congress had no power to prohibit slavery in the territories. Thus all of the intense debate that had attended the passage of the Kansas-Nebraska Act three years earlier, and indeed the debate that had attended the enactment of the Missouri Compromise nearly forty years earlier, became much ado about nothing. Whatever the vote in Congress, and whatever the majority of the people in the United States wished, Congress was powerless to prevent slaveholders from taking with them to the territories their "property"— i.e., slaves.

Horace Greeley's *New-York Tribune* editorialized with predictable rage:

> The long trumpeted decision . . . having been held over
> from last year in order not to flagrantly alarm and exas-
> perate the Free States on the eve of an important Presi-

dential election . . . is entitled to just so much moral weight as would be the judgment of a majority of those congregated in any Washington Bar-room.[3]

The nation was sufficiently aroused and divided over this question that no decision of the Supreme Court could "settle" it in any realistic sense of that term. Buchanan proved to be even more of a "doughface" than Pierce, and supported efforts by Southerners in Congress to deny the settlers in Kansas an effective vote on whether the state constitution should or should not recognize slavery. Even Douglas rebelled at this excess, and for doing so he was branded by some as a "traitor" to the South.

The Illinois legislature that was chosen in 1858 would decide whether or not Douglas would be returned for another term to the United States Senate, and from the ranks of the Republicans a formidable challenger arose. Abraham Lincoln was a lawyer by profession and during the Mexican War had served one term in the United States House of Representatives as a Whig. His speech to the Illinois Republican convention in June 1858 became famous for its use of the phrase "house divided":

If we could first know where we are and whither we are tending, we could better judge what to do and how to do it. We are now far into the fifth year since a policy was initiated with the avowed object, and confident promise, of putting an end to slavery agitation. Under the operation of that policy, that agitation has not only not ceased, but has constantly augmented. In my opinion it will not cease until a crisis shall have been reached and passed. "A house divided against itself cannot stand." I believe this Government cannot endure permanently half slave and half free. I do not expect the Union to be dissolved—I do not expect the house to fall—but I do expect that it will cease to be divided. It will become all one thing or all the other. Either the opponents of slavery will arrest the further spread of it and place it where the public mind shall rest in the belief that it is in course of ultimate extinction, or its advocates will push it for-

ward till it shall become lawful alike in all the States, old
as well as new—North as well as South.[4]

During the summer and fall Lincoln and Douglas conducted a
series of seven debates at different cities in downstate Illinois, which
became justly famous for the high quality of the oratory of both
candidates. Viewing these debates from the perspective of the
present day, one can only marvel at their literacy and at their
detailed treatment of the issues. In the little town of Ottawa, Illinois, twelve thousand spectators sat or stood in the hot August
sun for three hours while the candidates conducted their first debate. The next debate was held in Freeport, located in the northwestern corner of the state. Here fifteen thousand people attended
and listened for three hours in cloudy, chilly weather. Lincoln put
a series of questions to Douglas; one of them was "Can the people
of a United States Territory, in any lawful way, against the wish
of any citizen of the United States, exclude slavery from its limits
prior to the formation of a State Constitution?" Douglas, in a
roundabout way, answered yes; the institution of slavery could
not exist without a body of positive law to support it, he said, and
if the legislators of the territory refused to enact such laws slavery
would be effectively excluded. This answer won Douglas votes in
Illinois, but it was to cost him the presidential nomination of a
united Democratic party in 1860. The Democrats narrowly maintained control of the Illinois legislature in the election of 1858, and
Douglas was returned for another term in the Senate.

Lincoln was not the only Republican to predict an impending
crisis as a result of the conflict over slavery. In the spring of 1858,
William Henry Seward of New York, who had now shed his Whig
allegiance and become a Republican, spoke in terms of an "irrepressible conflict" between the free-labor states of the North and
the slave-labor states of the South. Men like Seward and Salmon
P. Chase of Ohio, who had now left the Democratic party to become a Republican, were viewed as more radical or extreme on
the slavery question than was Lincoln. They had their counter-
parts in the South; extreme proslavery men, such as Robert Rhett
of South Carolina and Robert Toombs of Georgia, who took the
view that slavery was a positive good, as compared to the North-

ern system of wage labor, and that Congress should enact a federal slave code to support the institution of slavery in the territories.

Men such as this, as well as many other people of more moderate views, were shocked and outraged when in October 1859 the fanatical abolitionist John Brown and a group of his followers seized the federal arsenal in Harpers Ferry, Virginia (later to become part of West Virginia). News of the sacking of the arsenal was sent by telegraph to Washington, and Colonel Robert E. Lee and a detachment of eighty marines were sent by train over the Baltimore and Ohio Railroad to capture Brown and his followers and retake the arsenal. This they did in rather short order, leaving all but two of Brown's force of eighteen men dead or wounded. Brown survived and declared that he had hoped to seize the arms of the arsenal and use them to start a slave uprising.

Brown was tried and convicted for treason to the state of Virginia, and was hanged in Charles Town after having discouraged efforts of his Northern supporters to abduct him. Some New England abolitionists praised his act, but most Northern antislavery leaders condemned it with little or no reservation. But less than two years later, Massachusetts volunteers who arrived in Washington in response to President Lincoln's call to fight for the Union would be singing "John Brown's Body" to the tune to which Julia Ward Howe later put the words of the "Battle Hymn of the Republic."

As the year 1860 opened, politicians North and South looked to the upcoming party conventions at which candidates for president would be nominated. The Democrats were the first to hold theirs, in April in Charleston, South Carolina. The leading candidate was Stephen A. Douglas, whose turn, it seemed, might have finally come. He had twice lost his party's presidential nomination to men far less able than he was: in 1852 to Franklin Pierce, and in 1856 to James Buchanan. But in 1860 events once more conspired against him. He had the support of a majority of the delegates to the convention, but the Democratic party then and for many years afterward operated under a "two-thirds rule," which required that the actions of the convention be approved by two thirds of the delegates voting. "Popular sovereignty" had turned sour for the Southerners; they had won the legislative battles in Congress about Kansas, but Kansas was now in the hands of a

Free Soil legislature that had followed Douglas's "Freeport Doctrine" and refused to recognize slavery. The Southerners demanded a plank endorsing a federal slave code for the territories, but the majority of Northern delegates refused. At this point the delegates of eight Southern states withdrew, and the convention was recessed to meet again in Baltimore in June.

The prospects for the Republican nominee increased dramatically after the Democratic fiasco in Charleston. In early May a splinter group calling itself the National Constitutional Union met and nominated John Bell of Tennessee for president and Edward Everett of Massachusetts for vice-president. It sought to appeal to conservatives in both the North and the South as the only party that could preserve the Union; its only platform was a recitation of its devotion to the Constitution and to the Union. Its appeal would be limited to the border states. The Republican Convention gathered in Chicago on May 16.

A building had been specially constructed for the occasion. It was called the "Wigwam," and it seemed to represent Chicago's ebullient personality. Twenty years earlier the city had a population of less than five thousand; ten years earlier it had a population of less than thirty thousand; but now it had a population of one hundred twelve thousand. Located at the foot of Lake Michigan, so that all land traffic from the east to states such as Wisconsin, Iowa, and Minnesota would have to pass through it, it was already on its way to becoming the major rail center of the nation. And it was the railroads, now reaching out west of Chicago into the great breadbasket beyond, that shifted the commercial ties of that region from the lower Mississippi Valley and New Orleans to the ports of the East Coast.

Among the Republicans, Seward of New York was regarded as the leading contender. He had been in the lists of the antislavery cause at least since his election to the Senate in 1849, and several state conventions in New England and the upper Midwest instructed their delegates for him. But Seward also had drawbacks; people disliked the perceived manipulation of his cohort Thurlow Weed, and many felt that his long-standing opposition to the Know-Nothing movement might cost the party votes from that sector.

Salmon P. Chase had long been identified with the antislavery movement both in Ohio and to a lesser extent on the national scene; he had served both as senator from that state and as governor. But Chase had never gotten along with Ben Wade, the other Republican senator from Ohio, and as a result the Ohio delegation to the Republican convention was not united behind him. Edward Bates of Missouri, Simon Cameron of Pennsylvania, and Abraham Lincoln of Illinois were closely watched dark horses. Lincoln had traveled extensively during 1859 making speeches to Republican gatherings, and had attracted favorable attention for a speech he gave at Cooper Union in New York in February 1860. As the leading dark-horse candidate, he was in a position to profit should Seward falter.

On the first ballot Seward polled 173½ votes to Lincoln's 102; on the second ballot Lincoln pulled almost even with Seward, and at the end of the third ballot Lincoln received the necessary number of votes for the nomination. The following day the delegates nominated Senator Hannibal Hamlin of Maine for vice-president. The platform backed away from the ardent Free Soil rhetoric that had been employed in 1856. It asserted that freedom should be the normal condition in the territories, and went on to address other issues. Federal support for internal improvements and for a Pacific railroad were endorsed, as well as the enactment of a homestead law and a moderate protective tariff.

The Democrats reconvened in Baltimore shortly afterward to attempt to resolve their differences, but there were enough Southern fire-eaters and administration lackeys to deny Douglas the necessary two-thirds vote for the nomination. The party split was final: The Northern wing nominated Douglas for president and Herschel V. Johnson of Georgia for vice-president, while the Southern faction chose John C. Breckinridge of Kentucky as its presidential nominee, and Senator Joseph Lane of Oregon as its candidate for vice-president.

The results of the November presidential election surprised scarcely anyone. Lincoln received an absolute majority of the electoral votes—180—while Breckinridge received 72, Bell 39, and Douglas only 12. But the popular vote told quite a different story: Lincoln, 1,866,452; Douglas 1,376,957; Breckinridge, 849,781; Bell, 588,879. Breckinridge carried every state in the Deep South, together with North Carolina, Delaware, and Maryland. Bell carried Virginia, Kentucky, and Tennessee. Douglas, in spite of his large popular vote, carried only the state of Missouri. Lincoln's electoral votes came entirely from the East and Midwest except for the states of California and Oregon. The sectional character of his victory was not lost upon the South.

Even as the popular returns from the presidential election were coming in in November, the South Carolina legislature was in session for the purpose of choosing presidential electors. On Wednesday, November 7, crowds thronged the streets of Charleston, the states' rights flag was hoisted over public buildings, and it was announced that the resident federal judge and the collector of the customs had resigned their offices. Within days the two South Carolina senators had resigned their seats in the national body. The legislature enacted a bill calling a convention to determine whether the state should secede from the Union: The election of delegates was to take place on December 6, and the delegates were to convene on December 17.

The wave of secessionist feeling swept other states of the lower South. In Alabama the legislature called for a convention to meet January 7; in Mississippi the plan was for an election of delegates on December 20, to convene in January; Florida provided for an election on December 24, and a January convention. Georgia, more divided on the question, finally decided to elect delegates early in January for a convention to be held in mid-January. The Texas legislature called for a similar convention on February 1. By the end of the year 1860, the seven states of the lower South seemed headed for secession.

The reaction in the North to this development was mixed. Some viewed the frenetic activity in the Southern states as a bluff, the sort of threat that Southerners had previously made but would not actually carry out. Others viewed the actions more seriously, but felt that some sort of peaceful solution could be worked out to retain the Southern states in the Union. Horace Greeley's *New-York Tribune* opposed coercion of the seceding states, decrying "a republic whereof one section is pinned to the residue by bayonets." *The New York Times*, on the other hand, editorialized: "We would yield nothing whatever to exactions pressed by threats of disunion." Northern opinion appeared understandably ambivalent and fluid, and ripe for leadership. But Abraham Lincoln would not be inaugurated as president until March 4, and until that time leadership would have to come, if at all, from lame-duck president James Buchanan.

Buchanan was nearly seventy years of age and enfeebled by illness. He had always been inclined to temporize, and was very much subject to the influence of his Cabinet. But the Cabinet itself was divided. Three Southerners—Secretary of the Treasury Howell Cobb of Georgia, Secretary of War Jacob Thompson of Mississippi, and Secretary of the Interior John Floyd of Virginia, were strong supporters of their respective states and thought the president neither could nor should do anything to prevent the secession of the states of the lower South. Secretary of State Lewis Cass of Michigan, Attorney General Jeremiah Black of Pennsylvania, and Postmaster General Joseph Holt of Kentucky were Northern Democrats; they disliked the Republicans, but they were supporters of the Union and thought Buchanan should take whatever action was possible to preserve it.

Buchanan was in the process of drafting a message to Congress expressing his views on secession, in the course of which he was importuned by both sides of his Cabinet. Congress reconvened the first week in December, and the president sent the message that had resulted from the Cabinet deliberations. That message took the position that the Southern states had no right to secede, but that there was nothing the president could do to prevent them if the federal officers within the states should resign their offices. The message would have been more appropriate for a scholarly journal than as a recommendation from the president to Congress at this critical time.

When the delegates to the South Carolina convention were chosen on December 6, it was widely predicted that the convention would favor secession. There were three Union forts in Charleston Harbor, and as soon as the state seceded there would obviously be a confrontation between it and the federal forces manning these forts. Major Robert Anderson, commanding the federal troops, requested reinforcements, but Buchanan vacillated, torn first one way and then the other by his various Cabinet advisers. The South Carolina convention met on December 17, and on December 20, it voted to take South Carolina out of the Union.

In early December, Secretary Cobb resigned to return to Georgia. Shortly afterward Secretary Cass insisted that Buchanan reinforce the Charleston forts, and when the president refused to give him any assurances, Cass resigned. Buchanan named Jeremiah Black to succeed Cass as secretary of state, and at Black's urging appointed Edwin M. Stanton, a fellow Pennsylvanian, as attorney general.

Edwin M. Stanton would be one of the principal protagonists in the 1868 drama that resulted in the impeachment and trial of President Andrew Johnson. He was born in Steubenville, Ohio, in 1814, attended Kenyon College in that state, and was admitted to the practice of law in Ohio in 1836. He had a remarkably successful law practice, arguing and winning important patent and commercial cases for his clients. He pioneered the defense of "temporary insanity" on behalf of a husband who had killed his wife's lover. When Jeremiah Black became attorney general in Buchanan's Cabinet, he appointed Stanton as a special United States commissioner in California to sift through numerous disputed Mexican land grants and decide upon their validity. Stanton had returned from California only a short time before he accepted the position of attorney general in Buchanan's Cabinet.

Stanton's first day on the job was December 27, 1860, and it proved to be a very eventful one. That very morning the capital received word that Major Anderson had moved his garrison from Fort Moultrie in Charleston Harbor to the more defensible post of Fort Sumter. A Cabinet meeting had been summoned, and Stanton arrived late. The usual Cabinet division had occurred over whether Buchanan should order Anderson back to Moultrie in keeping with a pledge that members of the South Carolina congressional delegation claimed the president had made to them. Stanton's biographers describe this acrimonious scene:

> Floyd wrote out a demand that the federal troops be withdrawn from Charleston Harbor altogether. Black snapped out that if any English minister had ever advocated the apathetic surrender of a defensible fortress to the enemy, as Floyd was doing, he would have lost his head on the block. Stanton added that to give up Sumter would be a crime equal to Benedict Arnold's and that anyone participating in it would deserve to be hanged like Major André. Floyd and Thompson started angrily from their seats, but Buchanan, raising his hands depre-

catingly, said: "Oh, No! Not so bad as that, my friend—
not so bad as that!"[5]

The following day Secretary Floyd resigned, and the Cabinet
was firmly in the hands of Unionist sympathizers. Stanton and
Black urged the president to take a firmer stand in his reply to the
South Carolina commissioners, whom he had received privately
after that state had seceded, but again Buchanan vacillated. Eventually he took a stronger position, more to the liking of Black and
Stanton, and advised the commissioners of his refusal to remove
the federal troops from Fort Sumter.

Stanton had been understandably perturbed by the secessionist
influences exerted by the pro-Southern wing of the Cabinet of
which he was a member, and he did his best to counter their
influence with the president with his own views. But his concern
was such that he took another step, a step that reflects less favorably upon his character. He had been a Democrat all his life and
was a member of a Democratic Cabinet, but he decided to relay
news of the deliberations of the Buchanan Cabinet to Republicans
in Congress. The primary recipient of these dispatches, through
an intermediary, was William H. Seward, widely thought to be
Lincoln's choice for secretary of state in his forthcoming administration. Seward, in turn, advised Lincoln of the news he received
from Stanton. The crisis in the Buchanan Cabinet had actually
passed by the end of December, and that administration simply
performed what was essentially a caretaker function until it expired on March 4.

The vacuum in leadership left by the administration was filled
by efforts of Congress and of a "Peace Convention" to work out a
solution that would keep the states of the lower South in the Union.
Once Congress had reconvened in December 1860, each house
made an effort to find a way to dissuade the states of the lower
South from leaving the Union. On December 18, the Senate voted
to form a Committee of Thirteen, to which were appointed able
representatives from each section of the Union. The principal ar-
chitect of compromise on this committee was Senator John J. Crittenden of Kentucky, who proposed six amendments to the
Constitution designed to avert the breakup of the Union. Among
Crittenden's proposals was one that would restore the line of the
Missouri Compromise as the boundary between free and slave ter-

ritories, and one that would have protected slavery against abolition even by constitutional amendment where it already existed.
His plan was the only one that received extensive study by the
committee, and during its deliberations there was much evidence
of popular support for it from the Northern states and the border
states. Seward of New York was the leading Republican on the
committee, and he and the other four Republicans naturally looked
to President-elect Lincoln for guidance. Lincoln was adamant that
the Republican party should brook no proposals by which slavery
could be further extended into the territories; and in December,
he wrote to Elihu B. Washburne of Illinois:

> Prevent, as far as possible, any of our friends from de-
> moralizing themselves and our cause by entertaining
> propositions for compromise of any sort on "slavery ex-
> tension." There is no possible compromise upon it but
> which puts us under again, and leaves us all our work
> to do over again. Whether it be a Missouri line or Eli
> Thayer's popular sovereignty, it is all the same. Let either
> be done, and immediately filibustering and extending
> slavery recommences. On that point hold firm, as with a
> chain of steel.[6]

When the committee voted on the proposal to restore the line
of the Missouri Compromise, it was defeated by a vote of 6 to 6,
with all of the Republicans voting in the negative. In late December, the committee reported to the Senate that it could reach no
conclusion. In early January Crittenden rose on the floor of the
Senate and proposed that his compromise should be submitted to
the people of every state for a popular vote, but because of opposition from both the Republicans and the Southerners his proposal
never came to a vote in the Senate.

In early December the House of Representatives had created a
special committee consisting of one member from each state to
consider the condition of the country, and it became known as the
Committee of Thirty-three. But this committee could muster no
majority for any particular proposal, and its deliberations proved
fruitless.

Up to this time the slave states of the upper South—Delaware,
Maryland, Kentucky, Virginia, North Carolina, Tennessee, and

Arkansas—had taken no action with respect to secession. On January 19, responding to a plea from the governor, the Virginia legislature invited all the states to send delegates to a convention which should meet in Washington on February 4. Former president John Tyler presided over the convention, and a number of elder statesmen participated in its work. But neither the states of the lower South nor four of the Northern states chose to send delegates, and its work was doomed from the start. Late in February it recommended to both houses of Congress a plan similar to the Crittenden Compromise, but neither house would act favorably on the proposal.

On the very day that the Peace Convention opened its meetings in Washington, delegates from the six states of the lower South met in Montgomery, Alabama, to launch the Confederate States of America. In a period of only a few days, they adopted a constitution, and elected Jefferson Davis of Mississippi president and Alexander Stephens of Georgia vice-president. On February 16, Jefferson Davis arrived in Montgomery, and as he alighted from the train he declared to those who had come to welcome him: "Our separation from the old Union is complete. No compromise and no reconstruction can now be entertained." Thus it was that when Abraham Lincoln was inaugurated on March 4, he confronted the fact of secession by the states of the lower South.

Between the time of his election and his inauguration, Lincoln had spent a good deal of time and effort in deciding upon his Cabinet. But, as he later told Gideon Welles, whom he named secretary of the navy, the Cabinet he nominated in March was almost identical to the Cabinet he first conceived on the day after he was elected. Lincoln faced a difficult task:

> Had the [Republican] party, in 1860, been a solid, well-established entity, strengthened by decades of tradition and loyalty, the objective would have been a difficult one. But the aggregation of which Lincoln had suddenly found himself the captain was something new—only four years old; and had never before won a national election. . . . The so-called party comprised several groups, under chieftains personally hostile and full of jealousy and rivalry, who had come together on one question only. The determination of Southern cotton planters to extend slav-

ery into the territories, and the appalling success their
program had achieved in the preceding fifteen years,
formed the danger that had brought under one standard
many otherwise conflicting forces, resolved to check the
aggression by political action.[7]

The senior and most eminent member of the Republican party
was Senator William H. Seward of New York, who represented
the large number of former Whigs who had crossed into the Republican camp. He and his supporters, such as Charles Francis
Adams (the son of John Quincy Adams) of Massachusetts and Tom
Corwin of Ohio, favored a conciliatory approach towards the
Southern states. Salmon P. Chase of Ohio was the leader of the
"radical" wing of the party, and his supporters included Thaddeus
Stevens of Pennsylvania and Charles Sumner of Massachusetts.
They were much closer to the abolitionists than was the Seward
wing, and much less disposed to conciliate the South.

Lincoln wished to have Seward as his secretary of state, and
Seward agreed to take that position. He anticipated that he would
be the "Prime Minister" in the new administration, and wished to
have a say as to who his Cabinet colleagues would be. He felt that
the Cabinet ought to be a "unit"—men who basically agreed with
one another as to the policy issues that would confront the administration—and that therefore the other wing of the party, headed
by Chase, should have little or no representation in that body.
Lincoln was perfectly willing to discuss this question with Thurlow Weed, Seward's longtime alter ego, who came to visit him in
Springfield, but he made it quite clear that Chase would have a
prominent place in the Cabinet. Lincoln was determined to form
a "ministry of all the talents" in which all of the quarrelsome factions of the Republican party would be represented. Seward appeared to acquiesce, but he and his cohorts continued to lobby
against the appointment of Chase. They insisted that the animosity between Seward and Chase was such that they could not sit
in the same Cabinet. Saying to his secretary, John Hay, that he
"could not let Seward take the first trick," Lincoln then proposed
a Cabinet slate that included Chase but excluded Seward. Although Seward wrote a curt note to Lincoln two days before his
inauguration, withdrawing his agreement to serve as secretary of

state, Lincoln refused to back down, and on the very day of the inauguration Seward capitulated and entered the Cabinet.

Seward was then almost sixty years of age, and had spent almost all of his adult life in politics. He was born and raised in upstate New York, and in 1838 was elected the first Whig governor of that state. He served two terms as governor, then retired to private law practice for six years, and was elected to the United States Senate in 1849 and reelected in 1855. There was no doubt as to his basic Free Soil principles, but he had by 1861 abandoned his views about the "higher law" and the "irrepressible conflict," and was willing to make great efforts to preserve the Union. He was a gregarious, companionable man, fond of sipping brandy and swapping stories, and he and Lincoln would develop a close personal relationship during the next four years.

Lincoln appointed Salmon P. Chase to be secretary of the treasury, the number-two post in the administration. Chase was then fifty years old, and had a checkered political career which had seen him first as a Democrat, then as a member of the Liberty party, then a Free Soiler, then again a Democrat, and now a Republican. In 1849 he was elected to the United States Senate by what many regarded as a corrupt bargain between Free Soilers and Democrats in the Ohio legislature. Unable to secure reelection to that office, he was twice elected governor of Ohio, and was again elected to the Senate in 1860. Chase was personally far less appealing than Seward; he was aloof, self-righteous, sanctimonious, and possessed of an almost insatiable ambition for high political office. This ambition led him on occasion to forsake his political party of the moment and his political allies, but to his credit it never led him to forsake his lifelong interest in bettering the lot of the slaves.

In addition to Seward and Chase, Lincoln named to his Cabinet Edward Bates of Missouri as attorney general, Simon Cameron of Pennsylvania as secretary of war, Caleb Smith of Indiana as secretary of the interior, Gideon Welles of Connecticut as secretary of the navy, and Montgomery Blair of Maryland as postmaster general. When he stepped onto the east portico of the Capitol shortly after noon on March 4 to give his inaugural address, he confronted a situation that would require all the talents of the ministry he had put together. The inaugural address had originally been drafted by Lincoln and revised by him on the basis of suggestions from Seward. Lincoln was by turns both firm and conciliatory. He admonished the seceding states:

> . . . [N]o state, upon its own mere motion, can lawfully get out of the Union— . . . *resolves* and *ordinances* to that effect are legally void; and . . . acts of violence, within any state or states, against the authority of the United States, are insurrectionary or revolutionary, according to circumstances. . . .
>
> The power confided to me, will be used to hold, occupy, and possess the property, and places belonging to the government, and to collect the duties and imposts; but beyond what may be necessary for these objects, there will be no invasion—no using of force against, or among the people anywhere . . .

But he concluded on an eloquent note of conciliation and hope:

> In *your* hands, my dissatisfied fellow countrymen, and not in *mine*, is the momentous issue of civil war. The government will not assail *you*. You can have no conflict, without being yourselves the aggressors. You have no oath registered in Heaven to destroy the government, while *I* shall have the most solemn one to "preserve, protect and defend it." . . .
>
> I am loath to close. We are not enemies, but friends. We must not be enemies. Though passion may have strained, it must not break our bonds of affection. The mystic chords of memory, stretching from every battlefield, and patriot grave, to every living heart and hearthstone, all over this broad land, will yet swell the chorus of the Union, when again touched, as surely they will be, by the better angels of our nature.[8]

- 11 -

*L*incoln would serve as president from March 1861 until his assassination in April 1865. The Civil War, which began with the firing on Fort Sumter a few weeks after he was inaugurated, and ended with the surrender of General Robert E. Lee at Appomattox a few days before he was assassinated, was the dominant event of his administration. At the beginning of the war, the president and the main body of Northern opinion regarded it as a war to preserve the Union. But as the war continued, this same body of opinion, and the president with it, came to view the freeing of the slaves as at least as important a goal as the preservation of the Union.

On the very day that Lincoln was inaugurated, a dispatch was received from Major Anderson at Fort Sumter, stating that his supplies were running low, and that substantial reinforcement would be required to secure the position of the federal troops. Anderson estimated that his food supplies could probably last no more than four weeks. Lincoln called his first Cabinet meeting on March 9, and put to each member the written question:

> Assuming it to be possible to now provision Fort Sumter, under all the circumstances, is it wise to attempt it?

The Cabinet members departed and returned a week later with written answers. Seward, Cameron, Bates, Welles, and Smith answered unqualifiedly no. Blair answered yes. Chase answered ambiguously and unhelpfully, saying yes, if peace could be maintained while doing so, but no if the provisioning of the fort would result in civil war. Lincoln, dissatisfied with this advice, sent his own emissaries to South Carolina to ascertain the situation there: The governor of South Carolina sent back word that any attempt to reinforce Fort Sumter would mean civil war. And should the North seek to coerce the states of the lower South that had already seceded, it was an odds-on bet that some of the slave states of the upper South—North Carolina, Tennessee, Arkansas, Virginia, Kentucky, Maryland, and Missouri—would also leave the Union.

Once more in late March the matter was discussed at a Cabinet meeting, in the context of a recommendation from General Winfield Scott that the evacuation of Fort Sumter, and Fort Pickens at Pensacola, Florida, could be justified. The Cabinet again voted, with Cameron absent; the remaining members were equally divided as to whether an effort should be made to hold Fort Sumter. On March 30 Lincoln ordered Secretary of War Cameron to prepare an expedition for the relief of Fort Sumter to be ready to sail within a week. After some confusion entailed by Seward's meddling in what was essentially the domain of the secretary of the navy, the expedition set sail from the Brooklyn Navy Yard. The ships appeared at the entrance to Charleston Harbor on April 12, but Confederate batteries prevented them from reaching the fort. The harbor batteries had begun early that morning to shell Fort Sumter, and on the following day, Major Anderson, his ammunition exhausted, surrendered the fort.

Events now moved even more swiftly. On April 15 Lincoln issued a call for 75,000 volunteers to put down the rebellion. Two days later, the Virginia Convention voted to secede, and three more slave states shortly followed her out of the Union: Arkansas, North Carolina, and Tennessee. There were now eleven members of the Confederate States of America. All but one of the senators and representatives from the seceded states resigned their seats in Congress. Andrew Johnson, senator from Tennessee and fervently loyal to the Union, alone refused to follow his state into the Confederacy. But while Johnson condemned secession, he was a co-author of the Crittenden-Johnson Resolution passed by Congress in the summer of 1861 expressing the view that the sole aim of the war was the restoration of the Union and not the interference with any state's domestic institutions. Johnson had been a

Democrat all his life, but he was a "War Democrat"—one who thought that the Union must fight and win the Civil War. Stephen A. Douglas, too, became a War Democrat. Though mortally ill, he had spoken to a giant rally in Chicago in the late spring and told them that "before God it is the duty of every American citizen to rally around the flag of his country." A few days later, he died at the age of forty-eight.

Seward, meanwhile, made one final effort to establish himself as "Prime Minister." On April 1 he sent Lincoln an extraordinary note, which included the following observations:

> First, we are at the end of a month's administration, and yet without a policy, domestic or foreign. . . .

> Fifth. The policy at home. I am aware that my views are singular and perhaps not sufficiently explained. My system is built upon this *idea*, namely that we must

> CHANGE THE QUESTION FROM ONE UPON SLAVERY, OR ABOUT SLAVERY, FOR A QUESTION UPON UNION OR DISUNION. . . .

The note went on to suggest that war be provoked with Spain and France because of their activities in Latin America, and concluded:

> But whatever policy we adopt there must be an energetic prosecution of it.

> For this purpose it must be somebody's business to pursue it and direct it incessantly.

> Either the President must do it himself, and be all the while active in it, or

> Devolve it on some member of the cabinet. Once adopted, debates on it must end, and all agree and abide.

> It is not my especial province.

> But I neither seek to evade nor assume responsibility.[1]

Lincoln replied to Seward's note on the day he received it, giving a patient and logical answer to each of Seward's points, and concluding with respect to the oversight of administration policy:

> If this must be done, I must do it. When a general line of policy is adopted, I apprehend there is no danger of its being changed without good reason, or continuing to be a subject of unnecessary debate; still upon points arising in its progress I wish, and I suppose I am entitled to have, the advice of all the cabinet.[2]

Seward did not give up easily, but he gradually came to realize that there *was* one man in charge of the administration, and that it was Abraham Lincoln.

Seward's proposals to provoke war with European powers in order to bring the Union back together were extreme, and the Union had all it could do during the Civil War to prevent England and France from formally recognizing the Confederacy. The ruling classes in both England and France had little love for the emerging colossus of the Western Hemisphere: France was already engaged in an effort to place a European prince, Maximilian, on the throne of Mexico, and England was the principal foreign purchaser of cotton from the South. Only when it became clear that the objectives of the North included not only the restoration of the Union but the abolition of slavery as well, did these countries finally turn their faces from any effort to aid the Confederacy.

The early engagements of the war in the eastern theater did not reflect favorably on Northern arms. In July 1861 Union forces under General Irvin McDowell were defeated by the Confederates at the First Battle of Bull Run, and some of the Union troops panicked and fled back to their encampments around the city of Washington. Lincoln replaced McDowell with General George McClellan, who had successfully defeated the Confederates at the Battle of Rich Mountain in what would later become West Virginia. McClellan had great skill as an organizer, and by regular drilling and strict discipline he made the Army of the Potomac into a first-rate military force. Unfortunately, however, he was loath to commit this force in battle. The Radical Republicans in

Congress grew impatient with him, and formed a Committee on the Conduct of the War to prod the president and the generals into action. Chaired by Ben Wade of Ohio, the committee became a forum in which the Radical Republicans found expression for their views as to war tactics and war aims.

Secretary of War Simon Cameron proved unequal to the greatly increased responsibility of his office in time of actual war. Well known in Pennsylvania political circles as a corrupt spoilsman, his failure in national office was due less to greed than to simple incompetence. Seeking to bolster his sagging prestige, with the help of his friend Edwin M. Stanton he placed in his annual report to Congress a recommendation that black troops be employed by the North. Lincoln instructed him to delete this passage, but it had already reached the press; the Radical Republicans denounced Lincoln and praised Cameron.

The president offered to appoint him as United States minister to Russia, and Cameron agreed to take that diplomatic post. Both he and Secretary of the Treasury Chase urged Lincoln to appoint Stanton as secretary of war. Lincoln, who had long felt that the War Democrats should be represented in the Cabinet, lent a sympathetic ear, and in January 1862 Edwin M. Stanton became secretary of war.

Lincoln took an expansive view of the authority conferred upon the president by the constitutional provision that made him Commander in Chief, and he would on several occasions lock horns with Congress over the extent of the authority of the two branches of government. Congress enacted two measures, called Confiscation Acts, which provided for the forfeiture of private property, including slaves, if used in aid of the rebellion. Lincoln refused to sign the second of these laws until changes were made in it to correspond with his view of the authority of the executive and of Congress in this area. Near the end of the war, he would pocket-veto the Wade-Davis Bill, which provided a method for the restoration of civil governments in the Southern states, because he believed that, although he could deal with this subject under his war powers, Congress did not have a similar authority.

The question of emancipation of slaves as a by-product of the war arose during its first summer because of actions taken by General John C. Frémont in the Western Department. That department consisted primarily of Missouri, which had not seceded from the Union and was regarded by Lincoln as a crucial border state, whose allegiance to the Union must be maintained. Frémont had not distinguished himself as a military commander of this department, but in August 1861 he nonetheless issued a proclamation establishing martial law throughout Missouri and providing that the slaves of all persons who took an active part in the field with the enemy should be freed. Lincoln would ultimately conclude that he had the authority to issue a similar proclamation as Commander in Chief, but he was not about to let a theater commander exercise that authority without his prior approval. He requested Frémont to revoke his proclamation; Frémont refused, and Lincoln then revoked it himself. Radical Republicans denounced Lincoln and praised Frémont.

The following year General David Hunter commanded an expedition that seized Port Royal, South Carolina, and some adjacent islands, and nonchalantly issued a proclamation declaring free all the slaves in South Carolina, Georgia, and Florida. Once again Lincoln had to intervene to revoke the proclamation.

After much prodding from both Lincoln and Radical Republicans in Congress, McClellan finally launched the Army of the Potomac on a campaign to capture Richmond, Virginia, the capital of the Confederacy. The result was the Peninsular Campaign, in which McClellan and his army marched up the peninsula between the James and the York rivers toward Richmond. They reached the outskirts of Richmond, but were driven back and ultimately returned to their base of operations around Washington. The Union fortunes were at a low ebb. Horace Greeley published a statement in the *New-York Tribune* in August 1862 criticizing the administration for showing more solicitude for upholding slavery than zeal to put down the rebellion.

Lincoln responded:

> My paramount object in this struggle is to save the Union, and is not either to save or to destroy slavery. If I could save the Union without freeing any slave, I would do it, and if I could save it by freeing all the slaves I would do it; and if I could save it by freeing some and leaving others alone, I would also do that. . . .[3]

But even as he wrote his letter to Greeley, Lincoln had already confided to his Cabinet that he thought the time had come for an Emancipation Proclamation. He had read his first draft to his Cabinet in July, and simply awaited a propitious moment after a Union victory to issue it. After the battle of Antietam, Lincoln published the Emancipation Proclamation, relying on his authority as Commander in Chief of the army and navy. Lincoln declared that effective January 1, 1863, all slaves within any state then in rebellion against the United States "shall be, then, thenceforward, and forever free." The proclamation had an ironic quality to it; it purported to affect only states in rebellion against the United States, and yet it was in these states that a proclamation of the president of the United States would carry no authority whatever. All of the slaves in states that had not seceded from the Union were left untouched by the Emancipation Proclamation.

The battle of Antietam was not a full-blown Union victory. McClellan, commanding the Union troops, had repulsed Robert E. Lee and Stonewall Jackson, but had allowed them to retreat across the Potomac without any pursuit. This time Lincoln and members of this Cabinet joined with the Radical Republicans in decrying McClellan's actions. Lincoln described McClellan as having "the slows," and sent him a detailed order requiring him to attack under certain circumstances. McClellan all but ignored the order, and in November 1862 Lincoln removed him from command.

The Radical Republicans in Congress were pleased with the Emancipation Proclamation, and pleased by Lincoln's removal of McClellan, but they still felt that top military and civilian posts in the government were held by those who did not have their hearts in the prosecution of the war. Chase represented to Senator William Pitt Fessenden of Maine that Lincoln was subject to "backstairs influence" in the form of Secretary Seward. In December 1862 the Republican senators met in caucus for two days, with the Radicals giving vent to their feeling that the conservative views of Seward were the dominant force in the Cabinet. The caucus adopted a resolution that mentioned no names but urged Lincoln to reorganize his Cabinet in order that there might be unified support of the war effort. Seward, learning of this resolution, tendered his resignation. Lincoln held a long meeting with the committee of senators appointed to present the resolution to him, and heard complaints about lack of consultation with the Cabinet in making decisions. The next day Lincoln called the senators back, and to their surprise they found all the members of the Cabinet except Seward present at the meeting. Lincoln inquired of the Cabinet members whether they had any criticism of the way the Cabinet functioned, and all—Chase very sheepishly—said they did not. The next morning Lincoln sent for Chase, who waited upon him in the presence of Welles and Stanton.

> Chase said he was so distressed by the happenings of the previous night that he had prepared his resignation. Lincoln's eyes lighted and he reached out for the paper Chase held in his hand. Chase seemed reluctant to let go of it, but Lincoln pulled it away from his, and reading it hurriedly, stole a grin at Welles and said: "This cuts the Gordian knot."[4]

Lincoln asked both Seward and Chase to withdraw their resignations, and they did. His Cabinet remained a "ministry of all the talents."

The dismissal of McClellan did not immediately improve the performance of the Army of the Potomac. Ambrose Burnside, who succeeded McClellan, was badly defeated at Fredricksburg, and in the spring of 1863 Joseph Hooker, who succeeded Burnside, was defeated at Chancellorsville. The fortunes of war were kinder to the North in the western theater. General U. S. Grant defeated the Confederates and captured Fort Donelson and Fort McHenry, and Union troops captured and occupied New Orleans after the navy had subdued the forts along the Mississippi River which guarded it. The commander of the Union army was Benjamin F. Butler, a Massachusetts politician and criminal lawyer whose first command had been at Annapolis, Maryland, in the spring of 1861. At that time he had moved one thousand troops to Baltimore and proclaimed that the troops were there to preserve order. He was then transferred to Norfolk, where he first proclaimed the doctrine that captured slaves were "contraband" of war and forfeitable to the Union just like other captured property used in aid of the rebellion. His tour of duty at New Orleans was tempestuous; he found it necessary to impose a harsh regime in order to govern a recalcitrant population. When he was removed from command there in 1864, he was known to the Southerners either as "Beast" Butler for his harshness, or "Spoons" Butler for the silverware he allegedly appropriated for his own use. Butler would later serve under Grant during the sieges of Petersburg and Richmond in the summer of 1864, but Grant was dissatisfied with his performance and at his request Lincoln again removed Butler from command. Butler was described by Lincoln's biographer Carl Sandburg as "heavy of body, with a well-rounded paunch, bald, sleepy-eyed with cunning, a cast in one eye. . . ."[5]

Butler, like Stanton, had undergone a complete political metamorphosis during the course of the Civil War. In 1860 he had been a member not merely of the Democratic party, but of the pro-slavery Buchanan-Breckinridge wing of that party. By 1864 he had become one of the darlings of the Radical Republicans, and was mentioned for a spot on the Republican ticket in 1864. He would be the lead prosecutor for the House managers at the Senate trial of Andrew Johnson in 1868.

During the summer of 1863, Union forces defeated the Confederates at Gettysburg, Pennsylvania, in what is generally regarded as the decisive battle of the Civil War. Henceforth there would be no major Confederate incursions into Northern territory, and the war would be fought in the South. In the very same week the Confederate fortress of Vicksburg, Mississippi, surrendered to the Union armies under Grant.

Lincoln and his advisers began to think of how to deal with those parts of the seceded states that were now occupied by Union forces. In December 1863 Lincoln announced a plan for amnesty that would exclude only those who had affirmatively supported the rebellion. Others were offered a full pardon with restoration of property rights (save those in slaves) if they would swear to uphold the Constitution, the Union, the Emancipation Proclamation, and laws and regulations dealing with slaves. Lincoln's announcement further provided that when, in any seceded state, one tenth of the number of voters who had participated in the election of 1860 had taken this oath, they could reestablish a loyal state government, and he would recognize it. His plan required that such new states should provide for the education of blacks, but did not require that they be allowed to vote. Lincoln's plan was condemned by peace Democrats in the North as too harsh, and by the Radical Republicans as too lenient.

In January 1864 General Nathaniel Banks, who had succeeded Butler in command at New Orleans, proclaimed that an election under Lincoln's plan would be held on February 22. Suffrage was limited to free white male voters who had taken the oath of allegiance required by Lincoln, and they distributed their eleven thousand ballots among three different candidates for governor. Michael Hahn, a prewar Douglas Democrat, was elected governor, and a convention was called to adopt a new constitution. Lincoln, writing to Hahn privately with respect to the qualifications for voters, said:

> I barely suggest for your private consideration, whether some of the colored people may not be let in—as, for instance, the very intelligent, and especially those who have fought gallantly in our ranks. They would probably help, in some trying time to come, to keep the jewel of liberty within the family of freedom.[6]

Lincoln's plan for the Reconstruction of seceded states, insisting as it did that slavery be ended, showed how far he, and the public opinion he reflected, had moved since the beginning of the Civil War on this question. In his message to Congress in December 1863, he urged that Congress propose an amendment to the United States Constitution abolishing slavery. Such an amendment had earlier been considered by Congress and passed the Senate but failed for lack of the required two-thirds vote in the House. In January 1864 the House approved the amendment by the necessary two-thirds margin and sent it to the states for ratification. William Lloyd Garrison hailed Lincoln in *The Liberator*, describing him as the "chain breaker for millions of the oppressed."

As Union forces continued to triumph in 1864, Lincoln employed his Reconstruction plan in three additional states now controlled by the Union Army—Arkansas, Tennessee, and Virginia. But the Radical Republicans in Congress had enough influence to assure that none of the members of Congress elected by these states would be seated. The Radicals were no longer satisfied with the condition that slavery be abolished in the seceded states, but insisted that an "ironclad" oath of past as well as future loyalty be sworn by anyone seeking to vote, and that the Confederate war debt be repudiated. These principles were adopted in the Wade-Davis Bill, which Congress enacted in July 1864. Lincoln killed the Wade-Davis Bill by a pocket veto, stating that he thought an inflexible commitment to a single plan of Reconstruction was unwise. Senator Ben Wade and Congressman Henry Winter Davis from Maryland, the authors of the bill, responded with the "Wade-Davis Manifesto," which denounced Lincoln's veto as an executive usurpation of legislative authority. Coming as it did at the beginning of the 1864 presidential election, the manifesto attracted little public support from the Republicans and none at all from the Democrats.

There was much dissatisfaction with Lincoln and his administration among both the peace Democrats and the Radical Republicans. For months Secretary Chase had shamelessly allowed a campaign to be carried on to supplant Lincoln with him as the party's presidential nominee in 1864, and he had not hesitated to use his Treasury patronage to bolster the campaign. But just as in 1860, his cold personality and his enemies within the party caused the effort to die a-borning. In June 1864 Chase submitted another one of his numerous resignations to Lincoln over a dispute about Treasury patronage, and much to his surprise Lincoln accepted this one.

During the spring, various Republican state conventions endorsed Lincoln for renomination. The Radical Republicans had first looked to Chase, then to Ben Butler, and even to John C. Frémont. But when the Republican Convention met in Baltimore in June, Lincoln won renomination "going away." But for reasons not entirely clear, the convention replaced Hannibal Hamlin with Andrew Johnson of Tennessee as its vice-presidential nominee. Lincoln approved the idea of having a War Democrat such as Johnson on the ticket in order to broaden its appeal, and the ticket was called the National Union ticket rather than the Republican ticket.

The Democratic party, split between its "peace" and "war" factions, postponed its convention until August in order to work out a compromise. It nominated none other than General George McClellan for president, on a platform calling for an immediate cease-fire and a negotiated peace. McClellan repudiated the peace plank, and sought to capitalize on Northern discontent with the seemingly interminable war. But fate smiled on the National Union ticket: General George T. Sherman finally captured the city of Atlanta after a long siege, and Admiral David Farragut won an important naval victory at the battle of Mobile Bay. The Union ticket did well in the October congressional elections, and in November Lincoln was decisively reelected president. He received more than 2 million votes to McClellan's slightly less than 1 million. He carried every state except Kentucky, Delaware, and New Jersey.

Shortly before the election, death had finally come to Chief Justice Roger B. Taney at the age of eighty-eight. He had served as Chief Justice for twenty-eight years, a term approaching in length that of his predecessor, John Marshall, who had served for thirty-four years. From 1801 to 1864 there had been only two Chief Justices, but there had been fifteen presidents. Several of Stanton's friends urged the president to name Stanton to the vacancy, but Lincoln demurred, saying that he could not find anyone to replace Stanton at the War Department. Stanton had proved to be a remarkably able and efficient secretary of war, bringing order and discipline to a department that had neither under his predecessor. General Grant, who by this time had been named Commander in Chief of all the Union forces, urged Stanton not to give up the War Department, and Stanton notified Lincoln that he no longer desired the Chief Justiceship. He lent his efforts to promote the candidacy of Salmon P. Chase, late secretary of the treasury.

To a man less magnanimous than Lincoln, Chase's incessant intriguing against him while he was secretary of the treasury would have ruled him out of consideration for such a desirable plum. But Lincoln thought Chase would be a good Chief Justice because he would be disposed to uphold the constitutionality of the greenback legislation and other innovative measures that had seemed necessary to effectively prosecute the war. Lincoln finally quelled his only doubt about Chase—whether he would give up his ambition for the presidency if he were appointed Chief Justice—and in December 1864 Lincoln sent his name to the Senate. Unfortunately, Chase was so bitten by the presidential bug that even the highest judicial office in the country would not deter him from seeking the presidential nomination in the future. Chase would preside over the trial of Andrew Johnson in the Senate in 1868: The Constitution provides that in case the president is impeached, the Chief Justice, rather than the vice-president, shall preside.

By the time of Lincoln's second inaugural in March 1865, the war was virtually over. Following tradition on that day, Andrew Johnson was sworn in as vice-president in the Capitol. He gave a speech that made an unfavorable impression on his listeners. He had been ill, and in the vice-president's office in the Senate building he had drunk two tumblers of whiskey before appearing to take the oath. To many of his listeners Johnson appeared to be drunk.

A procession then formed to move to the east portico of the Capitol, where Lincoln delivered his very brief second inaugural address. It concluded with these words:

> With malice toward none; with charity for all; with firmness in the right, as God gives us to see the right, let us strive on to finish the work we are in; to bind up the nation's wounds; to care for him who shall have born the battle, and for his widow, and his orphan—to do all which may achieve and cherish a just, and a lasting peace, among ourselves, and with all nations.[7]

Others in the North, however, contemplated more of a Carthaginian peace with the South than Lincoln did. Reconstruction—how the Southern states should be governed pending their return to the Union—and what should be done for the free slaves would be the principal issues facing the government for the next four years.

On April 9, 1865, Robert E. Lee surrrendered his army to U. S. Grant at Appomattox, Virginia, and the Civil War was for all practical purposes over. Only five days after that, Lincoln and his wife, Mary, attended a performance of the play *Our American Cousin* at Ford's Theatre in Washington. During the play John Wilkes Booth, an actor with Southern sympathies, stepped into the president's private box and shot him from a range of five feet. That same night, co-conspirators of Booth's attacked and wounded

Seward and his son Frederick. At the instructions of doctors, Lincoln was moved to a house across the street from Ford's Theatre on Tenth Street, and there his life hung in the balance during the early morning hours of April 15. Stanton was summoned, and he assumed charge of the situation in the house and notified other members of the government of what had happened. Secretary Welles and members of the president's family arrived and remained with him until he died shortly after seven o'clock in the morning. Stanton, not one for coining memorable phrases, exclaimed, "Now he belongs to the ages." And with Lincoln's death, Andrew Johnson became the seventeenth president of the United States.

-12-

Andrew Johnson was born in Raleigh, North Carolina, in 1808, and upon the death of his father three years later the family was left in abject poverty. At the age of fourteen he apprenticed himself to a tailor, where he first learned to read with the help of the shop foreman. In 1826 he, together with his mother and stepfather, made the arduous trip over the Appalachian Mountains into eastern Tennessee and settled in Greeneville. There he met and married Eliza McCardle, who taught him to write. At the age of nineteen he opened his own tailor shop and, though his successful political career would leave less and less time for his trade, he was unfailingly well groomed and well dressed throughout his life.

Eastern Tennessee had few slaveholders and few slaves, and its people were strong supporters of the Union. Middle and western Tennessee were quite different, particularly in the west, where a slaveholding plantation aristocracy was dominant. Johnson quickly entered public life in his adopted city of Greeneville, climbing the ladder of elective offices from alderman and then mayor of Greeneville to state representative, state senator, member of Congress, governor of Tennessee, and then United States senator from Tennessee. He was essentially a Jacksonian Democrat, who appealed to what would today be called the populist sentiments in the electorate.

In Congress he championed fiscal economy, and fought hard over an extended period of time for the enactment of a homestead law allowing settlers to acquire government land in the west for a nominal price. Like Edwin Stanton and Benjamin Butler, who would be arrayed against him in his impeachment trial, Johnson in 1860 had supported John Breckinridge, candidate of the slave-holding wing of the Democratic party, for president. Yet in December 1860 he had denounced secession on the floor of the Senate, and he was the only senator from any of the seceding states who retained his seat in that body. But at that time he did not think that the goal of the Civil War should be to abolish slavery. He was a co-sponsor of the Crittenden-Johnson resolution that passed Congress in 1861, declaring that in prosecuting the war the North had no desire to interfere with the domestic institutions of any of the states. In 1862 Lincoln appointed him military governor of Tennessee, which post he held until he became vice-president.

The adverse circumstances of his early life had left Andrew Johnson with something of a chip on his shoulder. His fellow Tennessean James Knox Polk described him in his diary as "very vindictive and perverse in his temper"[1] while Jefferson Davis said that he had an "intense, almost morbidly sensitive pride."[2] Now the nation waited to see how he would act as president. He had the most difficult burden imaginable thrust upon him by Lincoln's death, and the most broadminded and astute of statesmen would have had his hands full serving as the seventeenth president of the United States.

Lincoln had not been dead an hour when all the members of the Cabinet, except Seward and Hugh McCulloch, recently appointed secretary of the treasury, gathered in the back parlor at the house on Tenth Street. There they signed a letter prepared by Attorney General James Speed advising Andrew Johnson that he was now president. Secretary Welles and Speed were delegated to deliver the letter to Johnson. The Cabinet, bleary-eyed from lack of sleep, assembled at 11:00 A.M. in the Treasury Building to see Chief Justice Chase administer the oath of office to the new president. Johnson would use an office on the fourth floor of the Treasury Building for more than a month, in order to give Mary Todd Lincoln the time she needed to move out of the White House. After his swearing-in, Johnson requested the members of the Cabinet to meet with him at noon, and at that time asked all of them to remain in office. He said that he would follow Lincoln's policies; Secretary Welles commented that "all was vague and uncertain," as well it might have been.

The first session of Congress had as usual adjourned shortly after March 4, but although its members had dispersed, some of them returned to Washington upon hearing the news of Lincoln's assassination. While in the Senate, Johnson had served as a member of the Joint Committee on the Conduct of the War, and Senator Ben Wade of Ohio led a delegation of former colleagues of this committee to call on him on Sunday, April 16. Wade told the president that the committee had confidence in him. Johnson thanked them, and told them that his past actions would indicate his future policy: "I hold this: robbery is a crime, rape is crime; murder is a crime, and *crime* must be punished. . . . Treason must be made infamous and traitors must be impoverished."[3] Early the following week Johnson met with various delegations who were interested in hearing his views. Speaking at length to a group of visitors from Illinois, he seemed to espouse what one listener thought was a "radical policy." Similar views were expressed to an Indiana delegation. Leading Radicals such as Henry Winter Davis and Charles Sumner, after talking to Johnson, were satisfied that they would not be disappointed with his policies.

At a Cabinet meeting in early May, Stanton presented an outline of Reconstruction plans for Virginia and North Carolina. That night Stanton met with Charles Sumner, and the latter told him that he could not support any plan that did not give the vote to Negroes in the reconstructed states. Sumner would shortly find that the new president did not agree with him on this issue.

Meanwhile, when news was received of the terms of a truce that General Sherman had offered to Confederate General Albert Sidney Johnston, an emergency Cabinet meeting was called for eight o'clock in the evening of April 21. For although Lee's surrender at Appomattox had ended the fighting in the principal theater of war, Confederate soldiers in other parts of the South had not all laid down their arms. But the terms of truce Sherman had offered—terms designed, as he put it, to bring peace from the Potomac to the Rio Grande—shocked the members of the Cabinet. In exchange for the surrender of the last of the Confederate forces, Sherman had promised the recognition of existing Southern state governments once their members swore an oath of allegiance to the Union. He had also promised restoration of franchise and property rights for those who had not aided the rebellion, and a general amnesty for those who had.

Only a week earlier Sherman had told Grant and Stanton that
he would offer the same terms Grant had given Lee, and not get
into matters of policy. But Sherman's agreement dealt with the
most serious matters of policy, sounding more like the draft of a
treaty than terms of surrender. The president and all the members
of the Cabinet present agreed that Sherman's actions must be repudiated, and Johnson told Stanton to convey this information to
Sherman. Grant, who was a close friend of Sherman's, requested
that he be allowed to take Stanton's order personally to Sherman
in North Carolina, and his request was readily granted. The president had clearly shown that he was not disposed to offer excessively lenient terms of peace to the Confederates.

In May the Cabinet took up Stanton's plan for Reconstruction
of North Carolina and Virginia. As originally presented, it provided for a centralized Army Provost Marshal Corps to help govern the reconstructed states on an interim basis. But other members
of the Cabinet, lead by Welles, objected to this enlargement of the
army's responsibility, and it was dropped. Stanton's plan also provided for suffrage for all "loyal citizens"—with the understanding
that Negroes would be included—in order to conciliate Sumner
and his Radical allies in Congress. Johnson asked the individual
Cabinet members to express their views on this question, and with
Seward absent they divided equally. When Seward had recovered
sufficiently to attend Cabinet meetings, he opposed requiring Negro suffrage. Johnson reserved judgment on the question at the
conclusion of the Cabinet discussions.

On May 29, Johnson appointed a provisional governor of North
Carolina, and directed that the electorate for delegates to a state
constitutional convention should consist of white males. He also
issued a general amnesty proclamation, which excluded some civil
and military officers of the Confederacy, all persons who had violated their oaths of allegiance taken under Lincoln's 1863 plans,
and Southerners owning property worth $20,000 or more who
had voluntarily aided the rebellion. But those excluded could individually petition the president for a pardon.

During the summer, the president recognized a Union government in Virginia, and also extended the North Carolina plan to
Mississippi, Georgia, Texas, Alabama, South Carolina, and Florida. In August he advised the provisional governor of Mississippi

that he hoped the delegates to that state's constitutional convention would grant the vote to Negroes who could read and write and who owned $250 worth of property, "so as to completely disarm the adversary and set an example other states will follow." The Mississippi convention, however, did not follow Johnson's advice. In an interview in a New Orleans newspaper, the president suggested that Louisiana, like Massachusetts, impose a property qualification for voting that would apply to both races.

Congress in March 1865 had established within the War Department a Freedman's Bureau to assist former slaves in adjusting to their new lives. Part of the bureau's responsibility was to administer lands that had been confiscated by law from Southern Confederates, but the law was vague in many respects; the freedmen were to receive the title the United State could convey, but the United States could not convey title until there had been a forfeiture proceeding and then it could give an estate only for the life of the former owner. It was also uncertain what was to be done with the land while legal proceedings ran their course. General O. O. Howard, the commissioner in charge of the bureau, prepared a circular in July directing that lands that had not been fully confiscated be set aside for freed slaves. But at about the same time, Attorney General James Speed—who had voted in favor of Negro suffrage in the May Cabinet meeting—began to administratively limit the applicability of the confiscation law. Johnson therefore directed Howard to revise his circular so as to exclude lands belonging to Confederates whom he had pardoned.

Thaddeus Stevens, Charles Sumner, and Ben Wade grew increasingly dissatisfied with the president's Reconstruction policies, but since Congress was not in session they were powerless to do anything about them. They urged the president to postpone action until Congress met, or to call a special session, but he declined to do so. When Congress did convene in December, the president in his annual message stated that the Constitution gave to the states alone the authority to confer the right to vote, and that this question must therefore be left to the decision of the individual Southern states.

The leading Radical Republicans in Congress—Ben Wade, Charles Sumner, Zachariah Chandler of Michigan in the Senate, and Thaddeus Stevens in the House—believed firmly that any plan for the Reconstruction of the seceded states should include a requirement for Negro suffrage. But their view did not command the support of a majority of Republicans, to say nothing of Northern opinion as a whole. When the Civil War had ended in the spring of 1865, most Northerners would probably have been satisfied with a requirement that the seceded states ratify the Thirteenth Amendment abolishing slavery, and that high-ranking Confederate officials be disqualified from holding office in the new governments. But the events of the summer and fall gave pause to this body of opinion.

The governments organized under President Johnson's terms often elected to high office people who had actively supported the Confederacy. Many of these same governments enacted so-called Black Codes, which seemed to recognize only the letter of the Thirteenth Amendment, and imposed a variety of prohibition on Negroes—prohibitions against renting land, leaving masters whom they had contracted to serve, and giving evidence in court against whites. Many of the "moderate" and conservative Republicans had come to think by the end of 1865 that more than the abolition of slavery was necessary if the newly freed slaves were ever to make their own way in the South. Part of this change was based on moral feeling, and part on political considerations: If virtually all white Southerners, and only they, could vote, the Republican majority in Congress would disappear as soon as the representatives of these states were seated.

On the initiative of Representative Thaddeus Stevens, all questions relating to the seating of members elected from the recently reconstructed states were referred to a newly created Joint Congressional Committee on Reconstruction, which simply held the questions in abeyance. The result was that no senator or representative from these states were seated when Congress met in December.

The Senate Judiciary Committee was chaired by Lyman Trumbull, a scholarly and able Republican senator from Illinois. Under his leadership the committee reported to the Senate two bills designed to improve the lot of the newly emancipated slaves in the South. The first measure was a bill to extend the life of the Freedman's Bureau, which had originally been created just before Lincoln was assassinated. The bill passed both houses of Congress.

Senator William Pitt Fessenden of Maine, an influential Republican senator, discussed the bill at length with President Johnson, and came away from the discussion thinking that the president would sign the bill. But without previous consultation with them, Johnson read to his Cabinet on February 19 a veto message that had been drafted by Secretary Seward but made harsher in its tone by the president himself. It took the position that the authority of Congress to legislate for the seceded states was doubtful at best until these states were again represented in Congress, and that in any event the federal government had no authority to provide for indigents of any race. Enough Republicans in Congress stood by the president that his veto was sustained, but a number of them regretted this evidence of a widening breach.

The second bill introduced by Trumbull's Judiciary Committee was the Civil Rights Act, which defined national citizenship to include blacks, and gave them the right to acquire and hold property, make contracts, engage in ordinary occupations, and testify in court. These rights were hereafter to be protected by the national government, and suit would lie in the federal courts against anyone who violated these rights. The purpose of the bill was to render inoperative the Black Codes enacted in some of the Southern states.

Once again there was hope among some Republicans that Johnson would sign the bill, but on March 24 he told his Cabinet that he intended to veto it; he did, however, ask the opinion of various Cabinet members. Stanton, for one, though expressing disapproval of some portions of the bill, recommended that the president sign it. The president nonetheless did veto it, stating in his message that it represented an unwarranted centralization of authority in the federal government. Within the next two weeks both houses of Congress overrode the veto, and the Civil Rights Act became law.

Johnson was often cryptic and self-contained when discussing questions with small groups, but he had a penchant for off-the-cuff oratory to larger groups, a penchant to which he gave vent when speaking to a crowd who had come to serenade him at the White House on Washington's Birthday, 1866. He called the Joint Committee on Reconstruction "an irresponsible central directory," and upbraided both Stevens and Sumner as traitors to the fundamental principles of government. The president would indulge in this sort of rhetoric on other occasions in the next few months.

Two riots that occurred during the spring and summer did little to encourage the idea that all was going well with the governments of the newly reconstructed states. In April in Memphis, what began as a disturbance between discharged Negro soldiers and local authorities escalated into a race riot, in which a mob of whites attacked and killed a large number of Negroes. The mob was brought under control only by the intervention of the army.

In July another riot occurred in New Orleans. Radical Republicans in Louisiana wished to reconvene the state constitutional convention in order to enfranchise Negroes. Conservatives contended that such a move was illegal, and they threatened to use force to prevent it. The mayor of New Orleans asked General Baird, the local commanding general, for help in preventing the meeting. Baird replied that anyone had the right to assemble, and that he would use the army to protect that right. Baird in turn sought advice from Secretary Stanton, but he received no reply. State officials allied with the conservatives sought advice from the president, who responded that the military would not interfere with the civil authorities. The convention met at a hall in New Orleans at noon, but Baird, mistakenly thinking that it was scheduled to meet at 6:00 P.M., had provided no military protection. A mob gathered and fired upon black and white Radicals assembling to attend the convention. Forty were killed and one hundred wounded.

In June 1866 a group consisting largely of Democrats who agreed with Johnson's position sent out an invitation for a National Union Convention with delegates from all thirty-six states and the District of Columbia to meet in Philadelphia in August. The invitation declared that each state had the right to prescribe the qualifications of its own electors, and contained other recitals in a similar vein. Johnson supported the convention, and with his acquiescence Senator J. H. Doolittle of Wisconsin requested an endorsement from each Cabinet member. Within a month three members of the Cabinet resigned: Attorney General James Speed, Secretary of the Interior James Harlan, and Postmaster General William Dennison. Stanton, who disapproved of the convention, did not reply to Doolittle's request, but at a later Cabinet meeting expressed his feelings. The convention met in Philadelphia in the middle of August, and its proceedings opened with a procession of delegates two by two, one from the North and one from the South with arms linked together. Both the procession, and the resolutions adopted in support of Johnson's policies, provided grist for the mills of radical cartoonists such as Thomas Nast.

During the summer the Joint Committee on Reconstruction had finally put the finishing touches on the Fourteenth Amendment to the Constitution. Its suffrage provision was mild: If a state were to deny the vote to male inhabitants on a basis other than conviction of a felony or participation in the rebellion, its representation in Congress would be proportionately diminished. The sections of the amendment that were to have great importance in constitutional law were those that provided that a state could not deny to any person the equal protection of the laws, nor deprive any person of life, liberty, or property without due process of law.

Though the president has no constitutional role in the ratification of an amendment, Johnson nonetheless announced his opposition to the amendment and requested the opinions of the members of his Cabinet as to their view of it. Stanton made rather ambiguous comments in the Cabinet meeting, suggesting that he basically disapproved of it, and made even more ambiguous statements to the press. His sympathies by now were almost entirely with the Radical Republicans, and yet he could not bring himself to resign as did Speed, Dennison, and Harlan. He somehow envisioned himself both as a bridge between the president and Radicals in Congress, and as a bridge between the president and the army. This quite novel conception of the role of a presidential adviser and subordinate fitted in with the Janus-like role he had played in the last days of the Buchanan Cabinet.

During the summer Johnson took to the hustings to urge support for his policies. Using as a springboard a Chicago speech at the laying of the cornerstone to a monument to Stephen A. Douglas, Johnson began what is known as his "swing around the circle." Accompanied by Seward, General U. S. Grant, and others, he spoke in Cleveland, St. Louis, and other cities. The crowds that heard Johnson included opponents as well as supporters, and in his response to some of the jibes he frequently descended to the level of the hecklers. He criticized the Radical Republicans in

Congress, and in particular their failure to seat senators and representatives elected by the reconstructured states.

But the congressional elections in the autumn of 1866 proved to
be a boost for the Radical Republicans, and a defeat for Johnson.
The Republicans elected enough members to both the House and
the Senate to control each of those bodies by a two-thirds majority. If the voting was along party lines, the new Congress would
be able to override any veto the President sought to interpose.
The Radicals faced a threat from another quarter, however, when
in December the Supreme Court handed down its opinion in the
case of Ex Parte Milligan.[4] Lambdin P. Milligan was a "peace"
Democrat who during the Civil War had been charged with criminal offenses against the war effort. But instead of trying him before the regular federal court in Indianapolis, at Stanton's direction
he had been tried before a military tribunal and sentenced to death.
An order issued by the Supreme Court in the spring granted a
writ of habeas corpus to Milligan, and directed that he be freed
from military custody. The Court announced that it would hand
down its written opinions at the next term, which began in December 1866. In these opinions all nine members of the Court
agreed that Milligan could not constitutionally be tried before a
military tribunal when the regular courts were open for business
in Indiana. Five members of the Court, including two of Lincoln's
appointees—David Davis, who wrote the opinion, and Stephen
Field—were of the view that even Congress could not authorize a
military trial in such circumstances. Four members of the Court,
including three Lincoln appointees, Chief Justice Chase, Samuel
F. Miller, and Noah Swayne—were of the view that since Congress had not in Milligan's case authorized his trial by a military
court, it was unnecessary to decide the question of whether such
a trial would have been constitutional had Congress authorized it.
The opinion of the majority of the Court obviously cast a dark
cloud over the entire idea of military government in the South.

The Congress that convened in December 1866 was not the one
elected in November of that year but the lame-duck session elected
in November 1864. Nonetheless, the Radical Republicans, their
fortunes bolstered by the recent election returns, began to talk of
impeachment. In January 1867 Congressman James Ashley of Ohio,
a dyed-in-the-wool Radical, moved a resolution in the House to

investigate the conduct of Andrew Johnson. Against the wishes of Ashley and the Radicals, the resolution to impeach was referred to the House Judiciary Committee chaired by Congressman James Wilson of Iowa. Wilson was regarded as an able lawyer and was not a Radical.

In February, the Judiciary Committee began hearing testimony. Its operation was less like that of a grand jury, which investigates a particular incident to see if a criminal charge is warranted, than like that of the manager of a political candidate's campaign looking into what charges might be made against a political opponent. The committee sifted evidence at a slow, orderly pace that irritated Radicals such as Ben Butler and John Logan of Illinois, two Union generals serving their first terms in Congress, and they sought to discharge the Judiciary Committee and refer the investigation to a special committee. This effort was defeated on the floor of the House through the efforts of conservative and moderate Republicans.

The committee's deliberations during the year 1867 took place at a time when the relationship between Congress and Andrew Johnson moved from a widening breach to open confrontation. The Second Session of the Thirty-ninth Congress passed a series of laws designed to tie Johnson's hands before it adjourned on March 4, 1867. The first of these was the Reconstruction Act— the full title of which was An Act for the More Efficient Government of the Rebel States. (Today the title would probably be rearranged to make an acronym.) This represented Congress's first full-fledged attempt to totally supersede any executive plan in deciding the manner in which the Southern states should be reconstructed. It divided the states that had seceded into five military districts, with a commanding general of the army in charge of each. The commanding general was given authority to suspend or remove civil authorities who interfered with Reconstruction. The law provided that Southerners who would take a strict loyalty oath were to elect delegates to a constitutional convention, and that the convention must grant suffrage to blacks on the same terms as it was granted to whites, and must ratify the Fourteenth Amendment. Stanton alone of the members of the Johnson's Cabinet urged him to sign the bill; the president vetoed it, and his veto was overridden just before the March adjournment of Congress.

The second measure was the Army Appropriations Act, which had been suggested to congressional Republicans by Stanton himself. It provided that all orders from the president to the army must go through the General of the Army (U. S. Grant), and that this general could not be removed without the consent of the Senate. Johnson signed this measure into law with a protest as to its constitutionality.

The third measure was the Tenure of Office Act, which provided in essence that all federal officials whose appointment required Senate confirmation could not be removed by the president without the consent of the Senate. If the Senate was not in session, the president might suspend an official for misconduct, reporting his reasons to the Senate, but if the Senate when it reconvened did not concur in the suspension, the official retained his position. It was not clear whether the bill applied to Cabinet officers such as Stanton, who had been appointed to his Cabinet position not by Johnson but by Lincoln. In this respect the act provided that Cabinet officers "shall hold their offices . . . during the term of the President by whom they may have been appointed, and for one month thereafter, subject to removal by and with the advice and consent of the Senate." Johnson took this pending measure up with his Cabinet in February 1867, and the Cabinet unanimously advised him to veto it as being an infringement on the executive's appointment authority under the Constitution. Stanton assisted Secretary Seward in drafting the veto message that the president sent to Congress, but his veto was overridden and the bill became law.

No sooner had the Thirty-ninth Congress gone out of existence on March 4, 1867, then the Fortieth Congress—which had been elected in November 1866—convened. The newly reinforced Radical Republicans did not wish to leave the president on his own until December 1867, when the next regular session of the Fortieth Congress would convene, and so Congress agreed to meet again in July. Before then Johnson authorized Stanton to designate the military governors of the Southern districts whom he was required to appoint under the Reconstruction Act, and he proceeded to appoint those generals whom Stanton designated. During its March session, the new Congress had passed the first supplementary Reconstruction Act, making more specific the role of the military commanders in convening constitutional conventions in the seceded states. Johnson vetoed this bill, and Congress again overrode his veto.

In June Attorney General Henry Stanbery, appointed by Johnson to succeed James Speed, presented to the Cabinet for discussion opinions he had prepared as to the authority of the military commanders under the Reconstruction Acts. These opinions took a narrow view of the powers conferred on the commanders, limiting their authority to remove state officials, and holding that voter registrars could not look behind the statements made in the loyalty oath even if they believed the oath to be perjurious. Stanton expressed opposition to these views in Cabinet, but Johnson had them sent to the military commanders with the support of the rest of his Cabinet. When Congress reconvened in July 1867, it passed a second supplemental Reconstruction Act, the main purpose of which was to reverse the interpretation given to the earlier acts by the Stanbery opinions.

When the Thirty-ninth Congress had adjourned on March 4, the Judiciary Committee reported that it had made no definitive findings as to impeachment, and that the matter deserved further study. Meanwhile, an important development took place in the Senate. In March 1867, the position of president *pro tempore* of the Senate became vacant due to the retirement of Senator Lafayette Foster. Ordinarily it was essentially an honorary position, carrying little responsibility or authority. But under the law as it then stood, the president *pro tempore* of the Senate was the next person in line after the vice-president to succeed to the presidency. Since Andrew Johnson himself had succeeded to the presidency by virtue of having been vice-president, there was no sitting vice-president, and if Johnson was impeached and removed from the presidency the president *pro tempore* of the Senate would become president. Thus the decision of the Republican caucus as to who should succeed Foster could—and did—play a significant part in the trial of Andrew Johnson. The two candidates for the position were Senator Ben Wade of Ohio, who epitomized the views of the Radical Republicans, and Senator William Pitt Fessenden of Maine, who represented the views of moderate and conservative Republicans. The Republican caucus decided in favor of Wade by a vote of 22 to 7, and the following day the Senate ratified this choice.

The Judiciary Committee of the newly elected Congress continued to hold hearings; it met again in late June, and in July it
advised the full House that it was divided 5 to 4 on the question
of impeachment, and would not report until the December session
of the new Congress. At this time Congressman Thaddeus Stevens of Pennsylvania moved to the fore as one of the champions
of impeachment by the House. He had moved from Vermont to
Pennsylvania in the early part of the century, and practiced law
first in Gettysburg and then in Lancaster. He was a highly regarded lawyer, and always active in politics—first in the anti-
Masonic party, then the Whig party, and finally as a Republican.
He was elected to Congress in 1858, and by 1867 had served several terms as chairman of the House Ways and Means Committee.
He viewed Andrew Johnson as the "great obstacle" to a proper
Reconstruction of the Southern states.

After Congress had adjourned its session of July, Johnson finally decided to remove Stanton as secretary of war. Stanton had
become increasingly estranged from Johnson and the rest of his
Cabinet and had, sometimes surreptitiously and sometimes not,
collaborated with the congressional Republicans in their efforts to
thwart Johnson.

> By the spring and summer of 1867 it became evident
> that Stanton and the President were bitter enemies. In
> company with Grant, who was anxious to protect the
> army from interference by the courts and to simplify the
> task of military Reconstruction, the War Secretary was
> quietly sabotaging Johnson's Reconstruction policies.[5]

On August 5, the president's secretary arrived at Stanton's office with a terse message for him.

> Public considerations of a high character constrain me to
> say that your resignation as Secretary of War will be
> accepted.

Stanton replied that he declined to resign before the next meeting of Congress in December.

If he were to suspend or remove Stanton involuntarily, Johnson

needed to appoint someone to succeed him who would be acceptable to the Senate. The only conceivable candidate who would be
mutually acceptable was General U. S. Grant, and Johnson offered the position of interim secretary of war to the general. Grant
at first hedged, but later agreed to take the position. On August
13, the president sent Stanton another terse note:

> Sir:
>
> By virtue of the power and authority vested in me as
> President by the Constitution and laws of the United
> States, you are hereby suspended from office as Secre-
> tary of War, and will cease to exercise any and all func-
> tions pertaining to the same. You will at once transfer to
> General Ulysses S. Grant, who has this day been autho-
> rized and empowered to act as Secretary of War *ad in-
> terim*, all records, books, papers, and other public property
> now your custody and charge.

Stanton protested his suspension, but said that he had no alternative but to submit to "superior force," and turned the war port-
folio over to Grant. Even assuming that the Tenure of Office Act
applied to Stanton, Johnson consistently with the act could suspend Stanton from office until the next session of the Senate, which
would begin in December.

Before then, however, the Radicals would suffer electoral set-
backs in the off-year elections to Congress and state offices that
were held in October and November 1867.

> Only in Michigan and Kentucky did Republicans im-
> prove upon their showings of a year earlier. In eighteen
> other states electing officials, Republicans lost significant
> ground. In Massachusetts, the Republican share of the
> vote dropped from seventy-seven percent in 1866 to fifty-
> eight percent in 1867. The Democrats swept California,
> charging the Republican policy would inevitably mean
> the enfranchisement of the state's Chinese population. The
> Republican vote in New Jersey fell 1600 short of that
> polled in 1865. In Maryland, the Republican vote was

reduced from forty percent of the total to twenty-five
percent. Wade lost his Senate seat as Democrats won
control of Ohio's state legislature . . .[6]

The Judiciary Committee resumed its hearings in November,
and continued to compile a record of miscellaneous charges against
the president. Matters investigated included letters addressed to
Jefferson Davis with the president's signature (although the witness who testified about them was never able to produce the letters), misuse of patronage, wrongful use of the pardon power by
the president with respect to deserters in West Virginia, and even
the possible complicity of Johnson in the assassination of Lincoln.
The Judge Advocate General, Joseph Holt, produced the diary of
John Wilkes Booth for the committee and noted that eighteen pages
of the document were missing. The committee also examined
Johnson's private financial dealings and bank accounts. Finally in
November it heard from Representative Ashley, who presented to
the committee his theory that every vice-president who had succeeded to the presidency had played a part in bringing about the
death of his predecessor. This theory, of course, included such
unlikely conspirators as John Tyler, who had succeeded William
Henry Harrison in 1841, and Millard Fillmore, who had succeeded Zachary Taylor in 1850. Ashley was unable to supply any
concrete evidence to support his theory, and apparently neither
he nor his theory was taken seriously.

On November 25, the committee filed a report indicating that
it had reversed the view it had held in July, and now favored
impeachment by a vote of 5 to 4. The majority, consisting of five
Republicans—including John Churchill of New York, who had
changed his mind since July by reason of Johnson's veto of the
supplemental Reconstruction Act and his removal of Stanton—
listed seventeen charges against the president. Two Republicans,
including Chairman James Wilson, filed a minority report stating
that none of the charges listed by the majority were indictable
offenses, and therefore under the Constitution they could not be
the basis for impeachment. The committee's two Democratic
members agreed with the Republican minority as to the basis for
impeachment, but also indicated their support for the president's
Reconstruction policies.

In December 1867 the committee's report came before the House and was debated for two days. At the end of the debate, the motion to impeach Andrew Johnson failed by a vote of 108 to 57.

The Tenure of Office Act to which Johnson had referred when he suspended Stanton in August provided that the suspension should last only until the next session of Congress, and that if the Senate then refused to concur in the suspension, Stanton would resume his office. The Senate debated this question during the second week of January 1868, and on January 13 refused to concur in the suspension by a vote of 35 to 16. Grant acquiesced and relinquished the office, but the president was unwilling to accept the Senate decision. There were strong arguments to be made that the Tenure of Office Act did not cover Stanton, and that if it did, it was an infringement of the executive powers granted to the president by the Constitution. For the next month Johnson searched for someone willing to accept appointment to the War Department to succeed Stanton. Unable to persuade either Grant or Sherman to do so, he turned to General Lorenzo B. Thomas, the Adjutant General of the Army. On February 21, 1868, Johnson wrote and had delivered to Stanton this short note:

Sir:

By virtue of the power and authority vested in me as President by the Constitution and laws of the United States you are hereby removed from office as Secretary for the Department of War, and your functions as such will terminate upon the receipt of this communication.

Stanton was directed to turn over the office to Major General Lorenzo Thomas, the bearer of Johnson's note. Johnson sent a message to the Senate advising them of his removal of Stanton, and of his appointment of General Thomas as secretary of war *ad interim*.

The excited scenes which followed have often been described. When Stanton received the letter from Thomas, he sat down on a sofa and read it. He asked for time to remove his personal property, but after a while gave

Thomas to understand that he was not at all certain whether he would obey the order. Then he notified his allies on Capitol Hill.

The reaction in Congress was frantic. In the Senate the President's message arrived while Trumbull was delivering a speech. . . . A rush took place to the Vice-President's desk, and Sumner tore open the package. Then the Senators read the contents—the removal of the Secretary of War, the appointment of Lorenzo Thomas. . . . Summer promptly sent a one-word telegram to Stanton. "Stick," it admonished. Other Senators took a carriage to the War Department to urge the Secretary to hold fast. They also visited Grant to tell him that he had to support Congress. Upon the receipt of a note from Stanton that Thomas intended to oust him in the morning, Senator Edmunds introduced a resolution disapproving of the President's action. After the substitution of Henry Wilson's version specifically denying the President's power to remove the Secretary of War, it was accepted by twenty-eight Republicans and opposed by six—four Democrats, Doolittle, and Edmunds. Twenty Senators did not vote. . . .

In the House the uproar was even greater. When Colfax announced the receipt of Stanton's communication, excited little clusters of Congressmen formed. Thaddeus Stevens, leaning on Bingham's arm, moved about from group to group. "Didn't I tell you so?" he said again and again. "What good did your moderation do you? If you don't kill the beast, it will kill you." After some parliamentary maneuvering, John Covode offered a resolution that the President be impeached "of high crimes and misdemeanors." The resolution was referred to the Reconstruction Committee, and since it was late in the afternoon the House adjourned to take up the question on the following day. It was evident that the impeachment resolution would pass as soon as members had been given an opportunity to be heard.[7]

-13-

*H*igh excitement prevailed in Washington and throughout the country over the Washington's Birthday weekend in 1868. In the House of Representatives, the Reconstruction Committee, to which the Covode Impeachment Resolution had been referred the previous day, reported it favorably to the full House on Saturday, and that body debated it. The resolution made no effort to detail any charges against Johnson; it consisted only of the following:

> *Resolved*, That Andrew Johnson, President of the United States, be impeached of high crimes and misdemeanors in office.

The Senate received from the president the nomination of Thomas Ewing of Ohio to be secretary of war to succeed Stanton, but of course it took no action on that nomination. Stanton, meanwhile, urged on by his supporters, was maintaining a twenty-four-hour-a-day vigil at the War Department. Armed volunteers took turns stationing themselves in the basement of the building so that he would not be ousted by force.

On Monday, February 24, the House passed the Impeachment Resolution by a party vote of 126 to 47. The moderate and conservative Republicans, who had opposed impeachment only two months earlier, had finally been convinced of its necessity by Johnson's removal of Stanton. James Wilson, who had chaired the

House Judiciary Committee and who had opposed impeachment in December, said:

> Guided by a sincere desire to pass this cup from our lips, determined not to drink it if escape were not cut off by the presence of a palpable duty, we at last find ourselves compelled to take its very dregs.[1]

The Speaker of the House, Schuyler Colfax of Indiana, appointed the quintessential Radical Thaddeus Stevens, and John Bingham of Ohio, not identified with the Radicals, to notify the Senate of the House action.

Meanwhile, a committee of the House especially appointed for that purpose set about drafting the Articles of Impeachment. On February 29, the committee reported ten articles to the House, which after debate were reduced to nine. All were drawn to resemble a criminal indictment, and all but two were based on Johnson's alleged violation of the Tenure of Office Act by his action in removing Stanton on February 21. The second article was based on the theory that the appointment of Lorenzo Thomas as secretary of war *ad interim* was also a high misdemeanor. The ninth was based on a conversation Johnson had had with Major General William H. Emory about the constitutionality of the provision limiting the president's removal power contained in the Army Appropriation Act of March 2, 1867.

Stevens, never in good health, and now terminally ill, was disappointed at the technical nature of the charges, and urged Ben Butler to come up with an article that would more broadly reflect the congressional dissatisfaction with Johnson's performance as president. Butler proposed to the House an additional article grounded on Johnson's criticisms of Congress during his speeches in the "swing around the circle" in 1866, but this article was initially rejected by the House after debate. Wilson and Stevens then proposed another article, which was something of a catchall, including the removal of Stanton but citing the violation of other laws as well. This article was adopted, but this time eleven Republicans voted against it.

A committee of managers was chosen, including the moderates Bingham and Wilson, as well as five Radicals led by Thaddeus

Stevens, George Boutwell of Massachusetts, and Butler. Dissension broke out among the managers when it appeared that the two Radicals, Stevens and Butler, would have precedence over Bingham, which would mean that because of Stevens's illness Butler would be the actual head of the managers. Bingham declared, "I'll be damned if I serve under Butler," and the result was that Bingham became chairman of the managers. Butler persuaded all the managers but Wilson to resubmit his proposed article to the House, saying in response to criticism during the debate that he thought the idea that impeachment would lie only for an indictable crime "was dead and buried—I knew it stunk." This time the House agreed with Butler, and his article dealing with the speeches made by the president became the tenth.

Meanwhile, the Senate appointed a committee of seven—six Republicans and one Democrat, Reverdy Johnson—to recommend rules of procedure for the impeachment trial. The committee, on February 29, reported twenty-four proposed rules, several of which provoked debate in the Senate. The committee, chaired by Senator Jacob M. Howard of Michigan, referred to the Senate during the trial as a "high court of impeachment." The disagreement centered on whether or not Chief Justice Salmon P. Chase, who would preside, would have a casting vote as a presiding officer typically does, or whether he would simply be a moderator. Chase's views on the merits of the impeachment were at this time largely unknown, but the majority of the Senate agreed to delete the term "high court of impeachment." The rules proposed by Howard's committee also authorized Chase to rule on all questions of law and admissibility of evidence, with his ruling to stand unless overruled by a majority of the Senate. When some Radicals objected to this rule, an ambiguous substitute was accepted by the Senate.

The proposed rules also allowed each side one hour to argue questions of law that arose during the trial, a limitation that would seem excessively generous by the standards of the present day. But Senator Frederick Frelinghuysen of New Jersey argued not for less time but for more: He proposed that each side be allowed two hours. Die-hard Radicals such as Charles Sumner were determined that the trial should move rapidly, and Howard opposed any expansion of the one-hour limit. His position was sustained, but only by a vote of 20 to 24, eleven Republicans joining nine Democrats in favor of the two-hour limitation.

On March 4, the House resolved itself into a committee of the whole, and the entire body, led by Congressman Dawes of Massachusetts, followed the managers to the Senate chamber. There the *Journal* of the Senate records the following proceeding:

> The managers of the impeachment on the part of the House of Representatives appeared at the bar, and their presence was announced by the Sergeant-at-Arms.
>
> The PRESIDENT *pro tempore*. The managers of the impeachment will advance within the bar and take the seats provided for them.
>
> The managers on the part of the House of Representatives came within the bar and took the seats assigned to them in the area in from the Chair.
>
> Mr. Manager BINGHAM. Mr. President, the managers of the House of Representatives, by order of the House, are ready at the bar of the Senate, whenever it may please the Senate to hear them, to present articles of impeachment and in maintenance of the impeachment preferred against Andrew Johnson, President of the United States, by the House of Representatives.
>
> The PRESIDENT *pro tempore*. The Sergeant-at-Arms will make proclamation.
>
> The SERGEANT-AT-ARMS. Hear ye! Hear ye! Hear ye! All persons are commanded to keep silence, on pain of imprisonment, while the House of Representatives is exhibiting to the Senate of the United States articles of impeachment against Andrew Johnson, President of the United States.
>
> The managers then rose and remained standing, with the exception of Mr. Stevens, who was physically unable to do so, while Mr. Manager Bingham read the articles of impeachment. . . .

On the following day, March 5, at one o'clock in the afternoon, Chief Justice Salmon P. Chase entered the Senate chamber, accompanied by Justice Samuel Nelson, the senior associate justice of the Supreme Court. They were accompanied by a committee of three senators appointed for that purpose. When the Chief Justice had taken the chair, Justice Nelson administered the following oath to him:

> I do solemnly swear that in all things appertaining to the trial of the impeachment of Andrew Johnson, President of the United States, I will do impartial justice according to the Constitution and the laws; so help me God.

All of the senators had risen when the Chief Justice entered the chamber, and they remained standing while the oath was administered. The Chief Justice then proceeded to administer the same oath to each of the individual senators in alphabetical order, until he came to the name of Senator Benjamin Wade of Ohio. As Wade advanced toward the chair to take the oath, Senator Hendricks of Indiana questioned his right to sit because of the fact that if Johnson was removed from office, Wade as president *pro tempore* of the Senate would succeed to the presidency. The Senate adjourned for consultation on this question.

During the succeeding debate, no less than twenty-two of the forty-four senators present spoke. The argument of those who thought Wade should not sit was based on two theories: first, that a judge or juror who has an "interest" in a case is traditionally prohibited from sitting in that case, and, second, that the Constitution expressly provides that when the president is impeached, the Chief Justice, rather than the vice-president, shall preside. Since Wade as president *pro tempore* was in exactly the same position as the vice-president would ordinarily be—the first in line to succeed to the presidency—the implication from the Constitution was that he should not participate.

Those who took the opposite view pointed out that Senator Patterson from Tennessee, who had already taken the oath and who had not been questioned, was President Johnson's son-in-law, and that each state was entitled to have two senators present and participating in this proceeding just as it would have in the consideration of legislation. They also pointed out that the Senate could not disqualify one of its own members from participating in a matter; that was a question left to the judgment of the individual senator. Senator Hendricks, who had originally raised the question, ultimately withdrew it for procedural reasons, and the Senate adjourned. On the following day, Senator Wade, and the remaining senators, took the oath of office. The Senate, pursuant to the rules it had adopted for this occasion, ordered that Andrew Johnson appear before the Senate on Friday, March 13—one week hence.

On that day the managers again appeared, and the president's counsel appeared and took their seats for the first time. They were Henry Stanbery, recently resigned as attorney general to assist the president in his defense, Benjamin R. Curtis, former associate justice of the Supreme Court, who had written one of the dissenting opinions in the *Dred Scott* case, and Thomas Nelson of Tennessee. The president's counsel immediately moved for a forty-day period in which to prepare their answer to the Articles of Impeachment. Stanbery, arguing for the president, urged the importance of the matter and the difficulty of the legal work required in the preparation of an answer. Representative Bingham, speaking for the managers, strongly opposed any allowance of additional time to answer, and insisted that under the applicable rule the answer should be filed immediately. Stanbery replied:

> Mr. Chief Justice, the objection taken by the honorable managers is so singular that in the whole course of my practice I have not met with an example like it. A case like this, Mr. Chief Justice, in which the President of the United States is arraigned upon an impeachment presented by the House of Representatives, a case of the greatest magnitude we have ever had, is, as to time, to be treated as if it were a case before a police court, to be put through with railroad speed on the first day the criminal appears!

After some confusion, the Senate retired at two o'clock to consult and returned two hours later with a ruling that the president should be allowed ten days in which to file his answer. Bingham then moved that the trial commence on the day that the reply to the answer was filed, but this motion failed by a vote of 25 to 26. Representative Butler, speaking for the first time, objected to the

criticism of the trial proceeding at "railroad speed"—this is the age
of railroads and telegraphs, he said, and the old precedents based
on greater difficulty in communicating in traveling should not apply. In the course of his argument he said: "Sir, who is the criminal—I beg pardon for the word—the respondent at the bar?"

The Senate was thus introduced to the trial tactics of the lead
manager. Nelson replied for the president that "railroad speed had
not hitherto been a characteristic of legal proceedings, which should
be marked by calm and mature deliberation." The Senate ultimately decided that the trial should proceed as soon as the managers filed their reply to the president's answer with leave to the
president's counsel to seek additional time if it was required.

On March 23, the president's counsel filed their answer, and
William Evarts, now present with other counsel, moved for a thirty-
day continuance of the start of the trial. His motion was opposed
by Logan and Wilson, and the Senate defeated it by a vote of 12
to 41. Evarts then moved for a continuance of such reasonable
time as the Senate might grant, and at this point the Senate adjourned until the following day.

On Tuesday, March 24, the House managers announced that
they had filed a reply to the answer; the reply consisted of a standard one-paragraph document denying all the statements in the
answer. The Senate then took up again the question of what additional time should be allowed the president's counsel before the
trial actually started. Charles Sumner moved that the Senate proceed at once, but this motion failed by a vote of 23 to 29. The
Senate then resolved to retire for consultation, which it did at 1:25
P.M. The consultation and debate took approximately two hours,
and the result was that the trial was ordered to begin the following
Monday—six days hence.

These initial proceedings demonstrated, as no amount of ab-
stract argument could, how difficult and unwieldy it is for a body
consisting of fifty-six members to rule on what are routine procedural questions in a normal trial. Ordinary courts have standard
rules that govern some of these questions, but the Senate had only
a few precedents from impeachment trials that had taken place
long ago. The senators were also by nature loquacious; James
Garfield, future president of the United States and then a member
of the House of Representatives, said at a later point in the trial:

This trial has developed, in the most remarkable manner, the insane love of speaking among public men. . . . [W]e have been wading knee deep in words, words, words . . . and are but little more than half across the turbid stream. I verily believe that there are fierce impeachers here, who, if the alternative of conviction of the President, coupled with their silence; and an unlimited opportunity to talk, coupled with his certain acquittal, were before them would instantly decide to speak.[2]

On March 30 at one o'clock in the afternoon the trial itself began. Ben Butler opened for the managers, and as if to illustrate Garfield's point, he spoke for a period of three hours during which there was one ten-minute recess. His principal points were that impeachment need not be based on an indictable offense or crime, but could be based on an abuse of power, and that the Senate was not a court when sitting to try an impeachment, and therefore a senator could not be properly be challenged or disqualified for "interest."

When Butler had concluded, the managers began the presentation of their documentary evidence and the calling of their witnesses to testify. This took five days, and at the close of the session on Saturday, April 4, Butler announced that the managers had substantially concluded the presentation of their case. Counsel for the president then requested and received a postponement until Thursday, April 9, to begin their case. Benjamin Curtis made the opening argument for the president on that day, and concluded it on Friday. Witnesses for the president were then called and heard on Friday and Saturday, and throughout the next week. The proceedings were slowed down by frequent arguments about the admissibility of evidence, a question which, under the rules of the Senate, had to be finally decided by the senators themselves. These delays particularly irked Sumner, who moved on Wednesday, April 16, that all testimony should be admitted in evidence without argument, with its weight to be decided by the Senate. This motion was laid on the table by a vote of 33 to 11. Later Sumner moved that the Senate, which had been sitting from noon until between four and five o'clock in the afternoon, should convene at ten o'clock in the morning and sit later in the afternoon, but this motion, too, was defeated. Henry Stanbery, one of the counsel for the president, became ill and was forced to drop out of the case.

On Monday, April 20, the president's lawyers announced that they had concluded the presentation of their case. After a long and contentious discussion about how many lawyers on each side should be allowed to participate in the closing arguments, these arguments began on April 22, with Representative John Logan leading off for the House managers. He told the Senate:

> We are not doubtful of your verdict. Andrew Johnson has long since been tried by the whole people and found guilty, and you can but confirm that judgment already pronounced by the sovereign American people.

Logan was followed by Representative George Boutwell, who spoke for the remainder of Wednesday and concluded his argument on Thursday. Then Thomas Nelson, one of the president's lawyers, began his argument, and continued it on Friday. He was followed by William Groesbeck, who spoke on Saturday. On Monday, April 27, Thaddeus Stevens spoke, discussing only the eleventh article, which he himself had drafted. On Tuesday, Representative George Williams of Oregon took up the case for the managers, and spoke for the remainder of that day. On Wednesday, William Evarts made his closing argument for the president, which lasted for the better part of three days. When he had finished, Henry Stanbery, remarking that his doctors had urged him not to do so, spoke for a few minutes at the end of the session on Friday, and spoke more extensively the following day. He found it necessary to have a young associate read the latter portion of his argument because of indisposition on his part.

On Monday, May 4, Representative John Bingham made his closing argument on behalf of the House managers. His argument, like that of Evarts, took the better part of three days. When he finished in the middle of the afternoon on Wednesday, spectators in the galleries broke out with applause and with cheers. Order, however, was restored:

> THE CHIEF JUSTICE. Order! Order! If this be repeated the Sergeant-at-Arms will clear the galleries.

This announcement was received with laughter and hisses by some persons in the galleries, while others continued the cheering and clapping of hands.

MR. GRIMES. Mr. Chief Justice, I move that the order of the court to clear the galleries be immediately enforced.

The motion was agreed to.

THE CHIEF JUSTICE. The Sergeant-at-Arms will clear the galleries.

[Hisses and cheers and clapping of hands in parts of the galleries.] If the offense be repeated the Sergeant-at-Arms will arrest the offenders.

MR. TRUMBULL. I move that the Sergeant-at-Arms be directed to arrest the persons making the disturbance, if he can find them, as well as to clear the galleries.

THE CHIEF JUSTICE. The Chief Justice has already given directions to that effect. [The Sergeant-at-Arms, by his assistants, continued to execute the order by clearing the galleries.]

The session of May 7 was taken up with a long discussion of procedural matters and an executive session for deliberation was scheduled for Monday, May 11, with the vote on the articles of impeachment to be taken on Tuesday. But on May 12 Senator Chandler of Michigan advised the Senate that his colleague Senator Howard was delirious and ill and would not be able to attend again until May 16. He therefore requested, and obtained, a postponement of the vote on the Articles of Impeachment until that date.

The central charge made against Andrew Johnson was that he had unlawfully removed Stanton in February 1868. Articles I, IV, V, VI, VII, and VIII accused him of violating the Tenure of Office Act by the removal. Articles II and III accused him of acting contrary to law when he designated Lorenzo Thomas an interim secretary of war in place of Stanton. Article IX accused him of having attempted to induce General William Emory to disobey the Act of Congress requiring Senate approval for the removal of the General of the Army. Article X was based on the disparaging public statements made by Johnson about members of

Congress and Congress as a body in various speeches. Article XI, drafted by Thaddeus Stevens, was a potpourri which attempted to cast a broader net by lumping together several of the charges contained in the earlier separate articles.

When all of the evidence was in, and the arguments of the lawyers on both sides concluded, the essence of the case turned on the Tenure of Office Act. The articles not based on that act proved to be either factually flimsy or legally highly questionable. To convict under Articles II and III, the Senate would be required to conclude that statutes passed in 1792 and 1795, dealing with the president's authority to appoint acting or interim heads of departments, had been impliedly repealed by a statute passed in 1862. A more technical inquiry can hardly be imagined, and as a separate basis for removing a president from office it bordered on the absurd. The testimony in support of Article IX showed that Johnson did no more than express to Emory doubts about the constitutionality of the law in question; even one of the most ardent of the impeachers in the Senate, Jacob Howard of Michigan, would have voted to acquit on this article. The evidence of what Johnson had actually said in his various speeches, introduced to support Article X, was confusing because no official transcript of the president's remarks had been made. But even more telling was the reliance of the president's counsel on the provision of the First Amendment to the Constitution stating that "Congress shall make no law abridging the freedom of speech." Finally, and perhaps most important, with respect to each of these articles it was very difficult to argue that any of the acts charged were "high crimes or misdemeanors" of the sort required by the Constitution for impeachment and conviction.

The presentation of evidence on the articles based on the Tenure of Office Act had been anticlimactic, since anyone who had read a major newspaper published in the United States knew exactly what Andrew Johnson had done. On February 21, 1868, he had notified Stanton that he was removed as secretary of war, and on the same day he had notified the Senate to this effect. The president's counsel mounted a threefold defense to the charges based on the violation of this act: (1) Stanton was not covered by the Tenure of Office Act; (2) if he was covered by it, the point was a very doubtful one and should not be the basis for removal of the president from office; and (3) if Stanton was covered by the language of the act, the act violated the constitutional power to "take care that the laws be faithfully executed" granted to the chief executive by Article II of the Constitution.

The Tenure of Office Act, as previously noted, was enacted in March 1867 to prevent Andrew Johnson from removing persons holding offices for which Senate confirmation was required for appointment. One of its sections expressly provided that violation of its terms should be a "high misdemeanor." The measure had originated in the Senate, and that body had exempted Cabinet members from the bill's requirement that removal could be had only with the consent of the Senate. The House amended the bill to include those officers. The bill went to conference between the two houses, and the Senate conferees refused to accept the House amendment. The conference committee adopted a compromise provision that can best be described as opaque; based on it, the House conferees assured the House that the Senate had in effect accepted the inclusion of Cabinet members, while the Senate conferees told the Senate that members of Andrew Johnson's Cabinet who had been originally appointed by Lincoln were not covered. The operative section of the law read as follows:

> . . . Every person holding any civil office to which he has been appointed by and with the advice and consent of the Senate . . . is, and shall be entitled to hold such office until a successor shall have been in like manner appointed and duly qualified. Except as herein otherwise provided: *Provided* that the Secretaries of State, of the Treasury, of War, of the Navy, and of the Interior, the Postmaster-General, and Attorney-General, shall hold their offices respectively for and during the term of the President by whom they may have been appointed and for one month thereafter, subject to removal by and with the advice and consent of the Senate.

The lawyers on both sides had a field day with the "provided" language. Counsel for the president pointed out that unlike the members of the Cabinet whom Johnson had nominated himself, Stanton had been nominated by Lincoln and confirmed by the

Senate in 1862. He had stayed on in the position of secretary of war after Lincoln's death by Johnson's invitation, but he had not been nominated anew by Johnson. They pointed out that the opposite construction would fasten on an incoming president all of his predecessor's Cabinet appointments if the Senate did not confirm the new president's Cabinet appointments within the first month of his tenure. Two Republican senators who voted to convict on other articles—Timothy Howe of Wisconsin and John Sherman of Ohio—refused to convict on Article I because it was based solely on the Tenure of Office Act. They had both participated in the Senate debate as to the meaning of the Conference Committee Amendment.

The House managers replied that while the president's counsel's arguments might be true in the case of a president elected in his own right, it was not so in the case of a vice-president who succeeded to office upon the death of a president. Such an individual, they said, was not serving his own term as president, but was serving out the term of his predecessor. Thus Stanton was entitled to the protection of the act until one month after March 4, 1869, when Lincoln's second term would expire. After the manner of lawyers, they and their opponents then proceeded to marshal arguments pro and con on the thoroughly abstruse question of whether Andrew Johnson—concededly the president of the United States—was serving his own term as president or was simply serving out Lincoln's term as president.

The managers also relied on the resolution hastily passed by the Senate on the day Johnson had notified that body of his removal of Stanton, a resolution declaring that the president's action was contrary to law. They further pointed to the fact that when Johnson had suspended Stanton from office in August 1867 and submitted his reasons for doing so to the Senate, he obviously assumed that the Tenure of Office Act applied to Stanton.

The president's counsel made essentially two replies to these arguments of the managers. The first, and most telling with respect to the Republican senators who ultimately voted to acquit, was this: If the manager's position on the meaning of the proviso in the Tenure of Office Act was correct, it was still a highly debatable question; the president should not be convicted of intentionally violating a law that took a Philadelphia lawyer to interpret.

The second reply, though it persuaded none of the Republican senators who voted to acquit, was important in the history of American constitutional law. It was this: In order to "take care that the laws be faithfully executed," as the Constitution requires him to do, the president must be able to appoint subordinate officers in whom he can place his trust, and be able to remove them when they cease to have his trust. To require him to retain a subordinate official who has lost his trust, unless the Senate shall consent to the removal, infringes on this authority. This was in fact the advice that his Cabinet had unanimously given Johnson at the time he vetoed the Tenure of Office Act, and Stanton had helped Seward prepare the veto message.

This was not simply an exegesis on the written words of the Constitution, argued the president's counsel, but an interpretation that had been confirmed by the first Congress, many of whose members had been delegates to the Constitutional Convention. When that Congress had created the first Cabinet departments, the language of the bills creating them had authorized the president to remove the officers at his pleasure, but after debate, this language was stricken because, in view of both houses, it wrongly implied that Congress had the constitutional authority to decide the manner in which the president might remove such officers. That authority, the members of Congress believed, had been confided to the president alone.

The managers conceded that this consideration of the matter by the First Congress was against them, but pointed out that the view had been questioned by later Congresses, and that even the practice of the executive branch had not been consistent. It was not easy to find an exact precedent for the removal of a Cabinet officer, because the great majority of officers holding that position had the good grace and good sense to resign when they lost the confidence of the president or disagreed with the policies of the administration. Counsel for the president pointed to the example of John Adams, who had removed Timothy Pickering as his secretary of state when the two disagreed about foreign policy. The House managers responded that on the very same day, Adams had sent to the Senate the nomination of a replacement for Pickering, but counsel for the president in turn replied that the nomination sent to the Senate referred to Pickering as having been "removed."

Finally, the president's lawyers made an argument on the constitutional question similar to the one they made about the coverage of the Tenure of Office Act: Even if the Senate should disagree as to the constitutional authority of the president to remove, the unanimous advice of the president's Cabinet when he was contemplating a veto of the act was that it was unconstitutional, and that surely the president had a right to have that question determined by the courts. The managers replied that this position would enable a president to wholly frustrate the will of the people as expressed in laws; the president could veto a measure, and if Congress passed it into law over his veto, he could then refuse to enforce it on the grounds that it was unconstitutional.

While the senators who constituted the impeachment tribunal considered these various arguments, speculation was rife in Washington and throughout the country as to the outcome of the trial. The Senate consisted of fifty-four members, forty-two Republicans and twelve Democrats. Just as in Chase's case, if all the Jeffersonian Republicans had voted to convict, he would have been convicted, so now if all the Republicans voted to convict, Johnson would be convicted. The corporal's guard of Democrats regarded the impeachment proceedings as purely political, and it was rightly assumed that all of them would vote to acquit. But it was apparent that there was not similar unanimity within the ranks of the Republicans. Under the Constitution, thirty-six votes were needed to convict, and the Republicans could afford the loss of only six of their own members. At least three influential and able Republican senators—William Pitt Fessenden of Maine, chairman of the Senate Finance Committee, Lyman Trumbull of Illinois, chairman of the Senate Judiciary Committee, and James Grimes of Iowa—were thought to be definitely lost to the impeachment cause. Half a dozen others were regarded as doubtful, although some of them were subjected to considerable pressure from constituents to vote for conviction. The following telegram was sent from Kansas to both senators from that state:

LEAVENWORTH, MAY 14. KANSAS HAS HEARD THE EVIDENCE, AND DEMANDS THE CONVICTION OF THE PRESIDENT.

D. R. ANTHONY, AND 1,000 OTHERS"[3]

Samuel Pomeroy, the senior senator from Kansas, had already made up his mind, but Edmund Ross, the junior senator, had not. Ross was offended by the Anthony telegram, and sent this reply:

GENTLEMEN:

I DO NOT RECOGNIZE YOUR RIGHT TO DEMAND THAT I SHALL VOTE EITHER FOR OR AGAINST CONVICTION. I HAVE TAKEN AN OATH TO DO IMPARTIAL JUSTICE . . . AND I TRUST I SHALL HAVE THE COURAGE AND HONESTY TO VOTE AC-CORDING TO THE DICTATES OF MY JUDGMENT AND FOR THE HIGHEST GOOD OF MY COUNTRY.

TO D. R. ANTHONY AND 1,000 OTHERS.

E. G. ROSS[4]

Whereupon D. R. Anthony and his 1,000 others replied:

HON. E. G. ROSS, UNITED STATES SENATOR, WASHINGTON, D.C.

YOUR TELEGRAM RECEIVED. YOURS IS DICTATED BY TOM EWING, NOT BY YOUR OATH. YOUR MOTIVES ARE INDIAN CONTRACTS AND GREENBACKS. KANSAS REPUDIATES YOU AS SHE DOES ALL PERJURERS AND SKUNKS.

D. R. ANTHONY AND OTHERS[5]

Andrew Johnson, meanwhile, was giving assurances through intermediaries to senators such as Grimes that he would nominate a secretary of war acceptable to them if he were acquitted.

On May 16, the day of the vote, there was electricity in the air at the Capitol:

The rush for tickets to the Senate galleries had been tre-mendous. Long before eleven, all the best seats were taken—a strange contrast to the scarce attendance on the floor when, at 11:30, the Senate was called to order. Slowly the Senators drifted in. By noon, the galleries were wholly occupied. The diplomatic box was full, thousands were milling outside the chamber, and the overflow extended to the terraces and streets beyond. Rarely in its history had the capital witnessed such tension.[6]

George Julian, who had been elected to Congress twenty years before, was still a congressman from Indiana and sat in the area designated for members of the House. He recalled that:

The galleries were packed, and an indescribable anxiety was written on every face. Some of the members of the House near me grew pale and sick under the burden of suspense. Such stillness prevailed that the breathing in the galleries could be heard at the announcement of each Senator's voice. This was quite noticeable when any of the doubtful Senators voted, the people holding their breath as the words "guilty" or "not guilty" were pronounced, and then giving it simultaneous vent.[7]

At noon the Chief Justice appeared and took his chair, and the managers and the president's counsel took their customary seats. But before the vote began, Senator Williams of Oregon moved that the vote should take place on the eleventh article, which was thought to be the one that would command the most support for conviction. This rather extraordinary departure from normal procedure passed the Senate by a vote of 34 to 19, with Grimes of Iowa not voting. Ominously, from the point of view of the House managers, the number of "ayes" was two short of that which would be required to convict. The Chief Justice then directed the secretary of the Senate to read the eleventh article, which was the potpourri drafted by Thaddeus Stevens. The following proceedings then took place:

The CHIEF JUSTICE. Call the roll.
The Chief Clerk called the name of Mr. Anthony.
Mr. Anthony rose in his place.
The CHIEF JUSTICE. Mr. Senator Anthony how say you? Is the respondent, Andrew Johnson, President of

the United States, guilty or not guilty of a high misdemeanor as charged in this article?

Mr. ANTHONY. Guilty.

(This form was continued in regard to each Senator as the roll was called alphabetically, each rising in his place as his name was called and answering "guilty," or "not guilty." When the name of Mr. Grimes was called, he being very feeble, the Chief Justice said he might remain seated; he, however, with the assistance of friends, rose and answered. The Chief Justice also suggested to Mr. Howard that he might answer in his seat, but he preferred to rise.)

When the roll call was complete, thirty-five senators had voted to convict, and nineteen senators had voted to acquit. Before the Chief Justice could proceed to the reading of the first article, which would be next in order, Senator Williams was again on his feet to move that the Senate adjourn for ten days, to the twenty-sixth day of May at noon. Before that proposal was voted upon, the Chief Justice formally announced the vote on the eleventh article and, repeating exactly the words of Aaron Burr in the Chase case fifty-three years earlier, said, "Two-thirds not having pronounced guilty, the President is, therefore, acquitted upon this article." The motion to adjourn for ten days before considering other articles then passed the Senate by a vote of 32 to 21.

During the intervening ten days, the Republican National Convention was held in Chicago and nominated Ulysses S. Grant as its candidate for president in the 1868 election. The convention also expressed its hearty approval of the impeachment proceedings against Andrew Johnson, and the thirty-five senators who had voted to convict him. When the Senate reconvened on May 26, Senator Williams was again on his feet, moving that the resolution previously adopted as to the order of reading and voting on the Articles of Impeachment be rescinded. After much parliamentary maneuvering, and further attempts to adjourn the Senate to a later date, it was agreed that the Senate should vote next upon the second article of impeachment. When the roll was called on that article, the vote was precisely the same as it had been on the eleventh article: thirty-five voted to convict and nineteen to acquit. The

Chief Justice announced that the president was acquitted upon Article II. The same vote obtained when the roll was called on Article III. At this point, Senator Williams moved that the Senate sitting as a court of impeachment adjourn sine die. This motion carried by a vote of 34 to 16, and the effort to convict Andrew Johnson ended without a formal vote ever having been taken upon eight of the articles presented.

-14-

*T*he Senate's vote to acquit the president on the eleventh article was front-page news in the nation's press, and more than one newspaper put out an "extra" edition to proclaim the result. Knowledgeable reporters rightly saw that this first vote on May 16 foretold the failure of the entire impeachment effort.

The Washington *Evening Star*, in an extra on May 16, carried these headlines:

THE EVENING STAR

EXTRA.

IMPEACHMENT.

THE GREAT DAY!

Scenes at the Capitol.

Intense Excitement!

The Vote!

The Eleventh Article to be Voted on First!

On this Question, Yeas 34. Nays 19!

The Vote Admitted to be a Virtual Acquittal!

The New York Times, in its morning edition of Sunday, May 17, told the story in these words:

IMPEACHMENT.

Final Vote in the Senate on the Eleventh Article.

The President Acquitted of the Offences Charged.

Adjournment of the Court Without a Further Vote.

An Investigation to be Made of the Bribery and Corruption Charges.

Special Dispatch to the New-York Times.

Washington, Saturday, May 16.

Other newspapers were more overtly partisan. *The Chicago Republican* in its edition of Monday, May 18, carried these headlines:

WASHINGTON.

The Acquittal of the President on the Eleventh Article.

Postponement of the Vote on the Remaining Counts.

Facts Connected with the Treachery of Senators Ross and Fowler.

More Developments Concerning the Schemes of the Chief Justice.

The Alleged Corrupt Means Used to Secure the Acquittal.

The Proposed Changes in the Cabinet.

[Special Telegram to the Chicago Republican.]
WASHINGTON, May 17.

The Philadelphia Inquirer, in its edition of the same day, gave its version:

NEWS FROM WASHINGTON.

An Important Day in the Nation's Annals

SATURDAY IN THE HIGH COURT

Scenes Upon the Floor and in the Galleries

INTENSE ANXIETY AMONG THE PEOPLE

How Doubtful Senators Were Scrutinized

ROSS, OF KANSAS, CLOSELY WATCHED

He Records His Vote "Not Guilty"

HOWARD, GRIMES AND CONKLING IN THEIR SEATS

The Eleventh Article in Full

A REVIEW OF THE PRESENT SITUATION

Probability of a Recess of Both Houses

SENATORS AND REPRESENTATIVES GOING TO CHICAGO

All Quiet in Washington

EFFORTS TO FORM A NEW POLITICAL PARTY

Missouri Representatives' Address to their Constituents

[SPECIAL DESPATCHES TO THE INQUIRER.]
WASHINGTON, May 17, 1868.

The House managers and their Radical Republican supporters in that body were sufficiently frustrated by the result to appoint a special committee of the House to investigate possible bribery and corruption on the part of the president's supporters, but the investigation turned up nothing of consequence. Other explanations must be sought for the failure of the impeachment.

In trying to determine why the effort to impeach Andrew Johnson failed in the Senate, we have a good deal more to go on than we do in the case of the acquittal of Samuel Chase. Thirty of the fifty-four senators who participated in the Johnson trial filed written opinions in which they explained their view of the proceedings and why they had voted the way they did. The three ablest and most respected of the seven "Republican recusants" who voted to acquit Johnson were William Pitt Fessenden of Maine, James Grimes of Iowa, and Lyman Trumbull of Illinois. Each of them was a major national figure in the Republican party; each of them had come to the Senate at the time of the Northern furor over the Kansas-Nebraska Act. All three had risen through seniority to important committee chairmanships.

William Pitt Fessenden was raised in Fryeburg, Maine, where began his long acquaintance with Daniel Webster. Fessenden graduated from Bowdoin College at the age of seventeen. He studied law and was admitted to the Maine bar at the age of twenty-one. He settled in Portland in 1827, and that remained his home until his death in 1869. He had a thriving legal practice extending throughout the state, and was active in Whig, and later Republican, politics. He was elected to the Senate in 1854, and with one brief interruption represented Maine in that body for the rest of his life.

Fessenden was a leading proponent of the antislavery cause in the Senate before the Civil War. He became chairman of the Senate Finance Committee in 1861, and labored mightily to draft and enact the legislation raising the money necessary to fight the Civil War. He served briefly as Lincoln's secretary of the treasury following Chase's resignation in 1864, but was reelected to the Senate by the Maine legislature in 1865.

Fessenden, in his written opinion, pointed out the essentially judicial character of the proceeding:

> Each Senator has solemnly sworn, as required by the Constitution, to "do impartial justice, according to the

Constitution and the laws," upon the trial. It needs no argument to show that the President is on trial for the specific offences charged, and for none other. It would be contrary to every principle of justice to the clearest dictates of right, to try and condemn any man, however guilty he may be thought, for an offence not charged, of which no notice has been given to him, and against which he has had no opportunity to defend himself.

Fessenden went on to discuss the understandings of the First Congress as revealed in the 1789 debates, and concluded that the Tenure of Office Act properly interpreted did not apply to protect Stanton's office. But he said that even if he were wrong on this point, the application of the act to Stanton was at least highly debatable, so that the president should not be removed from office because he had put the wrong interpretation on the statute:

> To depose the constitutional chief magistrate of a great nation, elected by the people, on grounds so slight, would, in my judgment, be an abuse of the power conferred upon the Senate, which could not be justified to the country or the world. To construe such an act as a high distant misdemeanor, within the meaning of the Constitution, would, when the passions of the hour have had time to cool, be looked upon with wonder, if not with derision.

With respect to the tenth article, which was based on the speeches made by Johnson, Fessenden said:

> To deny the President a right to comment freely upon the conduct of co-ordinate branches of government would not only be denying him a right secured to every other citizen of the republic, but might deprive the people of the benefit of his opinion of public affairs, and of his watchfulness of their interests and welfare. That under circumstances where he was called upon by a large body of his fellow-citizens to address them, and when he was goaded by contumely and insult, he permitted himself to transcend the limits of proper and dignified speech, such

as was becoming the dignity of his station, is a matter of deep regret and highly censurable. But, in my opinion, it can receive no other punishment than public sentiment alone can inflict.

Finally, Fessenden replied to the urging of the managers that the Senate heed the clamor of public opinion demanding Johnson's conviction:

To the suggestion that popular opinion demands the conviction of the President on these charges, I reply that he is not now on trial before the people, but before the Senate. . . . The people have not heard the evidence as we have heard it. The responsibility is not on them, but upon us. They have not taken an oath to "do impartial justice according to the Constitution and the laws." I have taken that oath. I cannot render judgment upon their convictions, nor can they transfer to themselves my punishment if I violate my own. And I should consider myself undeserving of the confidence of that just and intelligent people who imposed upon me this great responsibility, and unworthy of a place among honorable men, if for any fear of public reprobation, and for the sake of securing popular favor, I should disregard the convictions of my judgment and my conscience.

James Grimes of Iowa had been born in New Hampshire and attended Dartmouth College for three years. At the age of nineteen he moved to Burlington, Iowa, and was admitted to the bar. He became active in politics, and was elected governor in 1854 as a Whig. During his term important strides were made in improving the public institutions of the state. He was elected to the Senate in 1859, and reelected in 1865. At the time of the impeachment trial he was chairman of the Senate Committee on Naval Affairs. During the trial he suffered a stroke and resigned the following year.

In his opinion, Grimes discussed in some detail the understanding evinced by the First Congress in 1789, to the effect that removal of high officials in the executive branch should be the sole

prerogative of the president. Like Fessenden, he concluded that
the Tenure of Office Act did not protect Stanton in his office, and
that Johnson was at least entitled to treat it as a debatable question. In concluding he said:

> Nor can I suffer my judgment of the law governing this
> case to be influenced by political considerations. I cannot
> agree to destroy the harmonious working of the Consti-
> tution for the sake of getting rid of an unacceptable Pres-
> ident. Whatever may be my opinion of the incumbent, I
> cannot consent to trifle with the high office he holds. I
> can do nothing which, by implication, may be construed
> into an approval of impeachments as a part of future po-
> litical machinery.

Trumbull of Illinois had been born in Connecticut; he ultimately settled in Belleville, Illinois, and was admitted to the Illinois bar. He was active in Illinois politics as a Democrat, and was
elected to the Senate in 1855. By the beginning of the Civil War
he had switched his allegiance to the Republican party, and during the Reconstruction Era, he was chairman of the Senate Judiciary Committee. He was probably the most scholarly of the three,
but in the words of one biographer, "his colorless public personality denied him the kind of support on which spectacular careers
are built."

Trumbull concluded his opinion on the impeachment with these
words:

> Once set the example of impeaching a President for what,
> when the excitement of the hour shall have subsided,
> will be regarded as insufficient causes . . . and no future
> President will be safe who happens to differ with the
> majority of the House and two-thirds of the Senate on
> any measure deemed by them important. . . . In view
> of the consequences likely to flow from this day's pro-
> ceedings, should they result in conviction on what my
> judgment tells me are insufficient charges and proofs, I
> tremble for the future of my country. I cannot be an
> instrument to produce such a result; and at the hazard of

the ties even of friendship and affection, till calmer times shall do justice to my motives, no alternative is left me but the inflexible discharge of duty.

It is impossible to doubt that each of these three senators held the views they stated not merely with sincerity but with deep conviction. But deep conviction was also expressed on the other side of the question by Charles Sumner of Massachusetts, who, although he objected to the entire idea of the senators' filing opinions in the case, nonetheless filed one thirty-four pages long, with a fourteen-page appendix. He began by describing the impeachment proceedings as the "last great battle against slavery." He said that "Andrew Johnson is the impersonation of the tyrannical slave power. In him it lives again."

He went on to arraign those who had spoken against conviction as essentially pettifogging lawyers, who did not really understand the meaning of impeachment:

> The formal accusation is founded on certain recent transgressions, enumerated in Articles of Impeachment, but it is wrong to suppose that this is the whole case. . . . It is unpardonable to higgle over words and phrases when, for more than two years the tyrannical pretensions of this offender, now in evidence before the Senate, as I shall show, have been manifest in their terrible, heart-rending consequences.
> . . . [I]t is important to understand the nature of the proceeding; and here on the threshold we encounter the effort of the apologists who have sought in every way to confound this great constitutional trial with an ordinary case of Nisi Prius and to win for the criminal President an Old Bailey acquittal, where on some quibble the prisoner is allowed to go without the day.

Further on in his opinion, he denounced in great detail the essentially judicial nature of the proceedings, in which charges were specifically delineated and debated, saying, "Next to an outright mercenary, give me a lawyer to betray a great cause." He concluded in a passage that shows that he, too, fervently felt the justice of *his* side of the argument:

> Alas! For the Unionists, white and black alike, who have trusted to our flag. You now offer them a sacrifice to those persecutors whose representative is before you for judgment. . . . They are fellow-citizens of a common country, brethren of a common humanity, two commanding titles both strong against the deed. I send them at this terrible moment the sympathy and fellowship of a heart that suffers with them. So just a cause cannot be lost. Meanwhile may they find in themselves, and in the goodness of an overruling Providence, that rescue and protection which the Senate refuses to give.

Sumner obviously had a basically different approach to the nature of impeachment than did Fessenden, Grimes, and Trumbull. To the latter, it was an essentially judicial proceeding, in which specific charges were made against the accused, just as charges are made against an indicted criminal defendant, and then the Senate sits in judgment as to whether these charges have been proved to their satisfaction. To Sumner, on the other hand, impeachment was much more like a vote of confidence in the government under a parliamentary system. The overriding issue for him was not whether Andrew Johnson had violated the Tenure of Office Act, but whether Andrew Johnson should continue to be president in view of his repeated obstruction of the reconstruction policies of the Radical Republicans. Here we hark back to Senator William Giles's stated view of impeachment at the time of the Chase trial: "We want your office in order to give it to a better man."

Not only all of the "recusant Republicans" who voted to acquit Johnson but most of the Republicans who voted to convict him accepted, or at least purported to accept, the judicial model of the impeachment proceeding. It remained for Sumner, who combined near-fanaticism with extraordinary ability, to frankly state the other view. But just as one would not want to see fastened upon parliamentary proceedings, in connection with a vote of confidence in the government, the often tedious and demanding requirements of a judicial trial, it is very difficult to reconcile Sumner's candidly political approach with the constitutional provisions dealing with impeachment. This, at any rate, was the view of those recusant Republicans who filed opinions in the case. Their acceptance of that view, and of the consequences that flowed from it, was surely the principal reason why they cast the critical votes to acquit Johnson.

Senator Joseph Fowler of Tennessee, another of the recusants, in his opinion stated another reason that influenced these senators. Explaining his interpretation of the proviso in the Tenure of Office Act to exclude Stanton from the protection of the Act, he said:

> The reason for this exception is this: the Senate considered the cabinet officers as the constitutional advisers of the President. They are and have always been regarded as the agents of the Executive. . . . The President has always had the right to select his own cabinet. It is a right guaranteed to him by the Constitution. The legislative department has no power either directly or indirectly to legislate a cabinet minister upon the President, or to remove him save by impeachment. The Senate knew and appreciated this view of the case, and did not desire to touch the long-established doctrine under which the government had flourished.

There were also factors external to the merits of the case that worked against the success of the impeachment, just as there were other factors that worked in its favor. One of the factors working against its success was an uneasiness, not only on the part of the Democrats but on the part of some Republicans, about having Senator Ben Wade of Ohio succeed to the presidency if Johnson was convicted.

> That Wade constituted a major stumbling block for the impeachers was widely recognized. His advocacy of women's rights, high tariffs, the advancement of labor, and—last but not least—black suffrage had not endeared him to the moderates. As early as February 28th the New York *Herald* predicted the failure of the trial not merely

because of the weakness of the case, but also because of "jealousy of Ben Wade and doubts as to his competency." Other papers agreed, and the pro-Johnson press never wearied of quoting Republican politicians and newspapers in disparagement of the Senator from Ohio.[1]

Chief Justice Chase had been cold to Wade since the latter failed to support his candidacy for the Republican nomination for president at the Chicago convention in 1860, and there were rumors afoot during the impeachment trial that Chase tried to influence one or more senators to vote for acquittal. These rumors were never proved, but Chase's overweening ambition for the presidency lent credibility to them.

Though it was not often referred to in the opinions of the senators as a critical fact, it was surely of some importance that Andrew Johnson seemed less a menace in May 1868 than he had in February of that year. Backstage negotiations conducted through his counsel had assured doubtful Republicans that the president would appoint a successor to Stanton as secretary of war who was satisfactory to them. Only ten months of Johnson's term remained to be served, and there was no prospect at all that he would receive the nomination of either major party as its candidate for president in 1868.

Finally, the tactics of the managers from beginning to end undoubtedly antagonized not only senators who were doubtful to begin with but some who leaned toward conviction at the beginning of the Senate trial.

> [The impeachment] was managed by a committee led by Benjamin F. Butler and Thaddeus Stevens, who exhausted every device, appealed to every prejudice and passion, and rode roughshod, when they could, over legal obstacles in their ruthless attempt to punish the President for his opposition to their plans. Ben Butler, now uglier and paunchier than ever, employed a device borrowed from Jenkins' ear in 1739: he illustrated an oration on the horrors of Presidential reconstruction by waving a bloody shirt which allegedly belonged to an Ohio carpetbagger flogged by klansmen in Mississippi.[2]

If there is one theme to be distilled from all of this as to why the impeachment failed, it is probably found in a letter written by Senator James Dixon of Connecticut to Fessenden after the trial was over:

> Whether Andrew Johnson should be removed from office, justly or unjustly, was comparatively of little consequence—but whether our government should be Mexicanized, and an example set which would surely, in the end, utterly overthrow our institutions, was a matter of vast consequence. To you and Mr. Grimes it is mainly due that impeachment has not become an ordinary means of changing the policy of the government by a violent removal of the executive.[3]

-15-

*L*ess than a year of Andrew Johnson's presidential term remained after his acquittal by the Senate, and no further clashes between the executive and Congress marked this period. Johnson offered himself as a candidate for the Democratic nomination for president in 1868, and at that party's convention in New York in July 1868, he received the second-highest number of votes on the first ballot. But his support thereafter steadily decreased, and the convention nominated Governor Horatio Seymour of New York as its candidate. Seymour lost to U. S. Grant in the presidential election that fall.

Johnson, bitter toward Grant, followed the examples of John Adams and John Quincy Adams and declined to attend the inauguration of his successor on March 4, 1869. He returned to his home in Greeneville, Tennessee, but his nature would not allow him to enjoy a life of quiet retirement. He had always been ambitious for public office, and now to that ambition was added a desire for vindication. He unsuccessfully sought election as United States senator from Tennessee in October 1869, and as a United States representative in 1872.

Such defeats would have discouraged a less determined man, but when the Democrats swept both houses of the Tennessee legislature in 1874, he again sought election from that body to the Senate. This time he was successful, and was sworn in amid great applause at a special session of Congress on March 5, 1875. The newly elected senator died suddenly a few months later while on a visit to his daughter. He was buried with suitable honors outside of Greeneville on a site he himself had selected, in full view of the mountains of eastern Tennessee.

The acquittal of Andrew Johnson by the Senate was of course a victory for the independence of the executive branch of the government, just as the acquittal of Samuel Chase sixty-three years before had been a victory for the independence of the judicial branch. But the nature and extent of that victory deserve further examination. It is conceivable that the impasse between Andrew Johnson and Congress was so unique that even had he been convicted, the conviction would never have served as a precedent for commencing impeachment proceedings against a later president. Perhaps the basis upon which the House managers proceeded, and upon which the senators who voted to convict acted, could have been limited to the removal of Andrew Johnson without posing a threat to the independence of the presidency as an institution.

The Civil War was a unique event in our history, and Andrew Johnson's presidency, beginning at the close of that war, partakes of that uniqueness. Brother had just ceased fighting brother in a fratricidal struggle. A majority in Congress, led by the Radical Republicans, was determined both to make the South pay a high price for its effort to dissolve the Union by force and to use the power of the federal government to aid the newly freed slaves. Many of the Radical Republican leaders had been elected to Congress during the decade before the Civil War, when the views of the Southern slaveholders and their Northern political allies were dominant. They had been subjected to verbal abuse and physical threats by their Southern colleagues in the House and Senate. When they finally had a substantial majority behind them in each house of Congress, they resolved to be stern, if not vindictive, toward the vanquished enemy.

But the other factors that combined to bring about the impeachment of Johnson were not unique. Andrew Johnson had succeeded to the presidency as a result of the assassination of Lincoln, and it could therefore be fairly said that he did not have an electoral mandate in his own right. But the same situation has occurred on seven other occasions in our history: John Tyler succeeded William Henry Harrison in 1840, Millard Fillmore succeeded Zachary Taylor in 1850, Chester Arthur succeeded James A. Garfield in 1881, Theodore Roosevelt succeeded William McKinley in 1901, Calvin Coolidge succeeded Warren G. Harding in 1923, Harry S Truman succeeded Franklin D. Roosevelt in 1945, and Lyndon B. Johnson succeeded John F. Kennedy in 1963.

Another factor leading to the impeachment of Andrew Johnson was that both houses of Congress were controlled by the Republican party, to whose policies he was opposed. But once again this factor was not unique to the presidency of Andrew Johnson. The following table shows the periods of time during which both houses of Congress have been controlled by one party and the White House by the other:

DATES	PRESIDENT
1841–1843	John Tyler
1849–1853	Zachary Taylor and Millard Fillmore
1879–1881	Rutherford B. Hayes
1895–1897	Grover Cleveland
1919–1921	Woodrow Wilson
1947–1949	Harry S. Truman
1955–1961	Dwight D. Eisenhower
1969–1977	Richard M. Nixon and Gerald Ford
1987–1989	Ronald Reagan
1989–1993	George Bush

Finally, there were not only profound policy differences between Andrew Johnson and Congress, but a determination on the part of each to insist on what it regarded as its institutional prerogatives. Johnson resolutely vetoed measures he felt were either wrong or unconstitutional, and he used his power of appointment to reward his friends. Congress retaliated by passing laws over his veto, and by enacting measures, such as the Tenure of Office Act and the Army Appropriations Act of 1867, designed to limit the president's power of removal. Johnson nonetheless proceeded to remove Stanton, thereby precipitating his impeachment.

While the way in which the conflict between Congress and the president manifested itself at this time may have been a worst-case scenario, it was by no means unique. Such friction first assumed major proportions in the administration of Andrew Jackson, and flared up again in the administration of John Tyler, a generation before the trial of Johnson. Serious policy disputes have occurred between Congress and those presidents who have come after Andrew Johnson. The nature of these disputes has naturally varied with the times. But underlying many of them has been a recurrent theme unrelated to the policy at issue: What is the significance of the constitutional grant of authority to the president that "he shall take care that the laws be faithfully executed"? More particularly, may Congress, in the light of this grant, require the consent of the Senate to the removal of a subordinate officer appointed by the president? The enactment of the Tenure of Office Act, which formed the basis for the charges against Andrew Johnson, was an extraordinary assertion of congressional authority, and it would remain on the books to bedevil Johnson's successors.

The Virginia dynasty of presidents, who served from 1801 until 1825—Thomas Jefferson, James Madison, and James Monroe—favored, consistently with their constitutional views, a weak chief executive. John Quincy Adams, who succeeded Monroe, was much of the same view. The result was that from 1801 until 1829 the occupants of the White House were not disposed to assert doubtful prerogatives as against Congress. But when Andrew Jackson—"Old Hickory," the hero of the Battle of New Orleans—succeeded Adams in 1829, the presidency had an occupant of a different stripe. Jackson brought with him to his office a hostility to banks in general, and in particular to the Bank of the United States. When Congress passed a bill renewing the charter of the Second Bank of the United States in 1832, it met with a firm rebuff from Jackson:

> On July 3rd Jackson received the bill. Hearing the news, Martin Van Buren, just back from England, went straight on to Washington, arriving at midnight. The General, still awake, stretched on his sick bed, pale and haggard and propped up by pillows, grasped his friend's hand. Passing his other hand through his snow white hair, he said firmly but without passion, "The Bank, Mr. Van Buren, is trying to kill me, *but I will kill it*!"[1]

Jackson vetoed the bill, and his veto was sustained. After he was decisively reelected in 1832, he decided not to wait for the charter of the bank to expire by its own terms, but instead to remove the government deposits from it on his own initiative.

The act chartering the bank confided the decision as to whether to deposit the monies of the United States in that institution not to the president but to the secretary of the treasury. William Duane, secretary of the treasury, opposed the immediate removal of the deposits. Jackson insisted that Duane carry out his request, but Duane refused to remove the deposits and also refused to resign as secretary of the treasury. Jackson then removed him, and appointed in his place Roger B. Taney, his attorney general. Taney thereupon removed the deposits in the fall of 1833.

In December 1833 Taney sent to Congress a report stating his reasons for withdrawing the funds of the government from the Bank of the United States. Henry Clay, influential senator from Kentucky and leader of the bank forces in that body, offered a resolution declaring that "the President, in the late executive proceedings in relation to the public revenue, has assumed upon himself authority and power not conferred by the Constitution and laws, but in derogation of both." This resolution passed the Senate by a vote of 26 to 20 in late March, and Andrew Jackson was outraged. Jackson sent to the United States Senate a long document entitled "Protest," which it refused to have entered on its *Journal*, but which took up the cudgels of the debate:

> The Act of 1816 establishing the Bank of the United States directed the deposits of public money to be made in that bank . . . "unless the Secretary of the Treasury should otherwise order and direct," in which event he was required to give his reasons to Congress. . . . It is not to be considered that this provision in any degree altered the relation between the Secretary of the Treasury and the President as the responsible head of the executive department, or release the latter from his constitutional obligation to "take care that the laws be faithfully executed."
>
> It can not be doubted that it was the legal duty of the Secretary of the Treasury to order and direct the deposits of the public money to be made elsewhere than in the Bank of the United States *whenever sufficient reasons existed*

for making the change. If in such a case he neglected or refused to act, he would neglect or refuse to execute the law. What would be the sworn duty of the President? Could he say that the Constitution did not bind him to see the law faithfully executed because it was one of his Secretaries and not himself upon whom the service was specially imposed? . . . Might he not be told that it was for the sole purpose of causing all executive officers, from the highest to the lowest, faithfully to perform the services required of them by law that the people of the United States have made him their Chief Magistrate and the Constitution has clothed him with the entire executive power of this Government? The principles implied in these questions appear too plain to need elucidation.[2]

To this assertion Daniel Webster, senator from Massachusetts, replied in that body on May 7, 1834:

At the end of the last session of Congress, the public moneys of the United States were still in their proper place. That place was fixed by the law of the land, and no power of change was conferred on any other human being than the Secretary of the Treasury. On him the power of change was conferred, to be exercised by himself, if emergency should arise, and to be exercised for reasons which he was bound to lay before Congress. No other officer of the government had the slightest pretense of authority to lay his hand on these moneys for the purpose of changing the place of their custody. All the other heads of departments together could not touch them. The President could not touch them.

. . . Now, Sir, it is precisely this which I deem an assumption of power not conferred by the Constitution and laws. I think the laws did not give this authority to the President, nor impose on him the responsibility of its exercise. It is evident that, in this removal, the Secretary was in reality nothing but the scribe; he was the pen in the President's hand, and no more.[3]

Jackson, anticipating the Senate's disapproval of Taney's actions in removing the deposits, did not send his nomination as secretary of the treasury to the Senate until near the end of the session. But the Senate, without debate, rejected his nomination, and Taney returned to private life. When a vacancy occurred on the Supreme Court because of the resignation of Justice Gabriel Duvall from Maryland, Jackson nominated Taney to be an associate justice of the Court. After much maneuvering, at the very end of the lame-duck session of Congress, a vote to indefinitely postpone—and thereby kill—Taney's nomination carried by a vote of 24 to 21. Thus the Senate exacted partial revenge for the actions of both Jackson and Taney.

The bitter fight between Congress and the president over the bank led to the formation of the Whig party, which championed the authority of Congress at the expense of the authority of the president. Indeed, its very name was taken from English political history, where the Whigs were the party championing the cause of Parliament against that of the king. But the Whigs ironically found themselves confounded a few years later by one of their own nominees. Martin Van Buren had succeeded his mentor Jackson as president in 1837, but his administration turned sour because of the Panic of 1837. It appeared that whoever the Whigs might nominate to oppose Van Buren would have a good chance of being elected president in 1840.

Henry Clay and Daniel Webster were the leaders of the Whig party in Congress, but neither of them was regarded as "electable." The Whig convention selected General William Henry Harrison of Ohio as its presidential candidate, and John Tyler of Virginia as its candidate for vice-president. Harrison, sixty-seven years of age, had had a rather checkered career. For twelve years, beginning in 1800, he had been governor of Indiana Territory, and while serving in that position had led the American militia to victory over Tecumseh and the Shawnee Indians at the Battle of Tippecanoe in 1811. He had later served briefly in both the House of Representatives and the Senate, and had been minister to Colombia under John Quincy Adams. But under the Democrats these political appointments no longer came his way, and he returned to farming at his home near Cincinnati. For a time he served as clerk of the court of common pleas in that city.

John Tyler was educated at the College of William and Mary in Virginia, and entered state politics at an early age. He served both as governor of Virginia and as United States senator from that state. He had opposed the removal of the government deposits from the bank, and at that time switched his allegiance from the Democratic party to the Whig party. The office of vice-president was not considered of much consequence, and the Whig convention in 1840 chose Tyler for that office both to add balance to the ticket and because Virginia was one of the most populous states in the Union at that time. The Whig convention deliberately decided not to adopt a platform, fearing that any attempt to draft such a document would tear the party apart before the campaign had even begun.

The Democrats placed an item in the *Baltimore American* designed to put Harrison in his place:

> Give him a barrel of hard cider and settle a pension of two thousand a year on him and, my word for it, he will sit the remainder of his days in a log cabin.[4]

Whig publicists seized on this item, and thus began the "log cabin and hard cider" presidential campaign of 1840. The Whig rallying cry was "Tippecanoe and Tyler Too," and as for Martin Van Buren, they chanted "Van, Van, is a used-up man." Nicholas Biddle, Jackson's old enemy, came out of retirement to raise funds for the Whig ticket, and advised the candidate's managers:

> Let him say not a single word about his principles or his creed—let him say nothing, promise nothing. Let the use of pen and ink be wholly forbidden.[5]

"Tippecanoe and Tyler Too" won the election in November 1840, and William Henry Harrison was inaugurated on March 4, 1841. One month later he was dead of pneumonia. The Cabinet met and summoned Tyler, who was at his home in Virginia, and he arrived in Washington on April 6. Some members of the Cabinet thought that Tyler should be sworn in as "acting president," or "vice-president, acting as president," but Tyler would have none of it, and he was sworn in as president by William Cranch, chief justice of the Circuit Court of the District of Columbia. The Whigs had won the presidential election, but now their president was not the presumably malleable Harrison, but the well-educated, politically experienced, and thoroughly independent Tyler. For the first time in United States history, a vice-president had succeeded to the office of president upon the death of the incumbent.

In the election of 1840 the Whigs had won, in addition to the presidency, solid control of both houses of Congress. The Whig leadership in Congress knew what it wanted in the way of legislation: the chartering of a new Bank of the United States, tariffs that would protect American manufacturers, and federal financing of internal improvements. They could, however, scarcely claim an electoral mandate for their program. In the presidential campaign they had deliberately avoided any policy debates in favor of slogans. Now "Tippecanoe" was dead, and they were quite uncertain what to expect from "Tyler Too."

The new president at first appeared conciliatory. He requested the members of the Cabinet appointed by Harrison to remain in office, and they agreed. The country awaited the convening of a special session of Congress, which had been called by Harrison for May 31, 1841. That session passed a public lands bill, and a bill raising tariff rates, both of which Tyler signed.

But he vetoed bills providing federal money for internal improvements, and a bill chartering a new Bank of the United States. Congress then passed a second bill, referring not to a bank but to a "fiscal corporation," which Tyler had given some reason to think would meet his objections. But after considering the second bill, Tyler vetoed it, too. He subscribed to the limited view of congressional authority that Jefferson had urged against Hamilton in their debate in Washington's Cabinet over the charter of the first Bank of the United States. Congress, in Tyler's view, had no power to charter such a bank. His veto was sustained by the votes of Democrats in Congress.

On September 11, 1841, a few days after the veto of the second bank bill, the Tyler Cabinet, with the single exception of Secretary of State Daniel Webster, resigned en masse. If there had been any presidential "honeymoon" for Tyler, it was over. He found himself very much in the position in which Andrew Johnson would find himself twenty-five years later. In order to broaden the appeal of the ticket, he had received the vice-presidential nomination of a party to whose principal views he did not subscribe. Through death he had succeeded to the presidency, and he found himself sharply at odds with the congressional majority of the party that had elected him.

A sizable group of congressional Whigs—it is uncertain just how many subscribed—purported to read Tyler out of the party. Their manifesto espoused the right of Congress to appoint the secretary of the treasury, restrictions on the president's authority to remove officials, and a constitutional amendment that would allow presidential vetos to be overridden by simple majorities in each house of Congress. When Tyler vetoed a tariff-extension bill in June 1842, Congressman John Minor Botts of Virginia offered a resolution in the House to appoint a special committee to investigate the conduct of the president with a view to impeaching him. Nothing came of this resolution, but a similar and more detailed one was brought to a vote in the House in early 1843, and there defeated by a vote of 127 to 83.

The Democrats regained control of the House of Representatives in the election of 1842, and there was no further threat of impeachment. But the Senate, which remained under Whig control, continued to battle the executive. Several of his Cabinet nominations were rejected. Two vacancies on the Supreme Court occurred during his administration, but the Senate repeatedly rejected or refused to act on the nominations he made to fill these offices. He finally succeeded in filling only one.

As the presidential election of 1844 drew near, Tyler again found himself in a situation similar to that in which Johnson would find himself twenty-five years later. He knew he was anathema to the Whig party on whose ticket he had been elected four years earlier and would receive no support from them for reelection. He thereupon made overtures to the Democrats, whence he had come. That party ignored him as an apostate, and chose James K. Polk of Tennessee as its presidential candidate. Tyler then considered running as a third-party candidate, but when that movement gained no support, he finally endorsed Polk. When he left office, he had exercised his veto power ten times; not a lot by present-day standards, but more than any of his predecessors except Jackson, who had vetoed twelve measures.

It can be seen from this brief account of the Jackson and Tyler presidencies that congressional frustration with the exercise of presidential vetoes was not a phenomenon that began with Andrew Johnson. The effort to limit the president's authority to remove his appointees from office, which was embodied in the Tenure of Office Act, was adumbrated by congressional opponents of Jackson and Tyler a generation before. That act, of course, remained on the statute books after the Senate acquitted Andrew Johnson, and continued to be a thorn in the side of succeeding chief executives.

When Ulysses S. Grant was elected president in 1868 with the full support of the congressional Republicans, it might be supposed that they would have quickly repealed the Tenure of Office Act now that there was a sympathetic president in the White House. One of Grant's first messages to Congress requested that it do just this. But even for Grant, Congress was unwilling to enact an outright repeal; it modified the law so that a president might suspend an official without giving reasons therefor if Congress was out of session. But the power to remove, and to suspend while Congress was in session, still depended on the concurrence of the Senate.

James A. Garfield, writing in 1876, described the consequences of the Tenure of Office Act as it existed at that time. He said:

> This evil has been greatly aggravated by the passage of the Tenure of Office Act, of 1867, whose object was to restrain President Johnson from making removals for political cause. But it has virtually resulted in the usurpation by the Senate of a large share of the appointing power. The President can remove no officer without the consent of the Senate; and such consent is not often given, unless the appointment of the successor nominated to fill the proposed vacancy is agreeable to the Senator in whose State the appointee resides. Thus it has happened that a policy, inaugurated by an early President [Thomas Jefferson], has resulted in seriously crippling the just powers of the executive, and is placed in the hands of Senators and Representatives a power most corrupting and dangerous.[6]

Garfield himself would be elected president in 1880, and be assassinated by a disappointed office-seeker after only a few months in office. Another future president, Woodrow Wilson, in his volume titled *Congressional Government*, written in 1885, described what he regarded as legislative usurpations of control of the nomination process. He said:

> This particular usurpation has been put upon a very solid basis of law by the Tenure of Office Act, which took away from President Johnson, in an hour of party heat and passion, that independent power of removal from office with which the Constitution had invested him, but which he had used in a way that exasperated a Senate not of his own way of thinking.[7]

Henry Cabot Lodge, who as chairman of the Senate Foreign Relations Committee immediately after the First World War would engage in a bitter struggle with President Woodrow Wilson over the ratification of the Treaty of Versailles, authored a biography of Daniel Webster in 1884, the year before Wilson wrote *Congressional Government*. Ironically enough, Wilson and Lodge agreed in their early years about the danger of congressional usurpation. Lodge described Jackson's struggle with Congress, and then commented:

> The conflict has gone on, and the balance of advantage now rests with the Legislature. This tendency is quite as dangerous as that of which Jackson was the exponent, if not more so. The executive department has been crippled; and the influence and power of Congress, and especially of the Senate, have become far greater than they should be, under the system of proportion and balance embodied in the Constitution. Despite Jackson's victory there is, to-day, far more danger of undue encroachments on the part of the Senate than on that of the President.[8]

Grover Cleveland, elected to his first term as president in 1884, protested bitterly to Congress over the operation of the Tenure of Office Act. In a message to Congress in 1886, he said:

I believe the power to remove or suspend such officials is vested in the President alone by the Constitution, which in express terms provides that "the executive power shall be vested in a President of the United States of America," and that "he shall take care that the laws be faithfully executed."[9]

The House of Representatives responded to Cleveland's appeals by voting to repeal the Tenure of Office Act, but the Senate balked. Finally, in 1887, it was repealed.

As we have seen, acrimonious differences between the president and Congress did not begin with Andrew Johnson, and they did not cease with him. And no one who has observed our national government in operation during the second half of the twentieth century can have any doubt that such differences continue to arise. While the passions engendered by the Civil War gave an unusual intensity to the antagonism between Andrew Johnson and Congress, the absence of those passions would not be sufficient to protect future presidents from the precedent that would have resulted had Johnson been convicted by the Senate.

-16-

One would have thought that with the repeal of the Tenure of Office Act, at least that bone of contention between the president and Congress would have been removed. But such was not the case. For in 1872 Congress had enacted a statute regulating the Post Office Department which contained the same requirement for removal of postmasters throughout the country as was contained in the Tenure of Office Act. They could not be removed without the consent of the Senate. This measure did not have the reach of the Tenure of Office Act, because it did not include Cabinet officers or other high-ranking advisers to the president. But it raised the same basic question as to the extent to which Congress could require the consent of the Senate before the president could remove lower-level officials in the executive branch.

This measure received little notice for many years, but in the administration of Woodrow Wilson it became the basis for a major constitutional decision by the Supreme Court of the United States. In 1913 Wilson had appointed one Frank Myers postmaster at Portland, Oregon, for a term of four years, and in 1917 he had reappointed Myers to that position. Each of these appointments was confirmed by the Senate. In 1919 postal inspectors had encountered what they believed to be irregularities in the management of the Portland post office, and as a result, Myers was asked to resign. He refused to do so, whereupon Postmaster General Albert Burleson sent him the following telegram:

. . . [O]RDER HAS BEEN ISSUED BY DIRECTION OF THE PRESIDENT REMOVING YOU FROM OFFICE OF POSTMASTER AT

PORTLAND EFFECTIVE JANUARY 31ST. I HAVE EXERCISED
AUTHORITY GIVEN IN §262, POSTAL LAWS AND REGULA-
TIONS, AND PLACED INSPECTOR IN CHARGE OF POST OFFICE.
THE RIGHTS OF THE DEPARTMENT IN SUCH CASES HAVE BEEN
FULLY DETERMINED BY THE COURTS. YOU MUST HAVE
NOTHING FURTHER TO DO WITH THE OFFICE.

                                        BURLESON

The President and the postmaster general never sought the consent of the Senate to Myers's removal. Myers insisted that his
removal was illegal, and sued in the Court of Claims to recover
the salary he would have received had he been allowed to serve
out his full four-year term. The Court of Claims ruled against him
in April 1923, and he appealed that decision to the Supreme Court
of the United States. He contended that the act of 1872 required
senatorial consent to his removal; the Senate had not consented,
and therefore his removal was in violation of the act. The government, defending against his suit, took the position that the act of
1872 was an unconstitutional infringement on the power of the
president.

The Supreme Court of the United States at this time was presided over by William Howard Taft, who was remarkable in more
than one way. He was a huge man, his weight as an adult having
varied from slightly under two hundred and fifty pounds to well
over three hundred pounds. He was also the only person who has
ever served as both president and Chief Justice. He came from a
prominent Republican family in Cincinnati, Ohio, and had held
many public offices. In Cincinnati he had been a judge of both
the state and federal courts; he had served briefly as solicitor general in Washington, and when Theodore Roosevelt became president in 1901 he appointed Taft to be governor of the Philippines.
In 1904 Taft became secretary of war, and a principal confidant
of Roosevelt. He succeeded his mentor as president in 1909, and
served one term in that office. During his four years as president,
he was able to appoint one Chief Justice and five associate justices
to the Supreme Court, which was a number exceeding the appointments of all of his predecessors except George Washington.
While he was signing the commission of Edward Douglass White,

whom he had appointed Chief Justice, he said to Attorney General George W. Wickersham:

> There is nothing I would have loved more than being Chief Justice of the United States. . . . I cannot help seeing the irony in the fact that I, who desired that office so much, should now be signing the commission of another man.[1]

Taft became a professor at the Yale Law School when he left the presidency, but his ambition for the Chief Justiceship remained. When Warren Harding was elected president in November 1920, he requested Taft to meet with him at this home in Marion, Ohio, to give him advice on the presidency. Taft, something of a stickler for protocol, explained to Mrs. Harding, while the president-elect was out of the room, "the necessity of insisting that all his friends, except the family, should call him Mr. President instead of Warren as they do now. . . ." During this conference Harding somewhat casually inquired of Taft whether he would accept an appointment to the Supreme Court. Taft replied:

> I said it was and always had been the ambition of my life. . . . But I was obliged to say that now under circumstances of having been President, and having appointed three of the present bench and three others and having protested against Brandeis, I could not accept any place but the Chief Justiceship. He said nothing more about it and I could not make out whether he concluded that was satisfactory or whether he did not further wish to commit himself. . . .[2]

Unfortunately for Taft, the office of Chief Justice was not vacant; it was still filled by the man whom he had appointed in 1910, Edward Douglass White. But in May 1921 White died, and the following month Harding appointed Taft to fill the position. The Supreme Court had acquired a presiding officer who had a great deal of governmental experience, and who would very probably be sympathetic to the position of the executive in any dispute between that branch and Congress.

The *Myers* case was argued to the Supreme Court in December 1924, and reargued in April 1925. The *Reporter of Decisions of the Supreme Court* noted: "In view of the great importance of the matter, the Reporter has deemed it advisable to print, in part, the oral arguments, in addition to summaries of the briefs."[3] The solicitor general, who customarily defends the constitutionality of a law enacted by Congress when it is challenged before the Court, took the position that the law was unconstitutional. Senator George Wharton Pepper of Pennsylvania, himself a highly regarded Supreme Court advocate, argued as *amicus curiae* in favor of the constitutionality of the law. Myers's attorney, of course, also took that position. The solicitor general in his brief referred to "[t]his great constitutional question—a question which has repeatedly been submitted to this Court, but which the Court up to the present hour has found it unnecessary to decide; a question of great delicacy, because it affects the relative powers of two great departments of the Government."

The opinion of the Court was delivered by Chief Justice Taft, who labored for more than a year on it. He received substantial help from the newest member of the Court, Harlan F. Stone, who had previously been attorney general under President Calvin Coolidge. Stone's biographer, Alpheus T. Mason, describes the opinion as being of "ridiculous length," and perhaps it was. The opinion of the Court comprised seventy-two pages, and the three separate dissenting opinions took an additional one hundred pages. The opinions were finally handed down in October 1926. The Court held that the effort by Congress to require the consent of the Senate to the removal of an officer in the executive branch violated the authority conferred upon the president by Article II of the Constitution.

It is obviously impossible to summarize even the main threads of these lengthy opinions. The essential difference between the majority and the dissenters was their respective reading of the provision of Article II providing that the president "shall take Care that the Laws be faithfully executed. . . ." Chief Justice Taft, for the Court, reasoned that in order to take care that the laws be faithfully executed, the president must be able to remove subordinate officials who in his view are not doing their job properly. To the dissenters, the clause meant much less; it meant that the president was to carry out the laws that Congress had passed, including a law that required consent of the Senate before the president could remove a subordinate official.

The Chief Justice relied heavily on what is referred to as the understanding of the First Congress, which it will be recalled was also relied upon by Andrew Jackson, by the recusant Republican senators who voted to acquit Andrew Johnson, and by Grover Cleveland. This understanding had been manifested in a debate in the House of Representatives in June 1789, when that body was considering the creation of the office of secretary of state to head a Department of Foreign Affairs. James Madison had proposed a bill to this effect, which recited that the secretary was "to be removable from office by the President of the United States." It was at first moved that this language be stricken, but that motion was defeated by a vote of 34 to 20. But Representative Benson of New York renewed the motion to strike the language "removable by the President" the following week, and after full discussion of its implications the motion carried by a vote of 31 to 19. The bill then passed the House and was sent to the Senate. At that time the deliberations of the Senate were conducted in secret, without any written report being made. The critical vote there on the motion to strike the objectionable language was 10 to 10, so that Vice-President John Adams was able to use his casting vote to carry the measure.

Chief Justice Taft in his opinion for the Court said:

> It is very clear from this history that the exact question which the House voted upon was whether it should recognize and declare the power of the President under the Constitution to remove the Secretary of Foreign Affairs without the advice and consent of the Senate. . . . [T]here is not the slightest doubt, after an examination of the record, that the vote was, and was intended to be, a legislative declaration that the power to remove officers appointed by the President and the Senate vested in the President alone, and until the Johnson impeachment trial in 1868 its meaning was not doubted, even by those who questioned its soundness.[4]

The dissenting opinions of Justice McReynolds and Justice Brandeis pointed out that subsequent laws establishing specific terms for offices created by Congress did provide for removal by the president, thereby implying that Congress might have provided otherwise had it chosen to do so. But Chief Justice Taft's opinion viewed the debate in the First Congress as having extraordinary weight because so many members of that Congress had themselves been delegates to the Constitutional Convention:

> The discussion was a very full one. Fourteen out of the twenty-nine who voted for the passage of the bill and eleven of the twenty-two who voted against the bill took part in the discussion. Of the members of the House, eight had been in the Constitutional Convention, and of these six voted with the majority, and two, Roger Sherman and Elbridge Gerry, the latter of whom refused to sign the Constitution, voted in the minority.[5]

Justice Oliver Wendell Holmes dissented from the Court's decision in three succinct paragraphs. His view was that the office of postmaster did not exist until Congress created it, the pay for its incumbent depended upon congressional appropriation, and it could be abolished by Congress tomorrow. Given these facts, he had "little trouble in accepting [Congress's] power to prolong the tenure of an incumbent until Congress or the Senate shall have assented to his removal. The duty of the President to see that the laws be executed is a duty that does not go beyond the laws or require him to achieve more than Congress sees fit to leave within his power."[6]

In closing his opinion, Chief Justice Taft said:

> When on the merits we find our conclusions strongly favoring the view which prevailed in the First Congress, we have no hesitation in holding that conclusion to be correct; and it therefore follows that the Tenure of Office Act of 1867, insofar as it attempted to prevent the President from removing executive officers who had been appointed by him by and with the advice and consent of

the Senate, was invalid, and that subsequent legislation
of the same effect was equally so.[7]

To a friend, Chief Justice Taft wrote of the *Myers* case, "I never
wrote an opinion that I felt to be so important in its effect." The
opinion, however, was more than half a century too late to assist
Andrew Johnson in his struggle with Congress. He had considered seeking a judicial test of the Tenure of Office Act in the
midst of that struggle, but the judicial process is both slow and
uncertain. Given the low esteem in which the Radical Republicans held the Supreme Court of the United States at the time of
the Johnson impeachment, and the natural demands for prompt-
ness in conducting the trial of the president, it is doubtful that
even a prompt effort on his part to test the law would have changed
the minds of those senators who voted to convict him.

The views of those in the Senate who voted to convict Johnson
for violating the Tenure of Office Act were not entirely in accord
with one another. Charles Sumner, in the remarks quoted earlier,
made clear his view that impeachment was a strictly political process, and that the question to be resolved was not whether the
president had violated the Tenure of Office Act, but whether in
view of the profound policy differences between him and Congress he should continue to be chief executive. He would have
converted the Impeachment Clause of the United States Constitution into a mechanism similar to that played by a vote of confidence in a parliamentary system. In such a system the head of
government is the prime minister or premier, who holds the office
only as long as he commands the support of a majority in Parliament. Had the parliamentary system been in effect in the United
States during Andrew Johnson's time, and had he been prime
minister rather than president, he would not have survived his
disagreement with Congress over the extension of the Freedman's
Bureau and the Civil Rights Act in early 1866.

But Sumner's view was not openly embraced by most of his
Republican colleagues in the Senate who joined him in voting to
convict. The best evidence of this fact is the refusal of the House
of Representatives to impeach Johnson in December 1867, at a
time when the vast differences between the president and Congress over Reconstruction were completely exposed to view. Un-

der Sumner's theory, Johnson should have been impeached and convicted at that time, but the majority of the House felt that Johnson had not then committed any "high crime or misdemeanor" which should subject him to impeachment. Johnson's removal of Stanton in February 1868 supplied that missing element.

But if an "impeachable offense" was necessary for the majority of the House, it is likewise true that this majority was willing to hold the president to a very strict standard. It is difficult to quarrel with the assessment of Senators Fessenden, Grimes, and Trumbull that it would be extraordinary to remove from office a president who violated a law when the meaning of the law as at best ambiguous, and when his Cabinet had unanimously advised him that it was unconstitutional. It is hardly likely that anyone would have thought that Woodrow Wilson should have been impeached and convicted for removing a postmaster in Portland, even if the Supreme Court had decided the *Myers* case differently. It was the fact that the officer removed was Edwin Stanton—a stalking horse for the Radical Republicans inside Johnson's Cabinet— that triggered the impeachment proceedings. Once the "trigger" had been activated, the House added counts about Johnson's speeches in 1866, and about his conversation with General Emory, both of which had been known of at the time of the earlier vote against impeachment.

Thus it seems fair to say that while those in the House and Senate who favored conviction would have not assented to Sumner's likening of impeachment to a parliamentary vote of confidence, they would have held the president strictly accountable for any violation of the law without regard to his moral culpability. The House managers in their repeated appeals to the court of public opinion suggested, in addition, that once the legal litmus paper had turned color, the question was not so much whether the president should be removed *because* of the offenses he had committed, but simply whether he should be removed for the public good.

Had these views prevailed, and Johnson been convicted, nothing like the parliamentary system would have descended upon this country. The president would still have been elected to a term of four years and not been in any way dependent on Congress for his election to that office. He would have continued to possess the constitutional right to veto bills passed by Congress. But to the traditional weapons of Congress in opposing presidential actions with which it disagrees—refusing to confirm appointments, overriding vetoes, demanding information from the executive—would have been added another one: the threat of impeachment. A specific violation of the law or breach of duty would be required for impeachment, but it would not have to be a serious one involving moral culpability. And once such a dereliction had been found, other charges of a far more nebulous nature could be added.

Probably the greatest significance of such a relaxed standard for impeachment would have been its usefulness simply as a threat—a sword of Damocles, designed not to fall but to hang. The traditional weapons of Congress against the executive, while they may frustrate the president in his effort to carry out his program, do not involve any threat to his continuation in office. Engagements like this may be likened to the trench warfare in France during the First World War: One side gains ground and the other loses it, but the result is only to move the line of demarcation between the forces a little bit. The president remains in office, to live to fight another day.

But the threat to a president of possible removal from office by impeachment and conviction is a horse of quite a different color. Presidents are willing to risk some of their prestige in the traditional trench warfare between themselves and Congress, but few wish to run a substantial risk of being removed from office. Future presidents of one party facing a Congress controlled by the opposite party could well think twice about vetoing bills with which they disagreed, and about resisting the inevitable efforts by Congress to poach on the executive domain.

To predict when such a threat might have been employed if Andrew Johnson had been removed, rather than acquitted, is a necessarily speculative endeavor. But surely there were several possible occasions. The Democrats gained control of both houses of Congress in the last two years of the administration of President Rutherford B. Hayes, a Republican. Hayes's own title to the office of president was clouded by the Compromise of 1877; the Democrats, still smarting from a conviction of Johnson, might have thought that turnabout would be fair play.

Forty years later, the Republicans gained control of both houses of Congress in the last two years of the administration of President Woodrow Wilson, a Democrat. This period was marked by bitter disagreement between the president and the Senate over the ratification of the Treaty of Versailles, and by the president's serious and incapacitating illness, during which many thought his wife was actually exercising the executive power. If impeachment had been made easier by Johnson's conviction, might not the Republicans have been tempted? And might they not also have been tempted during that part of Harry Truman's presidency when they had gained control of both houses of Congress? Truman was president only because Franklin Roosevelt had died in office, and there were profound policy differences between the president and Congress over important measures such as the Taft-Hartley Act. True, in none of these instances did one party have the necessary two-thirds majority in the Senate for conviction, but only a majority is required for the House of Representatives to impeach.

Andrew Johnson was not, of course, convicted; he was acquitted. His acquittal confirmed what had already been established by the acquittal of Samuel Chase in 1805. Impeachment would not be a referendum on the public official's performance in office; instead, it would be a judicial type of inquiry in which specific charges were made by the House of Representatives, evidence was received before the Senate, and the senators would decide whether or not the charges were proven. The Johnson acquittal added another requirement, as evidenced by the views of the Republican senators who voted against conviction. It was not any technical violation of the law that would suffice, but it was the sort of violation of the law that would in itself justify removal from office.

The importance of these acquittals can hardly be overstated. With respect to the chief executive, they have meant that as to the policies he sought to pursue, he would be answerable only to the country as a whole in the quadrennial presidential elections, and not to Congress through the process of impeachment.

This relatively narrow approach to impeachment has meant that it would be rarely resorted to against a chief executive. Only once in our history since the acquittal of Andrew Johnson has a serious move to impeach a president taken place, and that was against Richard Nixon. In 1972, Nixon, running for a second term, was opposed by George McGovern. In the November presidential election, Nixon defeated McGovern by a landslide in the electoral

college and by a large margin in the popular vote. The Democrats, however, retained control of both houses of Congress.

In June 1972, shortly before the Democratic Convention, a burglary took place at the headquarters of the Democratic National
Committee located at the Watergate complex in Washington, D.C.
The purpose of the break-in was apparently to bug—to place listening devices in—the committee offices. The persons who committed the burglary were not well known, but one of them, James
McCord, held the position of Security Coordinator for CREEP—
the Committee to Re-elect the President. Both the Washington
Metropolitan Police Department and the Federal Bureau of Investigation set about investigating the burglary. John Mitchell, until
recently attorney general and at that time chairman of CREEP,
stated that the burglars were not operating on behalf of CREEP.

During the next two years, it gradually became evident that
those involved in the burglary had ties to the Republican party,
and that efforts to frustrate the investigation of the burglary had
been made by persons on the White House staff. During testimony before a Senate committee looking into the matter, it was
revealed that all conversations in the president's offices had been
recorded on tape. A special prosecutor in the Department of Justice subpoenaed these tapes from the president, but he refused to
produce them on the grounds of executive privilege. In October
1973 the special prosecutor was fired at the direction of the president, and the House Judiciary Committee announced that it would
commence an investigation of whether Nixon should be impeached. The committee began its work in January 1974, and at
the end of July of that year it voted on five proposed articles of
impeachment which had been drafted by its staff.

The staff, perhaps at the behest of committee members, followed the same pattern that had been used by the House in the
Chase and Johnson impeachments. In Chase's case the original
impetus for impeachment came from his charge to the Baltimore
grand jury; the House used this as one count in the articles of
impeachment, but proceeded to add the counts related to the Fries
trial, the Callender trial, and the Delaware grand jury. In the case
of Johnson, it was the removal of Stanton that had electrified the
country and brought almost instantaneous impeachment of the
president. But the House, in drafting the articles, tacked on to the
counts based on Stanton's removal other counts dealing with

Johnson's conversation with General Emory and on his public speeches. Perhaps ironically, in Chase's case it was the count based on the charge to the Baltimore grand jury that produced the most votes to convict in the Senate and in Johnson's case it was the counts based on the removal of Stanton.

The impetus for Nixon's impeachment, of course, came from his alleged conduct in obstructing the investigation of the Watergate burglary. But here, too, the draft articles used that conduct as the basis of one count, and proceeded to add others. The second article charged that Nixon had abused the power of the presidency by, for example, ordering the Internal Revenue Service to audit the tax returns of his political enemies. Article III was based on the president's refusal to honor the subpoenas issued to him by the Judiciary Committee. Article IV charged that Nixon had made false statements to Congress about the bombing of Cambodia during the Vietnam War. The final charge was that Nixon had wrongly used public money to improve his home at San Clemente, and had also taken deductions on his income-tax returns to which he was not entitled. Just as with Chase and Johnson, what started out as a simple, focused charge would become a potpourri if approved by the Judiciary Committee.

There were thirty-eight members of the Judiciary Committee, twenty-one Democrats and seventeen Republicans. The committee approved the Watergate count by a vote of 27 to 11, the abuse of power count by a vote of 28 to 10, and the disobedience of subpoena count by a much closer vote of 21 to 17. It rejected the Cambodian bombing count by a vote of 26 to 12, and the public money–tax fraud count by the same vote. Eight Democrats voted yes as to all five counts and ten Republicans voted no as to each of them.

Before the committee could make its report to the full House of Representatives, its recommendations were overtaken by events. In late July the Supreme Court decided in the case of *United States* v. *Nixon*,[8] that the special prosecutor was entitled to examine the Nixon tapes. The tapes were turned over, and one in particular proved incriminating as to the charge of obstructing justice in connection with the FBI investigation of the Watergate burglary. This tape was made public on August 5, 1974, and President Nixon resigned on August 9.

The impetus for impeachment was thus aborted, and the full

House of Representatives never took up the report of the Judiciary Committee. The spotlight of national attention that shone on the committee's deliberations produced much reasoned discussion, both within and without the committee, as to the nature of impeachment. All members of the Judiciary Committee—even the ten Republicans who voted no on each proposed article—appear to have rejected the view that a constitutional "high crime or misdemeanor" must be an indictable offense under the criminal law. The first article—obstruction of justice in connection with the investigation of the Watergate burglary—nonetheless met this requirement. Much like the charge that Andrew Johnson had violated the Tenure of Office Act, it was based on specific incidents of presidential conduct. The second and third counts were not as clearly based in the criminal law, but they, too, dealt with particular incidents of presidential conduct, and not with policy differences between the president and Congress.

Because the proceedings never ripened into articles of impeachment voted by the full House, to say nothing of being tried by the Senate, it would be a mistake to read too much into them as precedents for the future. We cannot know which of the articles the full House would have accepted, or what other articles it might have added; we cannot know how the House managers might have tried their case to the Senate, or how the senators would have judged it. But as far as it went, the effort to impeach President Nixon was clearly directed to a judicial type of inquiry into specific acts he had performed as president, rather than the sort of "vote of confidence" that takes place in a parliamentary system. And the counts relating to the obstruction of justice and to the unlawful use of executive power were of the kind that would surely have justified removal from office.

Only once, then, in the more than one hundred thirty years since Andrew Johnson was acquitted, has there been a serious effort to impeach a president of the United States. And in that case, the counts adopted by the House Judiciary Committee were entirely consistent with the views of the recusant Republican senators who had tipped the balance in favor of Johnson in 1868.

-17-

*T*he Constitutional Convention that met in Philadelphia in 1787 borrowed many of its ideas from existing governments and from political philosophers. But it did make two original contributions to the art of government. The first was the idea of a presidential, as opposed to a parliamentary, system of government, wherein the executive is chosen by the electorate and is not dependent upon the confidence of the legislature for his office. The second was the concept of an independent judiciary, with the authority to declare invalid acts of the legislature that exceeded the limits imposed by the Constitution. The first of these was threatened by the impeachment and trial of Andrew Johnson in 1868, and the second was threatened by the impeachment of Samuel Chase in 1805.

Both proceedings took place at a time when the United States was undergoing a sea change in its political beliefs. The impeachment of Chase followed closely upon the capture of the presidency and of both houses of Congress by the Jeffersonian Republicans in the election of 1800. The impeachment of Andrew Johnson occurred in the aftermath of the Civil War, at a time when the Republican party—formed little more than a decade earlier—had established lopsided control of both houses of Congress. On each of these occasions, the passions of the victors ran high.

The Jeffersonian Republicans had smarted under the administration of Federalist president John Adams for more than one reason. The Sedition Act of 1798 was rightly thought by the Jeffersonians to have been used on occasion as a means of silencing hostile criticism of the administration by the opposition press. During the twelve years in which first Washington and then Adams had been in the White House, only Federalists had been appointed to public office. The crowning blow occurred during the lame-duck session of Congress in early 1801, when that body passed the Judiciary Act of 1801, and John Adams proceeded to appoint the Midnight Judges. Jefferson and his followers felt it grossly unfair that their popular mandate in the election of 1800, which enabled them to take over the presidency and Congress, should nonetheless leave the judiciary a bastion of hostile Federalism.

Sixty years later, when Andrew Johnson's course as president began to depart more and more widely from the views held by the Republican majority in Congress, passions were even more aroused. The Republicans felt their policies were vindicated by the victory of the North over the South in the Civil War, and they were determined that those who had rebelled against the government should not escape punishment for their acts. They were also determined that something must be done by the national government to help the newly freed slaves in the South, partly for humanitarian reasons and partly for political reasons. When Johnson vetoed measure after measure, and the power of the executive branch was brought to bear in favor of lenient treatment of the seceded states, the Republicans felt betrayed.

At such times it is easy for those heavily engaged in the struggle to see it as an apocalyptic confrontation between good and evil, when customary restraints must be cast off in order that evil may not triumph. Maxims such as "The end justifies the means" or "Any stick is good enough to beat the devil" are invoked. Provisions in the Constitution for judicial independence, or provisions guaranteeing freedom of speech to the president as well as others, suddenly appear as obstacles to the accomplishment of the greater good. The extreme example of this phenomenon is a lynch mob that believes that it has caught a brutal murderer red-handed, and wants to dispense with the normal processes of the law such as the presumption of innocence and right of trial by jury. Judges who hold their tenure during good behavior, and are therefore largely immune from the immediate force of public opinion, are trained to enforce these rights even in favor of criminal defendants whose guilt appears clear.

The framers of the Constitution placed the trial of impeachments not in any court but in the United States Senate. Alexander Hamilton, writing in "Federalist No. 65," justified the action of the framers in these words:

> Where else than in the Senate could have been found a tribunal sufficiently dignified, or sufficiently independent? What other body would be likely to feel *confident enough in its own situation* to preserve, unawed and uninfluenced, the necessary impartiality between an *individual* accused, and the *representatives of the people, his accusers?*

One might have looked at the Senate in 1805, and looked at it again in 1868, and have legitimately wondered whether it would live up to Hamilton's billing. The framers, and the authors of *The Federalist Papers*, had not envisioned political parties as we now know them. But they were very much on the scene by 1805, and even more so in 1868. Would the dominant role played by political parties make the Senate a partisan tribunal, which would be willing to undermine the fundamental principles of the Constitution in order to remove a political enemy from office?

Remarkably, in each of these two cases, the answer to that question proved to be no. There were undoubtedly political partisans on both sides of the aisle in each case, but each time enough members of the majority party balked at the demands for party unity to acquit both Chase and Johnson. We know much more about why the seven "recusant Republicans" voted to acquit Andrew Johnson than we do about why the minority of Jeffersonian Republican senators voted to acquit Samuel Chase. As to the former, by much the same line of reasoning, each of them decided that the trial was essentially a judicial proceeding, where the senators under oath were to decide whether or not the charges against the president had been proved. Deciding that they had not been proved, they followed the sound advice of the great English admiralty judge Lord Stowell, who said that "to press forward to a great principle by breaking through every other great principle that stands in the way of its establishment . . . is as little consonant to private morality as to public justice."[1] They followed their oaths and voted to acquit. It seems likely that the Jeffersonian

Republican senators acted for the same reason in voting to acquit Chase.

The importance of these two acquittals in our constitutional history can hardly be overstated. We rightly think of our courts as the final voice in the interpretation of our Constitution, and therefore tend to think of constitutional law in terms of cases decided by the courts. But these two "cases"—decided not by the courts but by the United States Senate—surely contributed as much to the maintenance of our tripartite federal system of government as any case decided by any court.

–Notes–

The excerpts from the Chase trial are contained in U.S. Congress. Senate. *Trial of Samuel Chase, Associate Justice of the Supreme Court of the United States, Impeached by the House of Representatives for High Crimes and Misdemeanors*. Washington, D.C.: Samuel H. Smith, 1805. The excerpts from the Johnson trial are contained in U.S. Congress. Senate. *Trial of Andrew Johnson, President of the United States, on Impeachment by the House of Representatives for High Crimes and Misdemeanors*. 3 Vols. 40th Cong., 2nd Sess., 1868. Washington, D.C.: U.S. Government Printing Office, 1868.

–CHAPTER 1–

1. William Plumer, "Diary," Plumer MSS., Library of Congress, February 8, 1805.

2. Ibid., February 12, 1805.

3. Letter of February 25, 1808, in William Wetmore Story, ed., "Life and Letters of Joseph Story, Associate Justice of the Supreme Court of the United States," 1:166, reprinted in Charles Warren, *The Supreme Court in United States History*, Vol. I (Boston: Little, Brown and Co., 1923), p. 465.

4. Pickering Papers MSS., XXVII, 46, quoted in Warren, op. cit., p. 281.

5. Warren, op. cit., p. 156.

6. Henry Adams, *History of the United States of America During the First Administration of Thomas Jefferson*, Vol. II (New York: Charles Scribner's Sons, 1898), p. 148.

7. Jefferson to Joseph H. Nicholson, May 13, 1803; quoted in Nathan Schachner, "Thomas Jefferson: A Bibliography," Vol. II, p. 778.

8. Quoted in Paul S. Clarkson and R. Samuel Jett, *Luther Martin of Maryland* (Baltimore: Johns Hopkins Press, 1970), p. 306.

9. Ibid., p. 305.

10. Ibid., p. 306.

11. 10 U.S. (6 Cranch) 87 (1810).

12. 17 U.S. (4 Wheaton) 316 (1819).

13. Clarkson and Jett, op. cit., p. 213.

14. Ibid., p. 280.

15. John Randolph to Joseph Hooper Nicholson, quoted in Richard E. Ellis, *The Jeffersonian Crisis: Courts and Politics in the Young Republic* (New York: Oxford University Press, 1971), p. 20.

16. Quoted in William Cabell Bruce, *John Randolph of Roanoke, 1773–1833*, Vol. I (New York: Octagon Books, 1970), p. 176.

17. Dumas Malone, in *Dictionary of American Biography*, Vol. XV (New York: Charles Scribner's Sons, 1935), p. 366.

18. John Quincy Adams, *Memoirs of John Quincy Adams*, Vol. I (Philadelphia: J. B. Lippincott and Co., 1874), p. 322.

-CHAPTER 2-

1. 17 U.S. 316, 4 Wheaton (February Term 1819).

-CHAPTER 3-

1. James D. Richardson, comp., *Messages and Papers of the Presidents*, I, 266 (June 21, 1798), quoted in Thomas A. Bailey, *A Diplomatic History of the American People*, 4th ed. (New York: Appleton-Century-Crofts, 1950).

2. Quoted in Richard E. Ellis, *The Jeffersonian Crisis: Courts and Politics in the Young Republic* (New York: Oxford University Press, 1971), p. 15.

3. *Marbury* v. *Madison*, 3 U.S. (1 Cranch) 137 (1803).

4. Thomas Jefferson to Abigail Adams, June 13, 1804, in Lester Cappon, ed., *The Adams-Jefferson Letters*, I, 270 (Chapel Hill, N.C.: University of North Carolina Press, 1959), quoted in Ellis, op. cit., pp. 32–33.

5. Thomas Jefferson, *Works of Jefferson*, Vol. IX, ed. Paul L. Ford (New York: 1905), p. 195.

6. Ibid., p. 340.

7. Henry Adams, *History of the United States of America*, Vol. II, New York: Charles Scribner's Sons, 1898), pp. 147–148.

8. Albert Gallatin to Thomas Jefferson August 10, 1801, in Henry Adams, ed., *The Writings of Albert Gallatin*, 3 Vols. (Philadelphia: 1879), quoted in Ellis, op. cit., p. 23.

–CHAPTER 4–

1. Russell Blaine Nye, *The Cultural Life of the New Nation (1776–1830)* (New York: Harper and Bros., 1960), pp. 127–128.

2. Frank M. Eastman, *Courts and Lawyers of Pennsylvania*, Vol. II (New York: American Historical Society, Inc., 1922), p. 314.

3. Ibid., p. 331.

4. *Gibbons* v. *Ogden*, 19 U.S. 448, 6 Wheat. (February Term 1821).

5. Eastman, op. cit., p. 379.

–CHAPTER 5–

1. Julius Goebel, Jr., *Antecedents and Beginnings to 1800* (Vol. I, *History of the Supreme Court*) (New York: Macmillan Publishing Co., 1971), p. 641.

2. Dumas Malone, *Jefferson and His Time*, Vol. IV (Boston: Little, Brown and Co., 1970), p. 212.

3. Malone, op. cit., page 214.

4. *Murphy* v. *Florida*, 421 U.S. 799 (1975).

5. Raoul Berger, *Impeachment: The Constitutional Problems* (Cambridge, Mass.: Harvard University Press, 1973), pp. 236–238.

6. Goebel, op. cit., pp. 644–645.

7. "[T]he law will not suppose the possibility of bias or favor in a judge. . . ." Blackstone's *Commentaries*, Vol. III, p. 361.

8. John P. Frank, "Disqualification of Judges," *Yale Law Journal* 56 (1947), pp. 605, 611, 612.

9. Charles Warren, *The Supreme Court in United States History*, Vol. I (Boston: Little, Brown and Co., 1923); Albert J. Beveridge,

The Life of John Marshall, Vol. III (Boston: Houghton and Mifflin Co., 1919); Edward S. Corwin, *John Marshall and the Constitution* (New Haven: Yale University Press, 1921); Gore Vidal, *Burr: A Novel* (New York: Random House, 1973). Dumas Malone, *Jefferson the President: First Term 1801–1805* (Boston: Little, Brown and Co., 1970). Henry Adams, in the second volume of his *History of the United States* (New York: Charles Scribner's Sons, 1898), took a somewhat harsher view of Chase's actions but does not suggest that Chase should have been removed from office by conviction.

10. Berger, op. cit., pp. 229, 250.

11. Stephen Presser, "A Tale of Two Judges," *Northwestern University Law Review* 88–91 (1978–79).

12. *New York Times Company* v. *Sullivan*, 376 U.S. 254 (1964).

-CHAPTER 6-

1. George L. Haskins, *Foundations of Power: John Marshall, 1801–1815* (Vol. II, *History of the Supreme Court*) (New York: Macmillan Publishing Co., Inc., 1981), p. 222.

2. Charles Warren, *The Supreme Court in United States History*, Vol. I (Boston: Little, Brown, and Co., 1923), p. 166.

3. Julius Goebel, Jr., *Antecedents and Beginnings to 1800* (Vol. I, *History of the Supreme Court*) (New York: Macmillan Publishing Co., 1971), p. 619.

4. Albert J. Beveridge, *The Life of John Marshall*, Vol. III (Boston: Houghton Mifflin Co., 1919), pp. 197–198.

5. Paul S. Clarkson and R. Samuel Jett, *Luther Martin of Maryland* (Baltimore: The Johns Hopkins Press, 1970), p. 221.

6. Ibid., p. 221.

7. William Cabell Bruce, *John Randolph of Roanoke, 1773–1883*, Vol. I (New York: Octagon Books, 1970). Original copyright 1922.

8. Henry Adams, *History of the United States of America During the First Administration of Thomas Jefferson*, Vol. II (New York: Charles Scribner's Sons, 1898), p. 238.

-CHAPTER 7-

1. John Quincy Adams, *Memoirs of John Quincy Adams*, Vol. I, (Philadelphia: J. B. Lippincott and Co., 1874), p. 365.

2. Ibid., p. 364.

3. *Richmond Enquirer*, March 12, 1805, quoted in Charles Warren, *The Supreme Court in United States History*, Vol. I (Boston: Little, Brown and Co., 1923), p. 292.

4. John Quincy Adams, op. cit., pp. 370–371.

5. *Harper's New Monthly Magazine*, Vol. LVIII, No. CCCXLVII (April 1879), "Dr. Mitchill's Letters from Washington: 1801–1813." The author of this article comments, "Among Dr. Mitchill's papers were found his notes of evidence in proceedings during this trial, amounting to forty folio pages, in his own handwriting. On these his judgment in both were determined."

6. 10 U.S. 87, 6 Cranch (February Term 1810).

7. Henry Adams, *History of the United States of America During the First Administration of Thomas Jefferson*, Vol. II (New York: Charles Scribner's Sons, 1989), p. 213.

8. William Cabell Bruce, *John Randolph of Roanoke, 1773–1883*, Vol. I (New York: Octagon Books, 1970), pp. 198–199.

9. John Quincy Adams, op. cit., p. 341.

10. *Ibid.*, p. 365.

-CHAPTER 8-

1. 5 U.S. 137, Cranch 137 (1803).

2. T. Jefferson to W. Giles, April 20, 1807, quoted in George L. Haskins, *Foundations of Power: John Marshall, 1801–1815.* (Vol. II, *History of the Supreme Court*) (New York: Macmillan Publishing Co., Inc., 1981), p. 265.

3. Joseph Borkin, *The Corrupt Judge* (New York: Clarkson N. Potter, Inc., 1962), p. 49.

4. *United States* v. *Manton*, 107 F.2d 834, 836.

5. Albert J. Beveridge, *The Life of John Marshall*, Vol. III (Boston: Houghton Mifflin Co., 1919).

6. Ibid., p. 177.

7. Ibid., p. 165.

8. Quoted in Charles Warren, *The Supreme Court in United States History*, Vol. I (Boston: Little, Brown and Co., 1923), p. 173.

9. Quoted in Warren, op. cit., p. 170.

10. Robert H. Jackson, *The Struggle for Judicial Supremacy* (New York: Alfred A. Knopf, 1941), pp. ix–x.

-CHAPTER 9-

1. Catherine Drinker Bowen, *Miracle at Philadelphia* (Boston: Little, Brown and Co., 1966), p. 201.
2. Samuel Eliot Morison, *The Oxford History of the American People* (New York: Oxford University Press, 1965), p. 405.
3. Robert Liston, *Slavery in America* (New York: McGraw-Hill Book Co., 1970), p. 108.
4. George Julian, *Political Recollections, 1840–1872* (New York: Negro University Press, 1970), pp. 72–74.
5. Allan Nevins, *Ordeal of the Union* Vol. I (New York: Charles Scribner's Sons, 1947), p. 343.

-CHAPTER 10-

1. James D. Richardson, comp., *Messages and Papers of the Presidents*, Vol. V (1849–1861), p. 43, published by authority of Congress.
2. 60 U.S. (19 How.) 393 (1857).
3. Quoted in Charles Warren, *The Supreme Court in United States History*, Vol. I (Boston: Little, Brown and Co., 1923), p. 27.
4. Abraham Lincoln, *The Collected Works of Abraham Lincoln*, Vol. II, ed. Roy P. Basler (New Brunswick, N.J.: Rutgers University Press, 1956), p. 461.
5. Benjamin P. Thomas and Harold M. Hyman, *Stanton: The Life and Times of Lincoln's Secretary of War* (New York: Alfred A. Knopf, 1962), pp. 96–97.
6. Quoted in Allan Nevins, *The Emergence of Lincoln*, Vol. II (New York: Charles Scribner's Sons, 1950), p. 394.
7. Burton J. Hendrick, *Lincoln's War Cabinet* (Garden City, N.Y.: Doubleday and Co., Inc., 1961), pp. 10–11.
8. Richardson, op. cit., Vol. VI (1861–1869), pp. 10–11.

-CHAPTER 11-

1. Abraham Lincoln, *Complete Works of Abraham Lincoln*, Vol. VI, ed. John G. Nicolay and John Hay (Lincoln Memorial University, 1894), p. 234.

2. Ibid., p. 237.

3. Quoted in Carl Sandburg, *Abraham Lincoln* (1 Vol.) (New York: Harcourt, Brace and World, Inc., 1954), p. 314.

4. Benjamin P. Thomas and Harold M. Hyman, *Stanton: The Life and Times of Lincoln's Secretary of War* (New York: Alfred A. Knopf, 1962).

5. Sandburg, op cit., p. 246.

6. Ibid., p. 499.

7. Carl Sandburg, *Abraham Lincoln: The War Years*, Vol. IV (New York: Harcourt, Brace & World, Inc., 1936), p. 93.

-CHAPTER 12-

1. Hans L. Trefousse, *Andrew Johnson* (New York: W. W. Norton and Co., 1989), p. 71.

2. Ibid., p. 117.

3. Hans L. Trefousse, *Impeachment of a President* (Knoxville, Tenn.: University of Tennessee Press, 1975), p. 7.

4. 71 U.S. (4 Wall.) 2 (1866).

5. Trefousse, *Impeachment of a President*, pp. 79–80.

6. Michael Les Benedict, *The Impeachment and Trial of Andrew Johnson* (New York: W. W. Norton and Co., Inc., 1973), p. 69.

7. Trefousse, *Impeachment of a President*, pp. 134–135.

-CHAPTER 13-

1. Michael Les Benedict, *The Impeachment and Trial of Andrew Johnson* (New York: W. W. Norton and Co., Inc., 1973), p. 105.

2. Garfield to J. H. Rhodes, April 28, 1868, Garfield Mss., quoted in Benedict, op. cit., p. 124.

3. David Miller DeWitt, *The Impeachment and Trial of Andrew Johnson* (New York: The Macmillan Co., 1903), p. 543.

4. Ibid., p. 544.

5. Ibid., p. 545.

6. Hans L. Trefousse, *Impeachment of a President* (Knoxville, Tenn.: University of Tennessee Press, 1975), p. 165.

7. George W. Julian, *Political Recollections, 1840–1872* (New York: Negro Universities Press, 1972), p. 316.

-CHAPTER 14-

1. Hans L. Trefousse, *Impeachment of a President* (Knoxville, Tenn.: University of Tennessee Press, 1975), p. 175–176.

2. Samuel Eliot Morison, *The Oxford History of the American People* (New York: Oxford University Press, 1965), p. 721.

3. Michael Les Benedict, *The Impeachment and Trial of Andrew Johnson* (New York: W. W. Norton and Co., Inc., 1973).

-CHAPTER 15-

1. Quoted in Arthur M. Schlesinger, Jr., *The Age of Jackson* (Boston: Little, Brown and Co., 1946), p. 89.

2. James D. Richardson, comp., *Messages and Papers of the Presidents*, Vol. III, pp. 83–84.

3. Daniel Webster, *The Papers of Daniel Webster: Speeches and Formal Writings*, Vol. II, ed. Charles N. Wiltsey and Allen R. Berolzheimer (Hanover, N.H.: University Press of New England, 1988), pp. 36–37.

4. Quoted in Marquis James, *Andrew Jackson* (New York: Grosset and Dunlap, 1937), p. 450.

5. Ibid., p. 451.

6. James A. Garfield, "A Century of Congress," *Atlantic Monthly*, July 1877 in *The Works of James Abram Garfield*, ed. Burke A. Hinsdale, Vol. II (Boston: James R. Osgood and Co., 1883).

7. Woodrow Wilson, *Congressional Government* (Boston: Houghton Mifflin Co., 1885), p. 49.

8. Henry Cabot Lodge, *Daniel Webster* (Boston: Houghton Mifflin and Co., 1884), p. 230.

9. Richardson, op. cit., Vol. X, p. 4964.

-CHAPTER 16-

1. Henry F. Pringle, *The Life and Times of William Howard Taft*, Vol. I (New York: Farrar and Rinehart, Inc., 1939), p. 535.

2. Ibid., Vol. II, p. 955.

3. 272 U.S. 56 (1926).

4. 272 U.S. at 114.

5. 272 U.S. at 114.
6. 272 U.S. at 177.
7. 272 U.S. at 176.
8. 418 U.S. 683 (1974).

-CHAPTER 17-

1. *Re Le Louis* (1817) 2 Dods. 210, 257.

-Bibliography-

Adams, Henry. *History of the United States of America During the First Administration of Thomas Jefferson*, Vol. II. New York: Charles Scribner's Sons, 1898.

Adams, John Quincy. *Memoirs of John Quincy Adams*, Vol. I, ed. Charles F. Adams. Philadelphia: J. B. Lippincott and Co., 1874.

Benedict, Michael Les. *The Impeachment and Trial of Andrew Johnson*. New York: W. W. Norton and Co., Inc., 1973.

Berger, Raoul. *Impeachment: The Constitutional Problems*. Cambridge, Mass.: Harvard University Press, 1973.

Beveridge, Albert J. *The Life of John Marshall*, Vol. III. Boston: Houghton Mifflin Co., 1919.

Billington, Ray Allen. *The Protestant Crusade, 1800–1860*. New York: The Macmillan Co., 1938.

Blue, Frederick J. *Salmon P. Chase: A Life in Politics*. Kent, Ohio: Kent State University Press, 1987.

Borkin, Joseph. *The Corrupt Judge*. New York: Clarkson N. Potter, Inc., 1962.

Bruce, William Cabell. *John Randolph of Roanoke, 1773–1833*, Vol. I. New York: Octagon Books, 1970.

Burns, James MacGregor. *Presidential Government: The Crucible of Leadership*. Boston: Houghton Mifflin Co., 1966.

Clarkson, Paul S., and R. Samuel Jett. *Luther Martin of Maryland*. Baltimore: Johns Hopkins Press, 1970.

Dewitt, David Miller. *The Impeachment and Trial of Andrew Johnson*. New York: The Macmillan Co., 1903.

Eastman, Frank M. *Courts and Lawyers of Pennsylvania.* New York: American Historical Society, Inc., 1922.

Ellis, Richard E. *The Jeffersonian Crisis: Courts and Politics in the Young Republic.* New York: Oxford University Press, 1971.

Franklin, John H. *From Slavery to Freedom,* 4th ed. New York: Alfred A. Knopf, 1974.

Goldsmith, William M. *The Growth of Presidential Power,* Vol. II. New York: Chelsea House Publishers, 1974.

James, Marquis. *Andrew Jackson.* New York: Grosset and Dunlap, 1937.

Julian, George W. *Political Recollections, 1840–1872.* New York: Negro Universities Press, 1972. (Originally published in 1884 by Jansen McClurg & Co.)

Labovitz, John R. *Presidential Impeachment.* New Haven: Yale University Press, 1978.

LaRue, Lewis H. *Political Discourse: A Case Study of the Watergate Affair.* Athens, Ga.: University of Georgia Press, 1988.

Liston, Robert A. *Slavery in America.* New York: McGraw-Hill Co., 1970.

Lodge, Henry Cabot. *Daniel Webster.* Boston: Houghton Mifflin Co., 1884.

Malone, Dumas. *Jefferson and His Time,* Vol. IV, *Jefferson the President: First Term, 1801–1805.* Boston: Little, Brown and Co., 1970.

Mayer, George H. *The Republican Party, 1854–1966.* New York: Oxford University Press, 1967.

Morgan, Robert J. *A Whig Embattled: The Presidency Under John Tyler.* Lincoln, Neb.: University of Nebraska Press, 1954.

Nevins, Allan. *The Emergence of Lincoln,* Vol. II. New York: Charles Scribner's Sons, 1950.

———. *Ordeal of the Union,* Vol. I. New York: Charles Scribner's Sons, 1947.

Peterson, Norma Lois. *The Presidencies of William Henry Harrison and John Tyler.* Lawrence, Kan.: University Press of Kansas, 1989.

Presser, Stephen B. "A Tale of Two Judges," *Northwestern University Law Review,* 88–91 (1978–79).

Sefton, James E. *Andrew Johnson and the Uses of Constitutional Power.* Boston: Little, Brown and Co., 1980.

Thomas, Benjamin P., and Harold M. Hyman. *Stanton: The Life and Times of Lincoln's Secretary of War.* New York: Alfred A. Knopf, 1962.

Trefousse, Hans L., *Andrew Johnson.* New York: W. W. Norton and Co., 1989.

——— *Benjamin Franklin Wade: Radical Republican from Ohio.* New York: Twayne Publishers, Inc., 1963.

——— *Impeachment of a President.* Knoxville, Tenn.: University of Tennessee Press, 1975.

——— *The Radical Republicans: Lincoln's Vanguard for Racial Justice.* New York: Alfred A. Knopf, 1969.

U.S. Congress. Senate. *Trial of Andrew Johnson, President of the United States, on Impeachment by the House of Representatives for High Crimes and Misdemeanors.* 3 Vols. 40th Cong., 2nd Sess., 1868. Washington, D.C.: U.S. Government Printing Office, 1868.

U.S. Congress. Senate. *Trial of Samuel Chase, Associate Justice of the Supreme Court of the United States, Impeached by the House of Representatives for High Crimes and Misdemeanors,* Washington, D.C.: Samuel H. Smith, 1805.

Vaughn, William Preston. *The Antimasonic Party in the United States, 1826–1843.* Lexington, Ky.: University Press of Kentucky, 1983.

Warren, Charles. *The Supreme Court in United States History,* Vol. I. Boston: Little, Brown and Co., 1923.

Weinstein, Allen, and Frank Otto Gatell. *American Negro Slavery.* New York: Oxford University Press, 1973.

Wharton, Francis. *State Trials of the United States During the Administrations of Washington and Adams.* Philadelphia: Carey and Hart, 1849.

Wilson, Woodrow. *Congressional Government.* Boston: Houghton Mifflin Co., 1885.

-Index-